WITHDRAWN

Essays on the Reconstruction
of
Medieval History

Edited by Vaclav Mudroch and G. S. Couse

ssays on the reconstruction of medieval history

McGILL–QUEEN'S UNIVERSITY PRESS

MONTREAL AND LONDON 1974

ONTRIBUTORS

NORMAN F. CANTOR, Distinguished Professor of History
State University of New York at Binghampton

GILES CONSTABLE, Professor of Medieval History
Harvard University

W. T. H. JACKSON, Professor of German
Columbia University

ARMAND A. MAURER, C.S.B., Professor of Philosophy
University of Toronto

ROBERT FOLZ, Professor of Medieval History
University of Dijon

SYLVIA L. THRUPP, Professor of History
University of Michigan

BERTIE WILKINSON, Professor Emeritus of History
University of Toronto

VACLAV MUDROCH, Associate Professor of History (†1969)
Carleton University

© McGill–Queen's University Press 1974
ISBN: 0 7735 0069 3
Library of Congress Catalog Card Number: 73-82844
Legal Deposit 1st quarter 1974
Design by Susan McPhee
Printed in the United Kingdom by
Hazell Watson and Viney Limited, Aylesbury, Bucks

ONTENTS

**REFACE** The following collection of essays has had a regrettably slow and fitful passage from conception to print. It originated in a series of seven public lectures on 'The Medieval World' presented at Carleton University in the winter of 1965. About the same time the initiator of this series, Professor Vaclav Mudroch, prevailed upon the eminent French medievalist Robert Folz to contribute a study of 'Charlemagne and His Empire' for publication along with the lectures. Progress toward that end was interrupted, however, by circumstances that have been profoundly saddening for Professor Mudroch's colleagues and friends. While he was editing the essays he began to suffer from an illness which turned out to be multiple sclerosis. This affliction obliged him eventually to abandon all academic activities, and it took his life finally on November 24, 1969, when he was forty-five years old. Meanwhile, at the request of Dean D. M. L. Farr of the Faculty of Arts at Carleton University, I undertook to complete the editorial work that remained to be done on the collection. Most of the originally submitted manuscripts were brought up to date, particularly with respect to their notes, in the spring and summer of 1968. Exceptional difficulties with two of them, however, have necessitated a further delay. The essays are now presented to the reading public in the conviction that, notwithstanding the tardiness of their appearance, they will prove to be a valuable contribution to the study

of the Middle Ages.

It will be observed that the essays in this collection go well beyond the depiction of one or other facet of the medieval world itself. In keeping with Professor Mud, roch's intention, our authors have centred their attention upon modern historical scholarship and its apprehension of the realities of the medieval past. They have done so, however, at two main levels of abstraction from such realities, and the essays have been grouped accordingly. The first four deal primarily with the changing condi, tions, preconceptions, lines of attack, and interpretations that have characterized the study of designated aspects of the Middle Ages. The remaining four present in a comprehensive fashion, and sometimes with reference to controversial questions, the fruits of more or less recent investigation within particular areas. In these two senses, then, the collection consists of essays in historiography.

I am gratefully conscious of assistance received toward the completion of this book. The Faculty of Arts at Carleton University has provided vital financial support. The authors of the essays have borne with good will the extra demands made upon them in consequence of the slowness of the collection's progress. My colleagues Professor J. G. Bellamy and Professor R. E. Reynolds have kindly put their erudition in medieval history at my disposal. Dr. G. H. Martin of the University of Leicester and Mr. R. E. Aksim, Carleton honours graduate in History, have helped with the translation of the essay by Robert Folz—a translation for which Professor Mudroch and I have been primarily responsible. And Mr. F. T. Kirkwood, another of our honours graduates in History, has taken a major part in preparing Professor Mudroch's essay for publication, has given me substantial editorial assistance with the other essays, and has helped in cor, recting the proofs. To these and others upon whom we have depended, my warmest thanks.

Finally I would presume to add a brief tribute of admiration and affection for Professor Mudroch on behalf of those who knew him. We are bound to be mindful of earlier hardships that he endured—his imprisonment, as a youth, in a concentration camp during the German occupation of Czechoslovakia; his eventual flight from post,war Czechoslovakia ac, companied by his stout,hearted wife but with meager material possessions and a doctorate in laws that could be of little practical value abroad; and his carrying out in

Canada of a second, long program of undergraduate and graduate studies, in history. Some of us will have had occasion thereafter to be impressed by the intensity of his devotion to scholarship, the multilingual scope and the solidity of his research, and the literary culture that graced his teaching and writing. All of us will have been captivated by his personal virtues. He was thoroughly unassuming and ingenuous, always co-operative, patient and cheerful: yet firmly committed to principles and deeply humane. While misfortune has cruelly cut short the fruition of his promise as a scholar, it has only served to confirm his stature as a man.

G. S. COUSE

he interpretation
of
medieval history

Norman F. Cantor

It was long the fashion for professors of medieval history in the United States and Canada to give stirring lectures on the 'medieval legacy'. They wanted to prove how much of our contemporary civilization was shaped by changes which occurred in western Europe between A.D. 300 and 1500. It was considered necessary to show how many of the institutions and ideas of the modern world originated in medieval Europe, leading to the inevitable conclusion that the study of medieval history was worthwhile. This attempt to defend medieval history as a legitimate subject is not necessary today. Historians no longer have to affirm as a credo that medieval western Europe produced a remarkably creative and complex civilization. We can take this fundamental fact for granted and devote our attention to the critical examination of the nature of this civilization. We do not have to waste our time exploding myths about the 'Dark Ages'; rather we can examine both the achievements and the limitations of medieval civilization, accounting for both its greatness and its failings, in the same way that we would analyse any society. Thus we can approach the interpretation of medieval history not from the standpoint of apologists or detractors, but rather from that of critical historians whose aim it is to come as close as possible to fulfilling the goal of historical study—establishing 'the way it was'.

The ultimate historical reality, we must assume, exists; but it is a thing very difficult for even the most critical and dispassionate mind to perceive. There are, no doubt, psychological and epistemological obstacles to historical perception, but within the framework of historiography itself there are also built-in limitations on the realization of that ultimate reality which we assume to exist. We see any given moment in the past through two prisms which simultaneously illuminate and distort reality, and the perception of reality depends on our critical evaluation of the vision provided by these two historiographical prisms. First we must consider the way in which contemporaries in any given society interpreted their own actions and categorized historical change which their own civilization experienced. Secondly, we must examine the way in which modern historians have interpreted this society or civilization of the past and evaluate the assumptions and categories which they have used to organize and interpret the known data of the civilization they are studying. Our knowledge of medieval history, then, depends first of all upon the historiographical categorization of medieval men themselves and then upon the interpretations of modern students of medieval Europe. Without a conscious realization that in coming to the study of medieval history we are working at all times within a double framework of contemporary and modern classifications, we will not be able to evaluate the general significance of the information we have, no matter how assiduous and painstaking our research. We are decisively handicapped from the start if we try to make any advances toward a deepening understanding of medieval civilization without a careful study of the twofold historiographical dimension of medieval history, both the contemporaneous and the modern. The advance in historical knowledge depends perhaps even more upon historiographical self-consciousness than upon laborious research into new documentary sources.

The view that I have propounded is not popular among medieval historians today. They wish to be free from the kind of historiographical criticism of their main categories and underlying assumptions that has been successfully used in other historical fields. I am not altogether sure that I know the reason for this resistance to historiographical criticism among medieval historians; but I expect it derives either from the shockingly naive assumptions of the pseudo-scientific variety, to the effect that the historian's mind does not, in very important ways, condition the making of generalizations about the nature of historical change, or from a suppressed realization that the assumptions and categories which the medieval historian uses cannot withstand critical evaluation. In any case, we should not allow the attitudes of the Establishment among medieval historians, particularly in the English-speaking world, to dissuade us from a critical examination of all the assumptions and categories which interpreters of the Middle Ages have used during the great flourishing of medieval scholarship in the past sixty or seventy years. Some of these assumptions and categories will readily bear critical scrutiny; others will easily be shown to be unfounded and delusive; while still others, valuable on a first examination, will appear, upon closer study, to be flawed by a basic ambiguity.

When the modern interpretations of medieval history are set alongside the ideas of history held by medieval writers themselves, it is remarkable how heavily our own historiographical conceptions are still conditioned by the medieval outlook. This gives encouragement to the trumpeters of the medieval legacy: they can proclaim that the medieval ideas of history were decisive for the development of historical thought in the West and that we are still in many ways thinking along the lines worked out by medieval writers. But further reflection may qualify our celebration of the medieval historiographical legacy. Is it altogether good for the progress of historical thought—and even taking a more limited end, for our grasp, ing of the medieval reality—that we should still be ostensibly operating within the framework of medieval historiographical categories? Perhaps we should break away entirely from the medieval legacy of historical thought and take wholly new historiographical dimensions as our starting point? On the other hand, it would not be easy to do this, for it is remarkable how much medieval people did achieve along the lines of general historiographical perception, although their actual historical writing is often disappointing. Even when, in modern historical thought, we seem to have departed from the medieval way of thinking, more careful exami, nation reveals the underlying medieval assumptions.

The most interesting and perceptive discussion of the medieval view of history is, after thirty years, still that found in R. G. Collingwood's *The Idea of History*.[1] Collingwood claimed that there were only two decisive turning points in the development of the idea of history: one at the end of the fourth century and the other at the end of the eighteenth century. More than half of our modern idea of history is the product of the first revolution in historical thinking, which occurs during the Latin patristic era. Collingwood believed that the Graeco-Roman historians had a cyclic view of history and that they were given to typology, the presentation of abstract types, rather than dealing with the complexity of real personalities and human events. Because of their belief that the course of historical change was merely an endless repetition of the same cycle and because they thought that the historical scene was merely a stage for the presentation of stereotypes, the outlook of the classical writers was fundamentally unhistorical, in Collingwood's view. He believed that Christian thought in the patristic era was a new departure. On the one hand linear history replaced cyclical flux, and going along with this was a new respect for the individuality of historical personalities and events. History proceeded along a straight line from the creation to the last judgment, and every event, every individual soul along this line was determined by divine provid, ence and therefore significant. Collingwood's view of the historiographical revolu, tion of the late fourth century was in large part confirmed by the more detailed studies made by C. N. Cochrane and T. E. Mommsen.[2]

By and large Collingwood's view of the changes brought about by Christian historical thought is correct, although he made the change of the historiographical ideas in the fourth century too abrupt and decisive. He failed to appreciate the emphasis in classical historiography upon the stresses and conflicts which real people undergo, presented with unsurpassed power by Thucydides and to a lesser degree by Tacitus. While overaccentuating the proclivity of classical historio, graphy to typology, Collingwood overrated the medieval Christian historians'

3

appreciation of real personality. Until the late eleventh century medieval writers were as much inclined towards typology as their classical predecessors, or more so. The categories of the typology have undergone some changes, so that the political types (the good citizen, the bad emperor, and so on) are replaced by theological figures (the saint, the monk, the anointed king). In early medieval historiography there is no appreciation whatsoever for the qualities of individual personalities. All people and all events are discussed only insofar as they relate to universal providential categories. Nevertheless, Collingwood is right in postulating a great turning point in historiographical thought in the fourth century. The Graeco-Roman thinkers were not much interested in history, and actually not very much history was written in classical civilization. Classical thinkers were not much concerned with history because they did not like to examine the flux and upheaval in their lives. The prevailing attitude to change was Plato's—only eternal, fixed ideas are real. Variety, flux are ephemeral, mere shadow of pure form. Anyone who believes this doctrine cannot write good history or, indeed, very much of it, because history describes change in human lives. Change to the classical thinkers was at best ephemeral and at worst an unreal mirage. The Greeks and Romans did not like to contemplate change because they were afraid of it. Their world was, in fact, a most unstable one, and, without a theistic providential faith such as the Hebrew prophets imparted to Christian thought, the classical thinkers could not make sense out of the historical world. The great advance in historical thinking that comes with the triumph of Christianity in the fourth-century Roman Empire is a new interest in history. Men were no longer afraid of change; in fact, they exulted in it, because every event brought the line of historical time closer to the end of the world. In other words, medieval men were eager to contemplate the significance of historical change because they believed in providence and they were not afraid to walk in the darkness of time. This does not mean that medieval Christian thinkers immediately began to write what we would regard as good history. But eventually they would, because they had decided that history led to a good end and therefore they could look at it as not only valuable but also all-important. For the first time, in the fourth century, thinkers who had been trained in the classical tradition had the courage to face historical change and think about it.

The historiographical revolution of the fourth century did not bring with it an escape from classical typology. Rather, the typology was reconstituted and entrenched in new Christian categories. Eusebius's Emperor Constantine is even more of an abstract type, an embodiment of a certain ideal, than the emperors portrayed by Tacitus or Suetonius. But the new Christian historiography did effect a departure from cyclical history in favour of linear history. St. Augustine was more responsible for this change than anyone. He condemned Origen's attempt to interpret sacred history in a cyclic form, by which Christ the saviour was born and suffered and died in each cycle of historical time. To Augustine this view was a contradiction of Jesus' humanity. He held, and all subsequent medieval writers agreed with him, that Christ, in partaking of the human form, lived in time and could only have been born once, suffered and died at one moment of historical time. All history, therefore, proceeded in a line from creation to the last judgment. Medieval historians therefore believed that all history took place as linear moments from the beginning to the end of the world. But not all events were to them of equal importance. Great events intercept, as it were, the straight line of history and stand out as significant moments. The incarnation was the most important of these events, and consequently Eusebius in the early fourth century already presented a time scheme by which all other events were related to this paramount moment. During the seventh and eighth centuries a scheme of dating which we still use, before and after the incarnation, was introduced into historical writing. Perhaps the time has come to introduce a third period of history, a post-Christian era starting at the end of the nineteenth century, for a world which is no longer so largely identified with Christianity.

The most significant aspect of medieval discussions of historical time was not, as so many modern writers have believed, the continuing faithfulness to linear history. It was rather the way in which linear history was qualified by a powerful tendency towards historical periodization, and this tendency is still with us in our own historical thinking. The medieval periodization of historical time was particularly marked during the later twelfth and the thirteenth and fourteenth centuries in eschatological doctrines which had far-reaching social and political implications. This kind of historical vision took a particularly hysterical form in the speculations of Joachim of Flora and the similar doctrines propounded by the radical wing of the Franciscan order. These eschatological ideas were widespread and they became central to the world view of a substantial part of the European population in the twelfth, thirteenth, and fourteenth centuries. Vast numbers of people, both educated and illiterate, believed that anti-Christ was taking over the rule of the world and that this would be followed by the second coming, the last judgment, the end of the world and historical time, and the eternity in which the saints would rule triumphant at the right hand of the Lord and the wicked would suffer just punishment. Such speculations are of course ultimately derived from certain doctrines in later Hebraic and early Christian thought, but in the later twelfth and thirteenth centuries they came to condition the way of life of vast segments of European society and inevitably made a deep impress upon the historical outlook of western civilization. People now achieved a consciousness of the possibility of great upheavals. They thought that they were witnessing a great dividing line in history, a significant moment intercepting the line of historical development. The days of their years were ones in which things would be turned upside down. Anti-Christ would sit on the throne of Peter, a communion of the saints would announce the coming of the Lord, and then would be seen the breaking up of the world. Thus, the medieval view of history was anti-cyclical in the sense that it rejected any possibility of recurrence of events. But it was not thoroughly linear, if by linear we mean that history proceeds along an undifferentiated, unmarked straight line in placid progress undisturbed by great upheaval. The medieval view of history evinced a strong belief in great upheavals which intersected the line of historical development and comprised the inauguration of new periods. We can best view the medieval idea of history as a line which occasionally rises above the flat plain and then falls again. The historical line is therefore hilly rather than straight.

It is a well-known theme in intellectual history that the Marxist view of the end of the historical process—the triumph of capitalism followed by the revolution or the proletariat under communist leadership resulting in a dictatorship of the proletariat, and then the withering away of the state—is a secularization of the medieval eschatological doctrine preached by Joachim of Flora and his disciples. What has not been so clearly perceived is how much of our general historical under-standing has been conditioned by the medieval propensity for periodization, in which the historical era is inaugurated by a great upheaval. Our comprehension of any segment of historical time depends upon the predication of periods, the demarcation of certain eras which start with some radical change in society and culture. It is not wrong to view the past through categorization by periods, but we must do this in a self-conscious and critical manner. We must realize how much this approach to the understanding of historical change was originally conditioned by the apocalyptical vision of medieval people. It is salutary to remember that, once a certain moment has been generally accepted as the beginning of a new era, historians will tend to bring to the study of this moment a foregone emotional attitude. They will look for all the data which illustrate historical change and will be blind to the information which reveals historical continuity and which, if carefully considered, might explode the whole concept of the beginning of a new era.

We can see the delusions and difficulties of historical periodization at work on medieval history itself. Historians no longer speak of the Middle Age but rather of the Middle Ages, which, like the medieval godhead, turn out to contain a trinitarian division—the early (300–1050), the high (1050–1300), and the late (1300–1500). Among many recent writers the very long early medieval period has come to be divided at the eighth century, so that we now have a fourfold periodiza-tion of medieval history. Before this periodization becomes infallible dogma, as indeed it already has in some quarters, it is necessary to ask some searching and perhaps embarrassing questions. It seems plausible to begin the medieval era with the accession of the first Christian Roman emperor, Constantine, in A.D. 312. But in doing this we have assumed that Christianity only achieves a crucial social importance when it unites with the Roman State. If the Christian Church is so fundamental to medieval history that we assume that the medieval era begins with the political triumph of the Church, ought we not also to consider the significance of the spiritual triumph of the Church? In other words does it not make more sense to begin the study of medieval history with the origins of the Church in the apostolic period? And would not so much of the burden of medieval history become clearer if we began with the examination of the nature of Christianity in the first three centuries A.D.? I think that this examination would be immensely valuable for the interpreter of medieval history and might yield some surprises to us. I suspect such an examination would show that there was a twofold nature in pre-Constantinian Christianity: an hierarchic, sacramental, authoritarian Christianity and an individualistic, illuminist, and eschatological faith. The historian en-counters these two conflicting lines of Christian religion in North Africa in the fourth century, to some degree also within early medieval monasticism, and writ large in the great conflicts between sacramentalists and anti-sacramentalists in high and late medieval Europe. Might the interpreter of medieval history then not realize that the struggle between hierarchic, catholic Christianity and Donatist, illuminative heresy, whether in the fourth century or in the twelfth century, springs out of ambiguity and tension within apostolic and post-apostolic Christianity? And if he reached this startling conclusion, how much validity then would he attribute to the accession of Constantine as the beginning of medieval history?

Moving now to the view of 1500 as the terminal date of medieval history, close examination makes this belief even less tenable than the use of 300 as the starting point for the medieval era. The crystallization of historical interpretation so as to mark the end of the medieval and the beginning of the modern world was an achievement of late nineteenth-century historiography. It may have been a useful classification a half century ago but it is now a real hindrance to our understanding of the period between 1300 and 1700. A fundamental dividing line has become fixed in historical thought at a point where it is not justified, and this makes it very hard for us to grasp the fundamental unity of the period between the early fourteenth and later seventeenth centuries.

The designation of 1500 as a fundamental dividing line in the history of western civilization was based upon the great Renaissance Myth, which in turn was simply based on ignorance. Under the pressure of greater historical knowledge it deserves to be consigned to the mythological scrap-heap. We still fall into apocalyptical emotionalism when we discuss the early sixteenth century—the modern era seems to be dawning on all sides. Luther inaugurates the great revolt against papal authority, capitalism flourishes, and the bourgeoisie rises; and these great events are tied in with the emergence of the modern state, the expansion of Europe, and the beginnings of modern thought. Yet we now have more than sufficient information to know how specious this view is. Luther's revolt against sacerdotal authority is only one in a long series that had been going on almost incessantly since the twelfth century. The power of the medieval papacy had already collapsed in the fourteenth century, and Luther was escaping from a sick and decadent institution rather than raising the standards of rebellion against the unified medieval Church. In the economic sense, capitalism had been rising steadily since the late tenth century; there is nothing particularly significant or novel about sixteenth-century capitalism. As far as the bourgeois ethos is concerned, it had come into existence not later than the twelfth century, and if the theses about the relation between religion and capitalism propounded by Weber and Tawney have any merits, they can be applied more plausibly to the bourgeoisie of the twelfth century than to the bur-ghers of the sixteenth. A sixteenth-century capitalist was no different from his twelfth-century predecessor in that, like the medieval merchant, he could not translate his economic wealth into political power, with the exception of a few very special areas in Europe. In 1500 political power was in the hands of leaders of landed society, as it had been in 1200.

If we turn to political history, we cannot find that 1500 makes much of a dif-ference. The states of the sixteenth century operated in very much the same way as the royal governments in France and England in 1300; what historians used to think was a new authoritarian monarchy in 1500 has turned out to be merely a revival of late thirteenth-century royal government after a century or so of political breakdown in France and England from about 1350 to 1450. Let it be said once and for all that the modern state did not begin in the early sixteenth century; it started either in the thirteenth century or in the nineteenth century, depending on our criteria. It is a well-known fact that the expansion of Europe began in the late fifteenth century. But recent research has shown that this did not bring about the immediate decline of the Mediterranean economy and the disintegration of the cultural and business unity of the Mediterranean world. The expansion of Europe contributed to sixteenth-century prosperity, but Europe did not really become an Atlantic community until the end of the seventeenth century, if in fact it ever has at all.

Historians were once inclined to proclaim 1500 as the beginning of modern thought, apparently assuming that modern thought is based on the ability to write Latin in a Ciceronian style. With deeper reflection and some very painstaking research we find 1500 no dividing line at all in intellectual history. We would have to say that what historians call 'modern thought' is distinguished by 'modern science', which in turn is marked by the stating of general propositions about nature in mathematical terms and by an appreciation of the experimental method. If this is so, then we discover that modern science has its beginnings in the reflec-tions of certain Franciscan scholars at Oxford in the later thirteenth century. The second stage of the history of modern science, when there is a real intellectual 'take-off', is the well-known period of the late sixteenth and seventeenth centuries. But between the work of the Franciscan scholastics and the achievements of Galileo and Copernicus we have the heyday of the Renaissance humanists, who were aggressively anti-scientific, so that the beginning of the sixteenth century marks a low point in the early history of modern science.

All these criteria lead to the conclusion that the end of an historical era occurred in either the early fourteenth or late seventeenth century, but that it is impossible to sustain the traditional date of 1500 as valid periodization. Historians of western civilization have the option either of positing a new distinct era transitional from the medieval to the modern world, from 1300 to about 1700, or of envisioning the medieval period as extending to 1700. It is only when, in the eighteenth century, we have the Industrial Revolution, the tremendous growth of population, and the emergence of democratic movements that we can say we find the beginnings of our modern industrial mass society. And since the eighteenth century marks the start of the long withdrawal from the Christian faith, it would be advisable, on intellectual grounds, to regard the early eighteenth century as a fundamental turning point. In religion, government, social organization, and economic institutions there is such similarity and continuity between the thirteenth and seventeenth centuries that we should, if we are to take historical periodization at all seriously, view the whole span of time from the ancient world until the early eighteenth century as one period in the history of western civilization. During this long span of time there were many upheavals but the fundamental conditions of society and culture remained unchanged—belief in the Christian religion or varieties of it, the domination of government and law by landed society, the recognition of the leadership of kings in the world, and the universal acceptance of the validity of an hierarchic view of the world. In 1650 these beliefs and conditions were still almost as effective as they were in 1250, but since 1750 they have been steadily undermined and eroded for better or for worse. Taking seriously the positing of historical periods means, therefore, that we should probably begin the medieval era with the foundation of the Christian Church in apostolic times and extend the history of medieval culture and society to the early eighteenth century. Otherwise we are playing with con-cepts which have no sound foundation in our current, fuller knowledge of the past.

Within the medieval period itself it has become fashionable to posit dividing lines in the eighth century and in the eleventh. The first of these historical periodiza-tions marks the First Europe, when the leaders of European society, particularly the papacy and the Carolingian dynasty, turn away from the Mediterranean world and, as the centres of civilization move inland to the Rhine valley and northern France, try to work out their own destiny as a distinct civilization separate from Byzantium and Islam. The mid-eleventh century is held to be the beginning of the High Middle Ages because we can find the first successful attempts at centralized royal government, the rise of an urban economy, and the beginnings of a vibrant creative intellectual life. The First Europe of the eighth century has been widely held to be dependent on economic and social change. As seen by Henri Pirenne this change came from without under the impact of the expansion of Islam on the western economy, cutting the Europeans off from the Mediterranean, now become a Moslem lake, and driving them back on their own resources.[3] As Pirenne's thesis has been slowly undermined by detailed research, historians like Lynn White have pointed to technological changes inside Europe as a starting point for social and cultural achievement.[4] It is significant that Professor White should have developed his thesis of the cataclysmic effect of the introduction of the stirrup and horseshoe and horse collar while he was the president of a women's college in California. If the culture and society of California are based on the automobile, then assuredly Carolingian civilization was the consequence of horsepower. The emergence of high medieval civilization in the mid-eleventh century has similarly been explained by economic and technological determinism: the rise of urban economies, the opening of European trade in the Mediterranean, the great boom in European population, and the more extensive use made of wind and water power.

That both economic and technological factors were important in the develop-ment of Carolingian and high medieval civilization cannot be gainsaid. But it is certainly worth questioning whether these factors were the starting point of historical change. How are we to account for the new optimism, energy, and determination which led the leaders of society in both the eighth and the eleventh centuries to want to create a better world, so that eventually they took advantage of material tools and economic institutions? It seems to me that the will to create a better society which makes the later eighth and the later eleventh centuries stand out in medieval history has its point of origin in fundamental shifts in religious life. The success of the missionary work of St. Boniface and his disciples in the mid-eighth century gave encouragement to kings and popes to reorganize society so as to bring their world closer to the ideal of a Christian community. Similarly the fulfil-ment of the Christianization of Europe in the eleventh century, marked by the appearance of a popular piety among the masses for the first time, inspired the papacy and various kings and dukes in different ways to perfect Christian society and realize something on earth which approximated the heavenly community.

What I am suggesting is that it was profound feelings about the nature of a Christian society rather than horseshoes and windmills which in both the eighth and eleventh centuries impelled men who held power and exercised leadership to attempt social melioration and political reorganization. The eighth century is distinguished from the previous three hundred years by an optimistic spirit inclined towards new forms of political and social organization; the late eleventh century is marked by an almost hysterical perfectionist view aimed, as Gerd Tellenbach has said, at setting up a right order in the world,[5] and this right ordering is manifested not only in the Gregorian reform but also in the Anglo-Norman monarchy and the Italian communes. These profound shifts in moral and emotional attitudes, once they had driven the leaders of society towards their progressive system-buildings, inevitably led men to make use of and improve upon their economic and technological resources. But if we are looking for the starting point of a new historical era in the eighth and eleventh centuries, I think we will be on surest ground when we examine the impact of missionary endeavours in the first instance and the impact of popular piety in the later one.

Periodization is the first fundamental historical category appearing in both medieval historical writing and in modern interpretations of medieval history which should be subject to a most careful re-evaluation. The second category worthy of such consideration is the treatment of personality. We have seen that Collingwood was somewhat in error when he said that the medieval Christian historians escaped from Graeco-Roman typology. The early medieval historians merely changed their typological criteria. Instead of the spirit of Rome, it was God's providence which controlled history. Instead of the good citizen, we now find the monastic saint, and the figures of Just King and Tyrant are now decided by the extent of a ruler's devotion to the Church. All medieval historical writing before the eleventh century is encased in this typological substantialism. Occasionally a recognizably real person, not an ideal type, will appear in the accounts of early medieval writers, often in a paradoxical way. Gregory of Tours presents Clovis as an ideal king but also as a savage. Einhard depicts Charlemagne as the ideal Christian emperor but also as a warlord who seems to relish bloodshed and as a cruel father who treats his daughters in an oppressive manner. This momentary departure from typological history is not the consequence of a change in basic assumptions but simply happens because the author's execution of idealized history breaks down in the face of his eagerness to tell a good story.

The medieval discovery of personality took place in the late eleventh and early twelfth centuries, as R. W. Southern's brilliant studies have made clear.[6] Individual qualities in human beings came to be respected and valued and to be written about in a careful and trenchant way. This discovery of personality is part of the great romantic movement of the eleventh and twelfth centuries, a movement so far-reaching in religion, social life, and literary imagination that its origins, its nature, and its consequences are not yet clearly known. Only the vague outline of this great upheaval in the way in which humanity thinks about itself and the world has in recent years come to be appreciated. We can see the new perception of personality coming into the work of the Anglo-Norman historians and also some writers of northern France and Italy in the late eleventh century. In Abelard's *History of*

My Calamities, we have a programmatic declaration of the new attitude in its most extreme form: Abelard wants to present himself to the world as a singular person with qualities whose combination makes him different from any one of his contemporaries and who fits into no conceivable stereotype of churchman or scholar.

Abelard's extreme anti-typological attitudes, the parallel and corollary of his questioning of Platonic philosophy, had great influence, but this does not mean that typology disappeared from medieval historical writings. I doubt, in fact, that typology can disappear from history, although for a biographer typology merely stands in the way of reconstructing a singular individual. Here lies the difference between history and biography. To the biographer the social and physical environments are simply the background for the actions of an individual, which are the important thing. The biographer wants to tell us how a certain individual came to terms with his environment, and these terms will be identical in no two people. The historian cannot accept the biographer's complete obliteration of typology. He understands that every personality is singular and unique, but he wants to find certain general common qualities which will appear in any group of men in a given situation. Without destroying consciousness of individual personality, the historian wants to find common qualities in men by which they will act in a similar manner in the same kind of environmental situation. The historian's task is therefore more difficult than that of a biographer. The biographer can concentrate on personality, while the historian always struggles to achieve a balance between general and individual traits.

This is a very hard thing to do well. Yet we find that in the second half of the twelfth century and during most of the thirteenth it is accomplished with a remarkable degree of skill. It is not sufficiently recognized that there were far more good historians writing in Europe between about 1100 and 1270 than in the whole Graeco-Roman era. Otto of Freising's account of Frederick Barbarossa is a very complex and valuable study of a great man. Otto tries to see Barbarossa both as an ideal emperor and saviour of society and as a unique person with a singular combination of talents and ambitions. Jocelyn of Brakelond's portrait of Abbot Samson is even more successful. Samson appears as a well-meaning, intelligent, but unintellectual organization man caught in a conflict between traditional ideals and the heavy and cruel burdens of office in a large corporation. He does as best he can, but inevitably he does not do well enough; he serves his office but not his calling. In Joinville's biography of St. Louis we find ourselves in the stylized microcosmic world of high and late medieval courtly life where the small ambitious merits and foibles of kings are immediately magnified in catastrophic proportion so as to affect the welfare of whole societies. In Matthew Paris's account of the struggle between the king and barons in thirteenth-century England, the leaders on both sides of the conflict have recognizable, distinctive human qualities, but already we notice the coming in of a new political typology which will by the seventeenth century evolve into the Whig view of history.

Twentieth-century historians of medieval Europe have been singularly weak and inept in dealing with personality. It is because they have generally failed to portray the leaders of medieval society as complex, singular, real people that medieval history has been so meaningless for the general reader. It must be recognized that the portrayal of personality in medieval history is a very difficult undertaking and a much harder task than confronts the historians dealing with modern people. It is unlikely that we shall ever be able to reconstruct the personalities of even the leaders of European society before the eleventh century. We are blocked by the typological abstractions which condition the contemporary accounts. Nor do we have before 1050, except in a very few instances, the personal letters which allow us to go beyond the typology of early medieval biographers. But with the new regard for personality that emerges in medieval biographical writing in the later eleventh century and with the vast amount of documentary sources, including contempo, rary correspondence, the historian of the high and late Middle Ages can, if he takes pains, make at least the leaders of European society—the kings and popes, the great nobles and bishops, and some of the outstanding scholars and popular religious leaders—live in our imagination as singular, distinct persons.

This is worth doing not only because it satisfies the historian's aim to describe the way it was, and not only because it makes medieval history more compre, hensible to the general reader, but also because the reconstruction of personality often illuminates critical turning points in medieval political, social, and intel, lectual history. Thus, for example, we are able to understand what happened to the Angevin monarchy in the early thirteenth century because the patient research and careful exposition in Sidney Painter's study at last has allowed us to see King John as a human being rather than as the archetype of tyrant, as he was portrayed by contemporary monastic writers who detested his taxation policies.[7] King John we find to be a not very pleasant or likeable person, but at least he is understandable to us. An extremely ambitious and authoritarian disposition, which allowed him to be in many ways an effective administrator, was vitiated in John's case by ob, vious mental illness. He was not only an unrestrained lecher but also a paranoiac, so that he denounced some of his tenants-in-chief as traitors and thereby forced these nobles to become his enemies. He also suffered from what we would call manic-depressive tendencies; at critical moments in his career he would go into a deep funk and become completely unable to function. Under these circumstances, it is not hard to see how John was beaten by both the king of France and a faction of the English barons, with enormous consequences for the history of the medieval English monarchy.

In a similar way, our understanding of the intellectual and religious history of the fourteenth century has been illuminated by K. B. McFarlane's biography of John Wyclif.[8] Wyclif's heretical pronouncements, which historians have so long considered from the point of view of abstract theological and political controversy, are shown to have some foundation in Wyclif's own personality. Wyclif the great heretic becomes a more plausible person to us when McFarlane shows that he was an insatiably unhappy man, a disgruntled academic who believed, rightly or wrongly, that he had not received sufficient recognition by his university. Wyclif therefore appears more human and at the same time less noble to us. This may be disturbing to those who wish to view him only as the idealistic forerunner of Protestantism, but when we can see him the way his colleagues at Oxford saw him, he becomes more credible and in a paradoxical way more sympathetic in our eyes. We know from the experience of our own era how often great movements arise from the delusions of brilliant but disordered minds, and if McFarlane's view of Wyclif is right, we would place Wyclif within this historical category.

Valuable studies of medieval personalities have rarely been made, not because of the lack of material nor even because of the difficulty of attack, but because nearly all the prevailing schools of medieval history in the twentieth century have devoted themselves to the study of ideology or institutions and have shown very little interest in personality. The great German school of *Ideengeschichte,* led by P. E. Schramm, Carl Erdmann, and Gerd Tellenbach, which has produced at least half of the best books on medieval history in this century, has tended to see indi-vidual people only as the bearers of great ideas about Church and kingship.[9] The Anglo-American school of political institutions has devoted itself to assessing the consequences of men's actions as they become congealed in administrative and legal documents but has shown very little inclination to reconstruct the aims, delusions, dreams, hopes, and fears which went into the making of these institu-tions.[10] While the Anglo-American institutional school has in effect given us a view of medieval civilization largely through the eyes of medieval lawyers, its members have not even attempted to study in any detail the personality of the medieval lawyer. If they did so, they might be led to question some of their facile conclusions about feudalism and representative institutions. The founder of the French social-economic-institutional school, Marc Bloch, showed a remarkable sensitivity to the drama and tragedy of human life,[11] but his disciples seem to be merely devoted to abstract classification of the varieties of social classes. I am not sure how much better we understand the medieval baron or peasant and the peculiar tensions of their lives simply because we are informed that in a certain French county in 1200 there were ten varieties of barons and fifteen varieties of peasants. But if the historian classifies, presumably he no longer has to think very hard.

It is the English school of F. M. Powicke, M. D. Knowles, and R. W. Southern which has shown the greatest interest in the study of medieval personality. Powicke's biography of Henry III, the splendid portraits of medieval churchmen in Knowles's monastic history, and Southern's studies of the leaders of piety in the eleventh and twelfth centuries have brought us very close to the way certain kinds of medieval men felt and thought.[12] What we have in the work of these great scholars is, however, too much of a filtered picture in which the ugliness, the agonies, and the confusions of even the lives of religious leaders have been screened by a kind of mystical veil. Powicke's thirteenth-century England comes to us trailing clouds of utopian glory, harmony, and beauty which were so fixed in the romantic vision of the unity of medieval civilization propounded in the late nineteenth and early twentieth centuries. Knowles is a kind of monastic Whig who runs through the gallery of medieval English ecclesiastical leaders handing out grades according to a scale of abstract Benedictine values. Southern's St. Anselm appears in every way as a serenely beatific saint. But there was another St. Anselm deeply involved in the bitter struggles over Church-state relations and also serving to inspire not only the Virgin cult in England but also the rise of Judeophobia and the blood libels. No two people will describe a mutual friend or enemy they know well in exactly the same way; no two historians can view St. Bernard or Abelard, Frederick II of

13

Hohenstaufen or Philip the Fair without highlighting certain aspects of the personalities of these men at the expense of others. But it should serve as a counsel of perfection for the biographers of medieval people to see these men in the round, in the same way that the institutional historian tries to fathom all the implications of feudalism or Roman law or representative government.

The student of medieval personality should also attempt to work out other typologies than the Christian ones which medieval writers themselves employed. The hardworking abbots involved in a myriad of secular obligations do not measure up well against the standards of the Benedictine Rule, but viewed as social leaders engaged in political and economic organization they assume a very different significance. The clever and ambitious secular clerks who staffed the new royal bureaucracies in the twelfth century were in most instances hardhearted and selfish careerists who would receive a negative rating on the scale of sanctity, but comprehended as the pioneers in the difficult art of governmental rationalization they must be seen as perhaps the most progressive and socially useful single group in twelfthcentury society. What is needed is a new typology of twelfth and thirteenthcentury personality in which Christian devotion will be only one among several criteria.

The third historiographical category which conditions both medieval historical writing and the work of modern historians writing about the Middle Ages is causality. Historical causation was not a great problem for medieval writers—they believed that everything that happened in history was the direct consequence of divine providence, and furthermore it was easy for the historian to ascribe providential significance to any particular event. This attitude makes much medieval historical writing very dull reading today. We may or may not believe that everything in history is ultimately decided by God, but we look for more immediate factors within the framework of political, social, economic, and intellectual history to 'generate', 'induce', 'influence', or 'cause' important changes. It is a widespread belief that medieval writers obtained their view of causation from St. Augustine's philosophy, but this is palpably untrue. St. Augustine did indeed say that everything that happens in time is divinely ordained, but he did not believe that we could know the ultimate providential significance of such great events as the fall of the Roman Empire. Medieval historians took their idea of causation not from Augustine but from the first great Christian historian, Eusebius, who followed the Biblical writers and ultimately the Old Testament prophets in trying to ascribe providential significance to every historical event.

The modern approach to historical causation, which finds causal factors within society itself and is thereby concerned with causation at the middle distance irrespective of the unknowable providential significance, was clearly formulated in eighteenthcentury thought. Thus Gibbon is still worth reading because he tried to explain the phenomenon of the decline of the Roman Empire not as a scourge of God but as stemming from defects in the empire itself. He tried to account for historical change from the context of history itself and left God out of the picture. His general conclusion that the decline of the empire can be attributed to immoderate greatness makes sense to us, while the medieval providential interpretation of these events gives us no satisfaction.

Gibbon's distaste for Christian theology no doubt compelled him to account for the decline of the Roman world in terms of a purely secular causation. But the trend away from the notion of providential causation was well under way in seventeenth-century historiography, and it constitutes the most important theme in the development of historical thought since the thirteenth century. With their delight in portraying personalities the historians of twelfth- and thirteenth-century Europe had already softened the harsh and simple providentialism of early medieval historiography. Medieval historiography never abandoned its original eschato-logical assumptions, but in the actual historical writing of the high Middle Ages the emphasis placed on personality forced the providential framework somewhat into the background. This tendency became far more pronounced in the historical literature produced by the fifteenth- and sixteenth-century humanists. To the humanists the fortunes of great men became the primary, almost the exclusive concern of historical literature. Government, economy, and society became merely the painted flat-backdrop before which the great actors in the theatre of history strutted their ambitions and passions. The general destiny of mankind was ignored by humanist historiography; it was the experience of great men alone which was worthy of narration, and therefore the only thing that changed in the humanist historical literature was the triumph or fall of great men. Without explicitly denying God's providential direction of history, the humanists removed providential causation from historical literature in favour of concentrating on the apparent free acts of colossal personalities.

The weakness of Renaissance historiography was its reduction of political and social institutions to lifeless and insignificant scenery. This deficiency became painfully apparent in seventeenth-century England, when the nature of political and social institutions was the prime subject of discussion among educated people. The motives of great personalities were found to be inadequate as explanations of the conflicts associated with these institutions, and there was an awkward, fumb-ling, but nonetheless quite marked tendency towards explaining historical events in general by political and economic causes. Thus the historians of seventeenth- and eighteenth-century England had to look, like medieval writers, beyond the actions of a few eminent personalities in order to account for change in history. But instead of divine providence determining the destiny of mankind, the causal agencies were now found within the context of history itself. It may be said, there-fore, that Renaissance humanist thought, with its overemphasis on a theatrical-great-man approach to historiography, turned out to be a blind alley in the development of historical causal thinking. The modern view of historical causation, emerging slowly in the seventeenth century and achieving its first triumph in Gibbon's *Decline and Fall of the Roman Empire,* was a secularization of the medieval providential view.

Although medieval historians never escaped from their proclivity to explain events by providential causation, the modern idea of causality is first clearly presented, although with reference to science rather than history, by the Franciscan philosopher William of Occam in the early fourteenth century. His view was that God's majesty is so far beyond human reason that, although God determined nature, we cannot rationally explain nature by reference to God. The knowledge of causation in nature is derived from observation and rational thinking along such lines as the law of falling bodies. Modern science was founded on Occamism and the modern idea of history arose out of the same attitude to causation applied to the world of history by Gibbon and other eighteenth-century writers.

In recent years philosophers have devoted a great deal of effort to the epistemological foundation of the concept of historical causation. Although they have congratulated each other on their progress towards a formulation of the nature of historical knowledge, what they have come up with so far is of little help to the historian, because they have dealt with only the simplest kinds of historical predication. Historians cannot, however, wait for philosophers to tell them what they are doing; they are too busy doing it. We know for instance, that there were tremendous changes in European political, economic, social, intellectual, and spiritual life between 1050 and 1300. It is the historian's task to reach plausible general conclusions as to how and why these changes took place.

We will never be on sure ground in explaining the course of medieval historical change as long as we study political, economic, and intellectual developments in isolation from one another. The only satisfactory and convincing explanations of the how and why of historical change are those based on a total view of a whole society and culture, no matter how difficult this is to do well. No explanation of the emergence of the modern state in twelfth-century Europe is meaningful if it confines itself to consideration of political, administrative, and legal institutions. Twelfth-century people were far more concerned about the Virgin Mary than they were about the idea of sovereignty or even the improvement in public taxation. The new monarchy of the twelfth century arises within a society seething with emotional and eschatological religious feelings. It is the historian's task to find the link between these two aspects of the twelfth-century world and furthermore to connect them with the dominant trends in other aspects of life—the educational revolution which produced the university, the beginnings of urbanization, the polarization of landed society, and the emergence of a distinct aristocratic ethos.

A great failing among twentieth-century historians of medieval Europe has been a widespread reluctance to look at the society as a whole and to explain historical change in terms of the interaction of various aspects of human motivation and conditions. Medieval historians have been reluctant to admit that imagination can sometimes illuminate the nature of historical change far more effectively than years of research in the archives. The one book which makes any sense of the bizarre political history of France and England in the late fourteenth and fifteenth centuries is Johan Huizinga's *The Waning of the Middle Ages,* which is not based on research in either English or French archives but is a study of the style of life and art in the court of Burgundy during a couple of decades in the fifteenth century.[13] After reading Huizinga, the historian of medieval government can perceive what went wrong with the English and French monarchies in the later Middle Ages. The kings themselves and the royal families lost their earlier consciousness of their distinct role and function in society. They absorbed fully the now highly stylized and decadent aristocratic ethos, were completely caught up in the deadly games of aristocratic life, and abandoned their position as social leaders. The consideration of a few literary and artistic works by the mind of a genius has thus provided more insight into the political crisis of the late Middle Ages than all the laborious accounts of the Hundred Years' War and the Wars of the Roses.

Of all the great scholars who have written about medieval history since the later nineteenth century, perhaps only two, F. W. Maitland and Marc Bloch, have consciously attempted a total understanding of medieval society, and have perceived the interaction of all aspects of medieval life. Maitland's history of the making of the common law makes sense to us because he tried to understand medieval legal institutions as the outcome of the trials and ambitions and failures of real men in recognizable human situations.[14] We can believe that this was the way it was because we can find relevance in our own experience to the social pressures under which the kings and justices of medieval England had to operate in making their decisions about legal institutions. Similarly the barons of twelfth-century France become recognizable people when Bloch considers them not as political and legal abstractions but as a distinct group of men with a certain level of intelligence and education, conditioned by certain family and societal traditions. When Bloch takes as much pains to discuss medieval people's sense of time as to analyse manorial economic organization, we are able to comprehend feudal society as a variety of human experience and not merely as a jumble of legal formularies.[15]

Only this kind of total history, this view of medieval society and culture as a whole, will open the way to the more profound understanding of the causes of historical change in the medieval world. When we no longer violate the real nature of human experience by separating men and events into isolated political, economic, intellectual, and religious categories, we will begin to understand the fundamental problems of medieval civilization.

Notes

1. First published in London, 1946, but based on lectures written in 1936.
2. See in particular C. N. Cochrane, *Christianity and Classical Culture: A Study of Thought and Action from Augustus to Augustine* (London, 1944), pp. 456–516, and T. E. Mommsen, *Medieval and Renaissance Studies,* ed. E. F. Rice, Jr. (Ithaca, N.Y., 1959), pp. 265–348. Cf. Georges Florovsky, 'The Predicament of the Christian Historian', in *Religion and Culture: Essays in Honor of Paul Tillich,* ed. Walter Leibrecht (New York, 1959), pp. 140–66.

3. Henri Pirenne, *Economic and Social History of Medieval Europe,* trans. I. E. Clegg (New York, 1937), pp. 1–12.

4. Lynn White, Jr., *Medieval Technology and Social Change* (Oxford, 1962), pp. 28–38, 67–68, and 76–78.

5. Gerd Tellenbach, *Church, State and Christian Society at the Time of the Investiture Contest,* trans. R. F. Bennett (Oxford, 1948), pp. 126–61.

6. For example, *The Making of the Middle Ages* (New Haven, 1953), pp. 219–57.

7. Sidney Painter, *The Reign of King John* (Baltimore, 1949).

8. K. B. McFarlane, *John Wycliffe and the Beginnings of English Nonconformity* (London, 1952).

9. For example, P. E. Schramm, *A History of the English Coronation,* trans. L. G. Wickham Legg (Oxford, 1937), *Kaiser, Rom und Renovatio: Studien zur Geschichte des römischen Erneuerungsgedankens vom Ende des Karolingischen Reiches bis zum Investiturstreit* (London, 1929), and *Der König von Frankreich* (Weimar, 1939); Carl Erdmann, *Die Entstehung des Kreuzzugsgedankens* (Forschungen zur Kirchen-und Geistesgeschichte, 6; Stuttgart, 1935); Tellenbach, *Church, State and Christian Society,* and *Der römische und christliche Reichsgedanke in der Liturgie des frühen Mittelalters* (Sitzungsberichte der Heidel-berger Akademie der Wissenschaften. Philosophisch-Historische Klasse, 1934/1935; Heidelberg, 1934).

10. For example, C. H. Haskins, *Norman Institutions* (Harvard Historical Studies, 34; Cambridge, Mass., 1918); R. S. Hoyt, *The Royal Demesne in English Constitutional History* (Ithaca, N.Y., 1951); Sidney Painter, *Studies in the History of the English Feudal Barony* (Johns Hopkins Studies, 61; Baltimore, 1943); J. R. Strayer, *The Administration of Normandy under Saint Louis* (Cambridge, Mass., 1932), and 'Laicization of French and English Society in the Thirteenth Century', *Speculum,* 15 (1940): 76–86; C. H. Taylor, *Studies in Early French Taxation* (Cambridge, Mass., 1939).

11. For example, *Feudal Society,* trans. L. A. Manyon (Chicago, 1961), *French Rural History: An Essay on its Basic Characteristics,* trans. Janet Sondheimer (London, 1966), and *Mélanges historiques* (2 vols.; Paris, 1963).

12. F. M. Powicke, *King Henry III and the Lord Edward: The Community of the Realm in the thirteenth Century* (2 vols; Oxford, 1947); David Knowles, *The Monastic Order in England: A History of Its Development from the Times of St. Dunstan to the Fourth Lateran Council, 940–1216,* 2nd. ed. (Cambridge, 1963), and *Saints and Scholars: Twenty-Five Medieval Portraits* (Cambridge, 1962); R. W. Southern, 'Lanfranc and Berengar of Tours', *Studies in Medieval History Presented to Sir Frederick Maurice Powicke,* ed. R. W. Hunt et al. (Oxford, 1948), pp. 27–48, 'St. Anselm and Gilbert, Abbot of Westminster', *Medieval and Renaissance Studies,* 3 (1954): 78–115, *The Life of St. Anselm, Archbishop of Canterbury, by Eadmer,* ed. and trans. R. W. Southern (Edinburgh, 1962), and *St. Anselm and His Biographer* (Cambridge, 1963).

13. Johan Huizinga, *The Waning of the Middle Ages: A Study of the Forms of Life, Thought and Art in France and the Netherlands in the XIVth and XVth Centuries,* trans. F. Hopman (London, 1924).

14. F. W. Maitland, *The History of English Law before the Time of Edward I* (Cambridge, 1923). See also his *The Forms of Action at Common Law* (Cambridge, 1909), and Sir Frederick Pollock and F. W. Maitland, *The History of English Law* (2 vols.; Cambridge, 1898). On Maitland's method, see R. L. Schuyler, 'The Historical Spirit Incarnate: Frederick William Maitland', *American Historical Review,* 57 (1952): 303–22.

15. Marc Bloch, *Feudal Society,* pp. 72–75.

he study of
monastic history
today

Giles Constable

The serious study of monastic history is now about a century old. With a few honourable exceptions in the seventeenth and eighteenth centuries—principally Dugdale and his collaborators in England, and D'Achéry, Mabillon, Martène, and their learned colleagues in the Congregation of St. Maur—historians before the middle of the nineteenth century considered monasticism to be of interest only to monks, antiquarians, and religious controversialists.[1]

There is no reference whatsoever in Gibbon's *Decline and Fall* either to St. Benedict or to Cluny, and St. Bernard of Clairvaux appears purely as a figure in the political history of the twelfth century. Gibbon's only account of monasticism is contained in a few pages at the beginning of chapter thirty-seven. It does not go beyond the fifth century and dwells heavily on the monks' superstition, slave-like obedience, and unnatural sufferings and devotions, which must have destroyed, Gibbon said, 'the sensibility both of the mind and the body'. 'A cruel unfeeling temper has distinguished the monks of every age and country,' he wrote, 'their stern indifference . . . is inflamed by religious hatred; and their merciless zeal has strenuously administered the holy office of the Inquisition.'[2]

These sentiments were characteristic of enlightened opinion, Catholic as well as

Protestant, in the eighteenth and early nineteenth centuries; and the historians of that age naturally saw no purpose in studying such a depraved and useless institution or in discussing its history in works which were designed to promote progress, tolerance, and liberty. According to the Englishman Samuel Maitland writing in about 1840, 'For centuries the general notion in this country has been that a monastery naturally, almost necessarily, is a place dedicated to idleness, gluttony, lewdness, hypocrisy, political intrigue, fraud, treachery, and blood.'[3]

Nor has this attitude entirely vanished even in the twentieth century. The eminent historian of monasticism G. G. Coulton was described by Dom David Knowles as having 'very deeply engrained, two atavistic prejudices which ever since the days of Wyclif have possessed a large section of his countrymen, the one a fear and distrust of ecclesiastical potentates in general and of Romans in particular, the other a conviction that monasticism is an unnatural institution which of itself always leads inevitably to disaster.'[4] Few educated people today would go as far as this, but many still feel that monasticism is intrinsically unsocial, anti-humanistic, and morally cowardly.[5] Milton expressed this attitude in a passage of the *Areopagitica* which is still often applied to monasticism: 'I cannot praise a fugitive and cloister'd vertue, unexercis'd and unbreath'd, that never sallies out and sees her adversary . . . .'[6] More prosaically, Dr. Johnson once said to an abbess, 'Madam, you are here, not for the love of virtue, but the fear of vice.'[7]

The reaction against this point of view came in the first half of the nineteenth century, partly as a result of the Romantic movement, which looked with favour upon all aspects of the Middle Ages, including the peculiarly medieval institution of monasticism. The first signs of this more sympathetic attitude can be seen in literature and the arts, but it soon touched historical scholarship. In England one of the first writers to defend monasticism was the Samuel Maitland whom I have already quoted and who was the grandfather of the great legal historian F. W. Maitland. In a series of articles that appeared in 1844 as a book entitled *The Dark Ages*, Maitland argued that the Middle Ages are called dark not because they were morally dark but because they are obscure and hard for us to understand. 'There is no subject in the history of mankind,' he declared, 'which appears to me more interesting, or more worthy of investigation, than the actual state of the Christian church during the dark ages.'[8] Most of the book is in fact an account, which can still be read with profit, of the social and cultural services of monks to Western civilization.

At the same time a new sympathy and concern for monasticism appeared on the continent. The first scholarly biography of St. Benedict was written by Peter Lechner in 1857.[9] The following year H. d'Arbois de Jubainville published his pioneering *Études sur l'état intérieur des abbayes cisterciennes*, which was largely based on documents from Clairvaux in the library at Troyes, where D'Arbois de Jubainville was archivist. Franz Winter's long and valuable studies on the Cistercians and Premonstratensians in northwest Germany first appeared between 1865 and 1871. The first critical edition of the Rule of St. Benedict was published in 1880. Meanwhile in Paris, in 1860, the liberal Catholic publicist and politician Montalembert published the first volumes of *Les moines d'Occident depuis saint Benôit jusqu'à saint Bernard*, of which the final volumes appeared posthumously in 1877. This is overtly the work of an apologist. It is uncritical, unanalytical, and almost entirely dependent for factual material on the works of Mabillon. Montalembert was a leading Romantic author, however, and a member of the French Academy. His work is written in an exalted style and addressed to a wide audience. It was trans- lated at the time it appeared into English and other European languages; and its highly sympathetic, not to say laudatory, tone both reflected and shaped the favour- able attitude towards monasticism that increasingly existed in cultivated circles all over Europe in the middle and late nineteenth century.

Even the rationalist historian Lecky praised the ideal of renunciation and the civilizing and charitable work of the early monks in his influential *History of European Morals from Augustus to Charlemagne,* which came out in 1869, though he disliked their 'passive obedience' and 'servitude', which he considered incompatible with free political institutions. 'However advantageous the temporary pre-eminence of this moral type may have been,' he wrote, 'it was obviously unsuited for a later stage of civilization.'[10] The Protestant historians Harnack and Workman, whose works on monasticism are still widely read today, likewise recognized the intrinsic value of the monastic ideal as well as the importance of monks in the history of European civilization, although they were still inclined to condemn as basically un-Christian its rejection of human nature and the world.

Scholarly work in the twentieth century has tended to divide along the line of what may be called the external and internal histories of monasticism. Secular scholars in particular have concentrated on the contribution of monks to social, economic, intellectual, literary, artistic, and architectural history.[11] An important group of German and Austrian historians working early in the century studied in detail the constitutional position of the monasteries in the Empire and their relations with the local ecclesiastical and secular authorities and with the pope and emperor.[12] The importance of monasteries in the development of territorial princi- palities in Germany, especially in the twelfth century, was emphasized by Hirsch and more recently by Theodor Mayer in his book entitled *Fürsten und Staat.*[13] Some modern constitutional and institutional historians have likewise stressed the interest of monasteries as self-governing communities and of the grouping of monasteries into self-regulating associations, in which power flowed from below as well as from above. These scholars have not for the most part, however, been interested in monasticism itself. There has indeed been a marked tendency to regard these external influences as incidental to the history of the monks themselves, who had no direct concern for the world outside their monasteries.[14]

The internal history of monasticism, which deals both with the organization of monastic life and with monastic spirituality, has not attracted the attention of many secular scholars. The authorities whose names come first to mind are all monks: Dom J.-M. Besse, who founded in 1905 the *Archives de la France monastique* and re-edited the great repertory of French monasteries compiled by Dom Beaunier in the eighteenth century; Dom Ursmer Berlière, whose *L'ordre monastique des origines au XIIe siècle* (first ed., 1912; third, 1924) is still the best brief history of Western monasticism; Dom Cuthbert Butler, whose *Benedictine Monachism* (first ed., 1919; second, 1924) has deeply influenced the interpretation of monastic history; Dom André Wilmart, the great textual scholar and student of monastic spirituality; and, among contemporary scholars, Dom Philibert Schmitz, who completed his seven-volume history of the Benedictine order a few years before his death in 1963; Dom David Knowles, whose four-volume history of the monastic and religious orders in England (1940–1959) is a monument of English historical scholarship; Dom Jean Leclercq ('that indispensable "all-rounder"', as he was recently called by Knowles),[15] whose researches during the past twenty years have thrown light on almost every aspect of medieval monasticism and who is at present engaged in the gigantic task—one at which even Mabillon produced less than his best work—of preparing a new edition of the works of St. Bernard; and Dom Kassius Hallinger, who in his *Gorze-Kluny* (1950) reinterpreted the history of monasticism in the tenth and eleventh centuries and who is editing a much needed *Corpus* of Benedictine customaries, of which the first two volumes appeared in 1963.

The principal periodicals on monastic history are likewise all edited by monks: the *Revue bénédictine* of Maredsous; the *Revue Mabillon* of Ligugé; the *Studien und Mitteilungen zur Geschichte des Benediktiner-Ordens und seiner Zweige* (St. Boniface's abbey in Munich); *Benedictina* (St. Paul Outside the Walls, Rome); and the new *Studia monastica* of Montserrat.[16] To these must be added the journals devoted to the history of particular orders, such as the *Cistercienser-Chronik*, the *Collectanea ordinis Cisterciensium reformatorum*, *Cîteaux in de Nederlanden* (now called simply *Cîteaux*), and the *Analecta sacri ordinis Cisterciensis*, not to mention the numerous journals concerned with the history of canons, such as the *Analecta Praemonstratensia*, and of the Mendicant orders. Several of these periodicals date back to the end of the nineteenth century, and all of them now publish serious and scholarly articles. Their very existence is a sign, therefore, of the great interest in monastic history today as well as of the predominant part in its study played by monks.

G. G. Coulton is almost the only outstanding secular Protestant historian of monasticism in the twentieth century. He was in some ways, however, more of a critic than an historian. His *Five Centuries of Religion*, although undoubtedly a work of great learning, stresses almost exclusively the dark side of monastic decline in the late Middle Ages. Coulton delighted in finding errors in the works of those whom he regarded as uncritical apologists for monasticism, such as Montalembert and especially F. A. (later Cardinal) Gasquet. Yet no avowed apologist could have written warmer praise of St. Bernard and St. Francis than Coulton; and no reader of his pages on these two saints can accuse him of being without sympathy for medieval monasticism.[17] I believe that in fact Coulton had a deep admiration for the ideal of monasticism but abhorred 'the spotted actuality'. He would indeed have made a good monastic reformer himself, believing as he did, with puritanical zeal, that no shame should be concealed and no crime unpunished.

Coulton is therefore no exception to the general rule that monasticism has been principally studied by those who are personally involved in it and has been on the whole neglected by disinterested secular historians. This situation has been accepted and even applauded by scholars outside the field. Eileen Power, who herself wrote a book on *Medieval English Nunneries* before turning to economic history, said in a review of Knowles's *Monastic Order* that, 'It is completely objective, but gains enormously from the fact that the author knows monasticism from the inside and brings to his work a depth and delicacy of understanding that only such knowledge can give.'[18] I do not dispute this judgment, but by using the word 'only' Miss Power suggested that monks alone are really suited for the study of monastic history. This is a limitation that she certainly would not have applied to other fields of history, and it implies a continuation of the point of view that sets monasticism aside from the rest of history and regards it as a special preserve of historians who are also monks.

Yet monks, who obey a written code and whose lives are oriented in terms of a fixed ideal, are not likely to be able to study impartially the origins and development of that code and ideal.[19] Even the Maurist historians, though always careful and sober in their judgments, were far from impartial in their attitude towards ancient and medieval monasticism. They were themselves dedicated to an ideal of monastic regularity with great emphasis on austerity and interior piety.[20] At least one recent historian has warned against the danger of seeing all monastic history through the ascetic spectacles of monastic purists such as D'Achéry, Mabillon, and Martène.[21]

The history of Benedictine monasticism during the past century has also heavily influenced the interpretation of its earlier history. This is not the place to study in detail the development of modern monasticism, but since the middle of the nineteenth century Benedictine monachism has made a recovery that historians in the future will doubtless regard as of major historical significance.[22] Most modern European states were founded on aggressively secular principles, and throughout the nineteenth century monks were systematically suppressed all over Europe. The last expulsion of monks from France took place in 1901. It is not therefore surprising that authors like Maitland, Lecky, Harnack, and Workman wrote of monasticism as almost entirely a thing of the past and as belonging to a previous stage of European history. In fact, however, the number of monks and monasteries all over the Christian world has multiplied many times over in the past hundred years. I have no exact figures, but the rate of increase may well be comparable with that in England during the century following the Norman Conquest, when the total number of monks, nuns, and regular canons is said to have grown from just over a thousand to somewhere between eleven and twelve-and-a-half thousand.[23] I cannot speculate here on the reasons for these phenomenal increases, either in the twelfth century or today; but they are clearly facts of prime importance in the history of monasticism.

Needless to say, this modern expansion met with heavy opposition, even in Catholic countries and within the Catholic hierarchy. Not all prelates, either in the past or today, are sympathetic to monasticism. At a time when there is a shortage of clergy for pastoral and missionary work, bishops are not always pleased to see dedicated young men disappear behind the walls of monasteries. Bishops and priests who themselves have no vocation for the monastic life, furthermore, often share with laymen the view that monks are anti-social and unwilling to face the problems of Christian life in the world. The leaders of the modern monastic revival have had therefore to justify themselves in the eyes of both the laity and the secular clergy. They have had to reconstruct from the history of monasticism a way of life that is at the same time basically and traditionally monastic and yet morally and socially acceptable in the modern world. It is no accident that so many modern monastic leaders have also been prominent scholars. One thinks of Guéranger (the founder and first abbot of Solesmes) in France, of Herwegen (the abbot of Maria Laach) in Germany, and of Gasquet, Butler, and Chapman (respectively prior, abbot, and abbot of Downside) in England. I do not wish to suggest that the works of these and other monastic historians are consciously tendentious. They are indeed often based on serious research. But their writers can hardly be expected to separate their own deepest spiritual and practical concerns from the subjects about which they are writing.

The influence of these concerns, and the consequent correlation of the results of research to the needs of monasticism, can be seen in both general attitudes and specific findings. Gasquet's emphasis upon the independence and seclusion of the individual Benedictine abbey, and on the complete absence of any direct social aim or action, was clearly influenced by the pressing need of monks in late nineteenth-century England for freedom from interference, either by bishops or by the abbot-president of the English Benedictine Congregation, and from the necessity of performing pastoral work.[24] Butler's emphasis on the moderation of Benedictine monasticism, and on its rejection of extreme austerity, served to allay the anti-monastic prejudices of many of his countrymen.[25]

Many issues of contemporary monastic life are deeply rooted in the past. The modern movement towards simplifying the liturgy is to a great extent a reaction against the ritualism of the liturgical movement inspired by Guéranger and other nineteenth-century Benedictines who were themselves reacting against the religious subjectivism of the early modern period.[26] The hostility of many modern historians to the elaborate liturgy at Cluny in the tenth and eleventh centuries is thus a reflection of their desire to simplify the liturgy today.[27] Guéranger himself, referring to the ninth-century liturgist Amalarius of Metz, complained of 'the incorrigible mania of the French for ceaselessly revising the liturgy'.[28] The issues of monastic priesthood and of monastic performance of pastoral work were no less hotly debated in the twelfth century than they are now.[29] The modern emphasis on the role of the laity in the Church has sharpened many of the problems associated with the history of lay-brothers (*conversi*) and the impact of laymen on monasticism from the tenth to the twelfth centuries.[30] A like effect is seen in works on monastic stability, manual labour by monks, abbatial elections, and other topics which are important not only in the history of monasticism but also in the life of monks today.

The study of monastic history has thus been shaped by a variety of factors that have tended to isolate it from the rest of history and to give it a distinctive character of its own. Some historians have even questioned whether a real history of monasticism is possible. As Newman said in his essay on 'The Mission of St. Benedict', written in 1858, 'Monachism was one and the same everywhere, because it was a reaction from that secular life, which has everywhere the same structure and the same characteristics.'[31] Harnack likewise asked, 'Of what variety are the ideals of poverty, chastity, and resolute flight from the world capable?... Is not the renunciation of the world essentially the abnegation of all development and of all history?'[32] And Knowles recently said that the principal difficulty of all historians of monasticism is 'to avoid confusing two processes which in the actual stream of time are interwoven but not intermingled: the living, permanent, unchanging spiritual idea or force . . . and the outward, historical shapes and forms which the idea and the life take when working in a world which has its own myriad influences of life and growth.'³³

This concept of monasticism as an immutable ideal, itself without history but with changing historical manifestations, raises fundamental questions about the nature, origins, and development of monasticism—questions to which there are no clear and generally accepted answers. Harnack, for instance, traced the spirit of self-sacrifice and renunciation through the early monks, the Benedictines, the Mendicants, and finally the Jesuits, whom he considered to be, 'the last and authentic word of Western monasticism.'³⁴ Workman went yet further and found the 'lineal descendants' of monasticism in the Puritans and Methodists, who seemed to him to share with the monks and friars of the Middle Ages the spirit of discipline, anti-sacerdotalism, and service to God.³⁵ Other scholars have emphasized the element of separation from the world as the essence of monasticism.³⁶ Yet it has recently been suggested that the term *monachus* derives not from μóνος (*solitarius*), as has been generally believed since the fourth century, but from μονάς (*singularis*) and that the early monk was therefore characteristically not so much a solitary or hermit as a one-of-a-kind ascetic.³⁷

Many historians have tended to see monasticism in fundamentally negative terms, as a reaction against secular society and the Church. Montalembert dwelt heavily on the evils of the Church in the fourth century, and for Newman the 'one idea' and 'one purpose' of monks was to be quit of secular life.³⁸ Ladner in his recent book on *The Idea of Reform* stressed the importance of monks in 'the ever repeated efforts by man to reassert and augment values pre-existent in the spiritual-material compound of the world'.³⁹ Some Protestant writers have gone further and seen monasticism not only as an effort to recover lost spiritual values but also as a protest against the Church. Harnack and Workman thus saw monasticism as something outside and sometimes opposed to the sacramental-sacerdotal Church, a non-Christian, dualist child grafted onto the Church in the third and fourth centuries.⁴⁰ This point of view was developed by Troeltsch and Von Martin into the influential theory of monks as a revolutionary sect-type, world-denying in contrast to the world-ruling Church.⁴¹

Historians who are themselves monks naturally tend to emphasize positive factors in the monastic spirit and to see themselves not only as within the Church but also as the highest expression of its ideal of Christian life. For them, the desire to leave the world was a fulfilment of the commands of the Gospel rather than a rejection of secular life. Needless to say, these commands were often crudely interpreted, but the fundamental motive was love of God, not hate of the world, fear, penance, or prudence.⁴² This ideal is in appearance highly individualistic, and most monastic theorists, especially in the East, have stressed the search of monks to achieve individual perfection. A number of theorists in the nineteenth and twentieth centuries, however, have developed an ecclesiological view of monasticism as part of the Church and as the living expression of the presence and action of the Holy Spirit in the Church.⁴³ Peter Damiani in the eleventh century saw the individual monk as the *ecclesia minor,* the fulfilment of the mystic union of love.⁴⁴

27

This view has been transferred to monasticism as a whole, which is seen not as a group of individual pneumatics but as the work of the Holy Spirit in the Church. According to Odo Casel, who together with Guéranger, Maur Wolter (the founder of Beuron), and Herwegen was one of the principal exponents of this view, 'It is the mission of Christian monasticism to maintain and safeguard the pneuma‑tic aspect of the Church.'[45] This view naturally emphasizes the liturgical activity and redemptory expiation of the monk exercising himself in the Church through prayer and penance.[46]

These differing views of the nature of monasticism have influenced the interpreta‑tion of the origins of Christian monasticism. Abbot Herwegen, for example, 'considered the appearance of monasticism above all not as the result of certain historical conjunctures . . . but as a substantial part of the Church, as an essential manifestation of its body born of the Spirit of Christ.'[47] Blazovich looked upon monasticism as a special way of life within the Church resulting not from protest but from a process of differentiation based on the varieties of individual religious dispositions.[48] In contrast to the older views of monasticism as the result of pagan practices or examples and of secular influences on the Church,[49] modern research has stressed the great role played by the Bible, and especially by the example of the apostles, in the life and thought of the early monks.[50] 'At the beginning of monasti‑cism,' wrote Steidle, 'stood the exemplar of the Old Testament "men of God", of the prophets, the exemplar of the apostles of Christ, of the martyrs, and of the angels.'[51]

Throughout their history monks have looked back for their origins and ideals to the Gospel and above all to the lost paradise of the life of the apostles in Jerusalem. There is a strong element in the monastic ideal of what Bainton has called 'Christian primitivism',[52] a wistful looking‑back to a golden age of the early Church, 'poor, simple, and penitential', as it was described by McDonnell, 'with interests and activities restricted to the spiritual domain'.[53] Cassian, for instance, maintained that monastic life was born in the earliest days of the Church and prolonged the *vita apostolica* over the centuries.[54] According to this view, masses of nominal Christians joined the Church in the fourth century as a result of its worldly success. This view of monastic history has been supported ever since the days of the historian Eusebius by the references in the works of Philo to the obscure community of Jewish ascetics in Egypt known as Therapeutae; and recently it has been sup‑ported by references in the Dead Sea scrolls to ascetic groups of the New Testament period, who may be antecedents of Christian monks.[55] There is no positive evidence to confirm this view, however; and for the time being Christian monasti‑cism must be viewed as having arisen in Egypt in the third and fourth centuries.

The development of monasticism has often been explained by metaphors. Individual monasteries in the Middle Ages were described as a ship, a city, Jerusalem, an earthly paradise, and by other images commonly applied to the Church as a whole.[56] Philip of Harvengt in the twelfth century compared the con‑temporary revival of monasticism, all in a single paragraph, to the coming of spring after winter, the fructification of a tree, the kindling of a furnace, the revival of a dead body, the stoking of a fire, and the manufacture of an artifact.[57] Newman compared the 'outward circumstances' of monasticism to 'some great natural growth' shaping itself to events 'from an irrepressible fulness of life within'; Workman saw it as a sea ebbing and flowing eternally around the unchanging rock of its ideals; and Butler at one point spoke of cycles within the growth of monasticism and of a smouldering old fire bursting into flame and reasserting itself within the soul of the monastic body corporate.[58] Almost all monastic historians make use of some mechanistic or naturalistic metaphors and of cycles of decline and reform.

Metaphors are doubtless useful in the writing of history, but they tend to short-cut, not to say short-circuit, the task of historical analysis. They are a kind of historical pathetic fallacy by which life, feeling, and behaviour are attributed to institutions that in fact have no life of their own. Monasticism is not a fire, a sea, a tree, or any kind of living body, nor is it a self-contained idea or entity that includes within itself its own development and means of change. A monastery has no life apart from the lives of its monks, and many monks, even in the Middle Ages, were raised in the secular world and turned to monasticism as a result of their experiences there. Monasteries are thus a part of, and essentially related to, the surrounding society, and the impetus to change comes from outside as well as inside their walls. I am therefore tempted to reverse the customary view that the ideals and motives of monks have remained one while their outer circumstances have changed, and to suggest instead that their inner life has changed while the institutional structure has remained remarkably stable. Benedict or Bernard, and perhaps also Pachomius and Basil, would recognize without too much difficulty the framework of monastic life today, but they would have very little in common with the monks. Indeed, the genius of Benedict's Rule seems to me to be precisely that its institutional frame has been able to contain the spiritual needs of very different periods.

Several scholars in recent years have stressed the need to study individuals as well as institutions in the history of monasticism;[59] and Paul Antin has coined the term 'monachology' to refer to the personal monastic view of individual monks as distinct from the institutional approach suggested by the term 'monachism'.[60] Monks make monasticism rather than monasticism making monks; and if the monastic institutions of a given period are not suited to the spirituality of that age, they will change, or even vanish, and new ones will be founded. There is an increasing willingness even in Benedictine circles to recognize what may be called the relativity of monasticism. According to Hilpisch, for instance, the balance of emphasis on renunciation (solitude), liturgy (prayer), and work (culture) in the history of Benedictine monasticism has varied and will continue to vary as a result of the influence of the 'Spirit of the Age' on the ideal of the Rule.[61] Leclercq in a recent article studied the 'elements of relativity' in the practice and theory of the Church, with particular regard to the priesthood of monks.[62] And the sociologist Blazovich asserted that, 'The distinction of what is essential and what is time-conditioned in the Rule is a task set to every generation, including today's.'[63]

Monasticism must therefore be studied from 'outside' as well as 'inside', and there is a real need for a sociological and comparative approach to its history. Some beginnings have been made towards the study of what may be called monastic ecology: the mutual relations between monasteries and their environment.[64] But this must be broadened into a consideration of the relation of monks to society not only in western Europe but in all countries where monastic institutions occur. Christian Courtois pointed out that the organization and success of monasticism in Gaul in the late fourth and early fifth centuries must be studied in social terms.[65] More generally, it is impossible to understand the different concepts and forms of monasticism in the Christian East and West without taking into consideration the differences in culture and society.

This broader and more personal approach to the history of monasticism has tended to break down the dichotomies of eremitism and cenobitism, action and contemplation, and wandering and stability, in terms of which the development of monastic institutions has often been explained. The strict distinction between eremitism and cenobitism, that is, of monks living in solitude from those in a community, and the accompanying view that cenobitism developed after and out of eremitism are important parts of the 'new look' of monasticism in the twentieth century, because almost all the extravagant features of monastic life and extreme examples of anti-social behaviour are associated with eremitism. The 'natural development' of monasticism has been depicted as from solitude to community life, where the monk, though cut off from the world, practises brotherly love within the monastery and thus sets before secular society an example of what Gasquet called 'Christian social sanctity'.[66] Almost all modern Benedictine commentators and historians, among whom Butler has been perhaps the most influential, have emphasized the community life and essential moderation of Benedictine monasticism in contrast to the earlier forms of monastic life. They have condemned eremitism, and the excesses believed to go with it, in terms worthy of an eighteenth-century rationalist and have branded as retrogressive any tendency for eremitism to emerge at the expense of the more advanced and socially acceptable form of cenobitism.[67]

The preference for cenobitism of many Western monastic historians is closely allied to their dislike of monasticism in the East, where monks have always tended to be more eremitical than in the West. Montalembert castigated the Eastern monks in a thoroughly unecumenical fashion for their decadence and lack of discipline. 'They ended up,' he wrote, 'like all the Eastern clergy, by becoming the slaves of Islam and accomplices in schism.'[68] Butler has almost nothing good to say about Eastern monks, and even Protestants like Harnack and Workman had no use for Orthodox monasticism. For Harnack, as for Butler, it remained in a stage of passive stagnation;[69] and Workman, while defending Eastern monks from the charge of extremism, none the less considered them 'amorphous' and 'prone to many of the diseases of hysterical subjectivism'.[70]

Recent research has shown that this view, even if not entirely without basis, needs to be greatly modified. Several scholars have demonstrated that the differences between the forms of monasticism in Egypt and the Near East in the fourth century were not of category but of degree. The great communities of Egyptian anchorites had some elements of common life, and there was no striking antagonism between adherents of the various forms of monastic life. Bacht has stressed the difficulty in finding any real line of demarcation between the ideals of Anthony and Pachomius, though he adheres to the view that cenobitism evolved out of eremitism.[71] Not all contemporaries welcomed this development, however, as

Vööbus has shown in his article on anti-cenobitic feeling among Syrian monks in the fourth and fifth centuries. 'The new forms were not satisfactory for the entire monastic movement,' he remarked.[72] There was thus a spectrum of forms of monastic life, ranging from complete solitude to strict common life, among which an individual could choose that which suited him best, rather than a rigid dichotomy between eremitism and cenobitism.

The study of both literary and archaeological sources in the past twenty years has also shown the importance of the co-existence of eremitism and cenobitism in the West and especially of an eremitical tradition *within* many cenobitic communities.[73] This usually took one of two forms: a monk might make long eremitical retreats between periods of life in a community or he might be a permanent recluse or anchorite and yet remain more or less attached to a monastery and under the control of its abbot. Scores of monasteries in the Middle Ages were surrounded by small hermitages whose inhabitants were associated with the community. There were of course many independent hermits, and not infrequently a group of hermits formed the historical basis for a cenobitical establishment. But it is clear that this was not part of an inevitable historical development from solitary to common life, since many monks left their monasteries, either temporarily or permanently, to live in solitude.

The situation in the West was not therefore entirely unlike that in the East. The difference again was of degree rather than of type. Jerome, Cassian, Benedict, Isidore of Seville, and other influential monastic theorists in the West were not opposed to hermits and anchorites.[74] St. Benedict's personal attitude towards eremitism is a matter of doubt, but the famous final chapter of the Rule suggests that he regarded cenobitical life as a preparation for a more perfect life in solitude.[75] Leclercq and others have emphasized that Benedict had no desire to break with the Eastern monastic tradition, and Rousseau referred to the Benedictine Rule as 'a Western adaptation of the old monasticism of the desert'.[76] In a recent article on *stabilitas loci* in Byzantine monasticism, Emil Herman has shown that in the East the technically illegal practice of monks leaving their monasteries without permission was sanctioned when their object was to live an eremitical life.[77] Thus the barriers between Eastern and Western monasticism are being broken down from both sides. No longer can the semi-eremitical and ascetic movements in Italy in the eleventh century—Camaldoli, Vallombrosa, Fonte Avellana—and north of the Alps at La Grande Chartreuse be regarded as reversions or the result of the re-introduction into the West of eremitical individualism and ascetic subjectivism from the East.[78] They re-emphasized elements that had always been present in the Western monastic tradition.

It is likewise a mistake to interpret monastic history in terms of a dichotomy between action and contemplation, either by identifying community life with action and solitude with contemplation or by presenting monasticism as essentially contemplative in contrast to the active life of men living in the world. In antiquity and the Middle Ages, action and contemplation were not divided in the way they often are today;[79] and the life of monks, though considered different from that of clerics and laymen, was not considered contemplative in the modern sense of the term.[80] Action and contemplation were considered complementary rather than mutually exclusive, and an active life of ascetic discipline and manual labour (not, of course, of secular activities or even of pastoral work in the world) was believed to be not only the preparation but also the indispensable basis for contemplation by monks. Even Cassian, who was almost alone among the early monastic theorists in equating action with cenobitism and contemplation with eremitism, insisted, following Evagrius, that contemplation depended on an 'active' conquest of vices.[81] For Gregory the Great and later for St. Bernard, the perfect life was a wedding of action and contemplation.[82] Aelred of Rievaulx saw the *vita actualis* or *activa* as a life of effort to conquer self-will and evil; it went hand in hand with a life of prayer and contemplation.[83] 'Certainly St. Aelred's monks could, in his own termino-logy,' wrote Squire, 'be accurately described as leading both the active and the contemplative lives, and it would seem that his view that action and contemplation are two activities of a single life was common teaching for his period and later.' The distinction between action and contemplation as applied to monasticism generally or to entire monastic communities is comparatively recent.[84]

The third cliché of monastic history is the dichotomy of stability and wandering. Nearly all early monastic legislators expressed their disapproval of monks who refused to stay in one place or obey a recognized superior;[85] and for many modern historians and commentators stability is the essence of Benedictine monasticism.[86] The fact is, however, that in both East and West many monks who were admired in their own time neither preached nor practised stability in the sense of remaining until death in a single monastery. They moved for many reasons: to escape the crowds attracted by their sanctity, to undertake pilgrimages and special missions, above all to seek a more austere life, either in another monastery or in solitude.[87] Leclercq in particular has investigated the concept of monastic peregrination in the sense not of pilgrimage but of ascetic exile.[88] The so-called missionary monks of the early Middle Ages were probably monks of this sort, who left their families and native land in search of penance, prayer, and martyrdom, and who kept moving precisely in order to avoid contracting ties with any one group or place. By wandering they constantly renewed and restored their separation from the world and maintained a *stabilitas in peregrinatione*. By the twelfth century, most monastic theorists opposed monastic peregrination, and the idea of stability in peregrina-tion was replaced by that of an interior peregrination, in which the emphasis was on leaving oneself rather than on leaving one's country. The great issue in the twelfth century was that of *transitus* from one monastery to another.[89] St. Bernard actually encouraged such moves when the second monastery was stricter than the first. Scholars have thus replaced the idea of stability of place with the more subjective concept of stability of order or profession[90] and have recognized that in practice there was a wider variety of legitimate forms of monastic life than the old idea of stability implied.

Among the most interesting of these various forms of religious life in the Middle Ages was that of the regular canons, whose importance has been shown by the works of Dickenson and Dereine.[91] Nothing is more difficult to define than a canon. Fundamentally they were ordained clerics organized into groups for the performance of the holy offices in cathedrals and other large churches. They might live separately, dividing the revenues of the church into individual prebends (in which case they were later known as secular canons); or they might live communally and according to a rule, hence the name of regular canons, whose way of life and spiritual ideals often resembled those of monks. A great deal of work still needs to be done on the history of regular canons in the early Middle Ages. They are frequently thought to have been of comparatively small importance in the period between the Carolingian Renaissance, when the rules for canons of Chrodegang of Metz and of Aix-la-Chapelle were compiled, and the Investiture Controversy, when the reformed papacy tried to enforce individual poverty on canons and the so-called Augustinian Rule, in various forms, was adopted by many groups of canons. In a recent article on the ideal of the *vita apostolica* among canons in the ninth, tenth, and eleventh centuries, however, Dereine has argued that this opinion is based on the denigration of the canons by monastic reformers of the period and that the canons in fact shared many ideals with the monks.[92] This view is strongly supported by Siegwart in his book on canons in the German-speaking areas of Switzerland, where the regular canons maintained a higher level of regularity, reforming activity, and spirituality than the monks.[93] He particularly stresses the close relations between monastic, canonical, and eremitical circles at this time and the number of monastic reformers who were trained by canons.[94] The same was true at Tours, where the famous old abbey of St. Martin became a house of canons early in the ninth century. Some of the canons, however, although living separately and supported by prebends, led lives of great austerity. The Blessed Hervé of Tours, for instance, who died in 1022, led a solitary life of silence and bodily mortification, though he was in touch with many of the monastic reformers of the day. His life is an example of what has been called the conpenetration of strict canonical and monastic ideals, which existed not only at this time but also in the twelfth century.[95]

From this evidence it is clear that monks in monasteries were not the only ones who withdrew from the world in the Middle Ages and that hermits, recluses, canons, lay brothers and lay men and women leading penitential lives, and wandering penitents, preachers, and pilgrims must be taken into consideration in a broad view of monasticism.[96] There was considerable variation in how the monastic ideal was expressed and carried out,[97] and an individual might during the course of his lifetime spend time not only in a community but also in a hermitage or as a canon, pilgrim, or penitent.

At the same time as the general concept of monastic history has broadened, many specific problems have been critically examined. I should like now to discuss three of these and to show their significance for the history of monasticism in the West.

The first is the problem of the Rule of St. Benedict, the *Regula Magistri,* and 'Benedictinism'. The *Regula Magistri* or Rule of the Master (so-named because the anonymous author is referred to simply as the Master) was universally regarded until the late 1930's as an expansion of the Rule of St. Benedict, written probably in the seventh century. In 1940, however, the revolutionary idea was proposed, and has gradually make headway in spite of the bitter opposition of conservative scholars, that the Rule of St. Benedict was written after, and to a great extent derived from, the *Regula Magistri.* During the past twenty-five years every possible type of scholarly technique and evidence, some of it highly specialized, has been brought to bear on the problem, and a vast number of different theories have been put forward; but no definite solution has been—or perhaps ever will be—found.[98] The whole issue was recently reviewed by Knowles, who concluded that: 'The thesis of the Master's priority may never be proved to demonstration, but it is hard to see that its opponents can ever regain the ground that they have lost in the past twenty-five years, and, unless some wholly unforeseeable discovery is made, the hypothesis that St. Benedict made extensive use of the previously existing Rule of the Master must remain as one enjoying a very high degree of probability.'[99]

From the point of view of later history, it does not perhaps matter very much whether or not St. Benedict copied from the *Regula Magistri*. For most of the Middle Ages his Rule enjoyed an absolute priority among monastic legislation in the West; and it is fair to say that the credit for this fact still belongs to Benedict, since what he excluded from the *Regula Magistri* is almost as important as what he included. His changes and additions bear without question the stamp of administrative genius. His Rule thus preserves its unique constitutional importance for the history of Western monasticism.

In other respects, however, the controversy has broad implications for the study of monastic history. The distinctiveness of St. Benedict as a spiritual master will never be seen in the same light as before. His monastic doctrine now appears as more dependent on the work of earlier theorists, especially in the East, and as marking far less sharp a break in monastic theory than was previously believed. Another blow has thus been dealt at the radical differentiation of Eastern and Western monasticism, and the way to a more ecumenical approach to monastic history has been opened.

Scholars can no longer concentrate so narrowly on the special character of Benedictinism and the historical importance of literal observance of the Benedictine Rule. According to Mabillon, indeed, the very term *Benedictinus* was not used before the fifteenth or sixteenth centuries.[100] Since then, as might be expected, the estimates of essential Benedictinism have varied according to the spiritual temper and monastic needs of the times. In the nineteenth century the main emphasis was on moderation—the *discretio* praised by Gregory the Great—and on the good nineteenth-century virtues of family life, work, obedience, and stability. Guéranger, for instance, laid great stress on the position of the abbot as the representative of God and centre of unity in the abbey and on stability, which he considered to be 'the entire Benedictine institution ... a revolution that saved the monastic order.'[101] The importance of the *opus Dei* in Benedict's Rule was also emphasized by the founders of the liturgical movement. More recently, Blazovich, following Gundlach, suggested that the essence of Benedictinism lay in its distinctive view of Christ;[102] and there has been a greater tendency to stress the subjective elements, such as solitude, in the Rule. As long as its origins and sources are a matter of doubt, however, it is hard to call any feature of the Rule uniquely Benedictine.

Almost since the day it was written, Benedict's Rule has required study and interpretation, owing both to obscurities and vaguenesses in its regulations and to changes in the meaning of terms. The term *conversatio morum*, for instance, is still the subject of dispute,[103] and the military expressions which have long given

Benedictine monasticism a somewhat martial tone probably in fact connoted service and obedience rather than warfare.[104] Yet more striking is the term *biblio-theca* in chapter forty-eight, which has been taken since at least the eighth century to mean 'library' but which very likely in fact meant the Bible: Benedict wanted his monks to read books from the Bible, not from the library, during Lent.[105] The age-old disputes over whether Benedictines were allowed to eat the flesh of birds were the result of obscurities in chapters thirty-six and thirty-nine of the Rule.[106] Other prescriptions were perhaps intentionally vague. The obligation of the abbot to consult with the entire community before doing *aliqua praecipua* (chapter three)[107] and the instructions for selecting a new abbot (chapter sixty-four) clearly required interpretation and adjustment in individual cases. Grundmann has recently pointed out the error of reading modern legal and political attitudes into chapter sixty-four and proposed that Benedict had in mind not a single legally binding electoral procedure but a variety of ways of discovering the will of God in the selection of an abbot.[108]

This need to interpret Benedict's Rule, and the consequent development of Benedictine monasticism, was the major reason for the second controversial issue I wish to discuss: the influence of Benedict of Aniane, the great Carolingian monastic legislator, and the character of reformed monasticism in the tenth and eleventh centuries. The role of the second Benedict is almost as disputed as that of the first. A few historians have regarded his work as a legitimate extension of the aim and spirit of Benedict of Nursia.[109] According to Hilpisch, for example, Benedict of Aniane was 'the first Benedictine'; he ended the period of mixed monastic rules and really put the Benedictine Rule into effect.[110] Many scholars and commentators, however, have deplored the narrow view of monastic life, the tendency towards uniformity and centralization, and the prolongation of the liturgy found in the monastic legislation inspired by Benedict of Aniane. Gasquet considered it a 'cast-iron system of uniformity . . . an idea wholly alien to the most elementary conception of Benedictine life.'[111] Dekkers said that Benedict 'resolutely took the road to ritualism'.[112] And Butler and Schmitz called his view of monasticism more oriental than Benedictine.[113] The critics of Benedict of Aniane admit that some of his reforms were necessary and that not all of his measures were without precedent;[114] but he summed up and centralized the features of Benedictine monasticism that had changed since the death of the founder and handed it on to the future in a new form.

The most impressive examples of this new form of Benedictinism were found in some of the reform movements of the tenth century and above all at Cluny, which is considered the culmination of Benedict of Aniane's influence. To his ideals of uniformity, centralization, and concentration on the liturgy, Cluny added exemp-tion from episcopal authority; and almost since the date of its foundation it has been criticized for its alleged independence, rigidity, and neglect of manual and intellectual activities. The role of Cluny in the monastic world of the tenth and eleventh centuries has been for a long time a subject of scholarly dispute and has often been exaggerated, owing in part to the late medieval usage of loosely referring to all black Benedictine monks as Cluniacs, whether or not they were officially affiliated with Cluny. The title of Ernst Sackur's influential book *Die*

Cluniacenser, which appeared in 1892–1894, has also been misinterpreted, although Sackur himself recognized the importance of other centres of monastic reform, particularly of Gorze in Lorraine and east of the Rhine. The belief in the prepon, derance of Cluny was fully overthrown only in 1950, however, with the appearance of Kassius Hallinger's *Gorze–Kluny,* which is probably the single most important work on medieval monasticism to come out since the Second World War. Not all of Hallinger's points are new, and some of his distinctions are too rigid, but he has established beyond doubt the variety of movements of monastic reform in the tenth and eleventh centuries.[115] He studied in great detail the differences in monastic attitudes and observances and showed in particular that the influence of Gorze was predominant in the Empire before the second half of the eleventh century. The 'problem of Cluny' has thus been reduced in scope but increased in complexity. In recent years it has been re-examined by a number of scholars, especially in Germany, who have studied not only Cluny itself and its monastic rivals in the tenth century but also, following in Hallinger's footsteps, the modified 'neo-Cluniac' movements in the Empire in the late eleventh and twelfth centu, ries.[116]

It is impossible to discuss in detail here the many questions that have been raised concerning the monastic reforms of the tenth century. Their organization, economy, and attitudes towards episcopal authority, secular powers, intellectual activity, and the liturgy have all been investigated with great care, even though the results have not always been conclusive. There has been a tendency to draw sharp distinctions between the various movements. Hallinger especially identifies Cluny with liturgy and the Lorraine centres with intellectual activity, a dichotomy character, ized by Hilpisch as *Kultkloster* and *Kulturkloster.*[117] Leclercq, on the other hand, has defended Cluny against the charge of emphasizing ritual to the exclusion of learning and literary culture.[118] Some historians have stressed the feudal aspects of Cluniac organization,[119] while others have considered it un- or even anti-feudal.[120]

The most sharply disputed issue has been the attitude of Cluny towards the Investiture Controversy in the eleventh century and the efforts of the papacy to reform the Church and the world. The traditional view was that the Cluniacs, led by Gregory VII, inspired the reform movement and were the principal opponents of secular control over ecclesiastical affairs.[121] The reaction against this view started in the late nineteenth century with the works of Cauchie and Sackur and was summed up in the well-known book on the Investiture Controversy by Gerd Tellenbach, who maintained that Cluny was primarily concerned with the liturgy and with monastic reform and that it was essentially non-political, and certainly not anti-imperial, since it relied heavily on secular support for its program of strict monastic seclusion. The monks of Cluny, he insisted, were not interested in the reform either of the Church generally or of lay society.[122] The belief that Gregory VII was a Cluniac was described by Bennett in his translation of Tellenbach's book as an 'entirely discredited legend'.[123] This view was rapidly accepted by historians, [124] and the prevailing opinion today is that Cluny took a conservative stand in the Investiture Controversy and even favoured the imperialists, who were by no means as hostile to monastic reform as they were to the radical program of Gregory VII.[125] There are signs, however, of a return to a more moderate position.

Borino has shown, for instance, that Gregory VII almost certainly had some Cluniac experience;[126] and Hallinger and Lemarignier, and most recently Violante, Schieffer, and Hoffmann, have strongly argued that although Cluny may not itself have played a leading part in the Investiture Controversy it helped to lay the basis for the reform movement by its influence on lay piety, its promotion of the independence of monasteries and individual churches, and its support of papal power and ecclesiastical centralization.[127]

The question of medieval monastic reform has thus been expanded to include every feature of monastic life and to involve every aspect of the history of the age. Nowhere is this more true than in my third controversial problem: the origins and character of the Cistercian order and its relation on the one hand to Cluny and on the other to the new religious movements of the eleventh and twelfth centuries. This is a vast problem, and I can touch here only on some of the principal points.[128]

The differences between Cluny and Cîteaux have been very variously assessed by modern historians. Some have seen the controversy as a spiritual dichotomy: a contrast in the way of observing the Rule, either according to the letter or in the light of tradition, or a contrast of liberty and ritualism, asceticism and humanism, eremitism and cenobitism, or simply unworldliness and worldliness. For some the Cistercians restored the pure Benedictine ideal, while for others the Cluniacs lived more in accord with the spirit, if not the letter, of the Rule, whereas the Cistercians revived the harsher spirit of pre-Benedictine monasticism.[129] For Leclercq the crisis was primarily economic. 'The "crisis of cenobitism",' he wrote, 'was in reality a crisis of prosperity.'[130] Wealth did not necessarily bring laxity, but it brought involvement in worldly affairs, and the best antidotes were poverty and solitude. For Cantor, on the other hand, the Cistercian withdrawal from the world was the result of the failure of the Gregorians to reform secular society.[131] In contrast to these broad interpretations, several German historians have laid great stress on the specific differences in liturgy and monastic observances at Cluny and Cîteaux. These material differences, according to Hallinger, created the psychological tension between the two orders. It was a contrast of Old and New in which Cluny, which had been the 'New' of the tenth century, became the 'Old' of the twelfth.[132] Others have pointed out the differences in organization—the so-called feudalism of Cluny as contrasted with the federalism of Cîteaux—and in the position of abbot, who at Cluny was a king and at Cîteaux a father.[133] Ernst Werner saw the reform in Marxist terms as the expression of economic and social changes in the feudal order and of the hate of the lower classes for the aristocratic bishops and Cluniacs.[134] Grundmann long ago demonstrated that there is no evidence to support this view. The monks in the reformed monasteries were not drawn primarily from the lower classes, and they were certainly not inspired by a desire to break with the established social order.[135]

These differing interpretations clearly reflect some of the views of monastic history that I have already discussed, above all the concentration on the essence of Benedictinism and the dichotomy of eremitism (austerity) and cenobitism (moderation). These views have also influenced the study of early Cistercian history, and particularly the importance assigned to each of the first three abbots of Cîteaux, Robert, Alberic, and Stephen Harding. Angelo Manrique, the father of Cistercian historiography, compared the roles of these three to those of the Trinity: to Robert belonged the first creation, to Alberic the *passio,* and to Stephen Harding the great diffusion of the order.[136] For a long time the claims of Robert were neglected by scholars on account of his reputation for spiritual instability and eremitical subjecti‑ vism, but his role as true founder of the Cistercians has been strongly asserted by Lenssen and Lefèvre.[137] Müller and Ducourneau, on the other hand, maintained that Alberic was the guiding spirit and element of perseverance in the founda‑ tion.[138] More recently Duvernay has argued, from a careful comparison of the customs of Cîteaux with those of Vallombrosa, that Stephen Harding was the real organizer of Cistercian monasticism and brought it into the main stream of monastic development of the eleventh and twelfth centuries.[139] There is no final solution to these differences in interpretation, which depend largely upon the relative weight given to individualism and organization in the early years of Cîteaux.

A scholarly bombshell almost of the proportions of the *Regula Magistri* contro‑ versy was thrown into the camp of Cistercian research by the Belgian scholar J.‑A. Lefèvre, who published between 1954 and 1959 a series of articles throwing serious doubt on the dating of the *Carta caritatis, Exordium parvum,* and other documents upon which the early history of Cîteaux was almost entirely based.[140] A few questions had already been raised in the 1930's and 1940's by the textual discoveries of Hümpfner and Turk, but the essential validity of these documents was as previously undoubted as that of the Rule of St. Benedict.[141] There was a sharp reaction in Cistercian circles to Lefèvre's challenge, and the fighting still continues. The details are too technical to examine here, and the solution of the main issues will have to await a complete study of the manuscripts and a systematic survey of the problem by an impartial scholar. As in the *Regula Magistri* contro‑ versy, however, it appears that the conservatives have had to give ground, even if the challengers have not proved all their points; and most serious scholars today accept that the early documents of Cistercian history—and the institutions they describe—developed over a considerable period of time and do not reflect the nature of the order at its beginnings.

These researches, while showing how little is really known about the origins of Cîteaux, suggest that it was less well organized and less distinctive than the Cistercians wished to believe later, following the phenomenal success of their order in the first half of the twelfth century. The relative positions of the mother‑abbey and the chapter‑general in the government of the order changed during its early years; and the order gradually achieved a degree of emancipation from the diocesan bishops, in spite of its early opposition to exemption.[142] Certain recent authors have pointed out the dependence of the Cistercian liturgy and observances on previous Benedictine usages,[143] while others (such as Duvernay in his study of Cîteaux and Vallombrosa) have shown its close resemblance, and possible debt, to other contemporary centres of monastic reform. Thus the study of early Cistercian history has moved towards a greater emphasis on development, continuity, and interrelationship. Presse, Ducourneau, and Lenssen were among the first to see that Cîteaux was not a negative but a positive movement, not a rejection of contempo‑ rary monasticism but a search for primitive purity and basic monastic values.[144]

They exaggerated the originality and uniqueness of Cîteaux, however, and Canivez, Lefèvre, Dimier, and Van Damme have all recently stressed that Cîteaux was part of a broad movement of return to the sources (*ressourcement*) and that the ideals of eremitical solitude and primitive monastic purity were not restricted to the Cistercians at this time.[145]

The Cistercian reform must therefore be studied in relation to the whole monastic movement, which was itself an aspect of the spiritual upheaval of the eleventh and twelfth centuries. It included not only the foundation of countless new monasteries and orders but also lay movements of spirituality and heresy of which the consequences for the medieval Church and society only later became clear. Grundmann in his important book on religious movements in the Middle Ages, which came out in 1935, and more recently Chenu and Delaruelle have emphasized the connections between the spiritual, monastic, and heretical movements of the twelfth century and their association with the Mendicants, who thus appear not as a radically new departure but as the culmination of a basic shift in medieval spirituality of which the first signs can be found in the eleventh century.[146] Personally I believe (though not all scholars would agree with me on this point) that the Cistercians were part of this movement and that in their origins they looked not only backwards to the Benedictine past but also forwards to the Franciscans and Dominicans, in whom the ideal of the *vita apostolica* ultimately emerged as a life combining evangelical poverty, charitable love, and wandering proselytism in the world.

The development of this apostolic ideal over the centuries, and particularly in the twelfth century, is the subject of a small book by Vicaire entitled *L'imitation des apôtres*.[147] I have already discussed the importance of this ideal among the early monks, for whom it meant a common life of personal poverty and prayer. Down until the twelfth century, indeed, the life of the apostles in Jerusalem was interpreted in purely monastic terms, without any commitment to engage in proselytism.[148] It was then gradually reinterpreted, partly by the canons,[149] so as to include pastoral work, and finally emerged in the thirteenth century as the ideal of the Mendicants, who found in the apostolic life of the New Testament the example for their own communities of poor itinerant preachers.[150]

This was not a sudden transformation, and its history can be traced in the use of various monastic slogans: *ecclesiae primitivae forma,* which was first used in the middle of the eleventh century to mean a common life of personal poverty, like the *vita apostolica,* but was revised in the twelfth century to include preaching;[151] *pauperes Christi,* which was commonly applied to monks in the eleventh and twelfth centuries;[152] and *nudus nudum Christum sequi,* naked to follow the naked Christ, which was taken from Jerome and expressed the ideals of the twelfth-century reformers.[153] The use of these terms corresponded to changes in the spirituality of the age, to a turning away from a purely ascetic ideal of Christian perfection,[154] and to the new devotion to the humanity of Christ. The ideal of imitating the apostles and saints was replaced by the ideal of the imitation of Christ, which was epitomized by St. Francis and the early friars.

This is an ideal that both cut across and incorporated many of the traditional monastic values and combined, in a new synthesis, action and contemplation, stability and peregrination, eremitism (in a broad sense) and cenobitism—even, in a way, East and West: St. Francis is one of the few medieval Western saints who is honoured in the East. It thus developed into a new vision of a life which is in but not of this world and which is open to laymen as well as to clerics and monks.

The emergence of this new ideal marks the end of the period when monasticism was universally regarded as the highest ideal of Christian life. In the later Middle Ages, Benedictine monasticism lived on and still played an important historical role, but it lost its spiritual supremacy in the Christian world, and the monastic order gradually merged into the clerical order as its regular branch.[155] During the Benedictine centuries, however, monks were considered to be a separate and superior order of society, and their ideals and activities must be taken into consideration by any historian of the period.

Notes

The following abbreviations will be used in the notes: *Anal. SOC* = *Analecta sacri ordinis Cisterciensis* (now called *Analecta Cisterciensia*); *Coll. OCR* = *Collectanea ordinis Cisterciensium reformatorum; Rev. bén.* = *Revue bénédictine; Rev. d'hist. ecc.* = *Revue d'histoire ecclésiastique; Rev. Mab.* = *Revue Mabillon; SMGBOZ* = *Studien und Mitteilungen zur Geschichte des Benediktinerordens und seiner Zweige.*

1. On Dugdale and the beginnings of medieval historical scholarship in England, see David C. Douglas, *English Scholars, 1660–1730,* 2nd ed. (London, 1951). There are many works on the Maurists, none of them entirely satisfactory. The principal source is Edmond Martène, *Histoire de la Congrégation de Saint-Maur,* ed. G. Charvin (Archives de la France monastique, 31–35, 42–43, 46–48; Ligugé–Paris, 1928–54); see also the brief account by David Knowles, 'The Maurists' (1959), reprinted in *Great Historical Enterprises* (Edinburgh, 1963), pp. 33–62. Mabillon above all deserves to be known as the father of monastic history. His works constitute 'the most valuable contribution, beyond all comparison, ever made to monastic history', according to G. G. Coulton, *Five Centuries of Religion* (Cambridge, 1929 [2nd ed. of vol. 1]– 1950), 1: xxvi, who was not inclined to be over-indulgent to monastic authors. Jean Leclercq, 'Pour une histoire intégrale du monachisme', *Analecta monastica,* 6 (Studia Anselmiana, 50; Rome, 1962): 1–2, recently stressed again that almost all the primary sources for the study of Benedictine monasticism down to the twelfth century are contained in Mabillon's great collections.

2. Edward Gibbon, *History of the Decline and Fall of the Roman Empire,* ed. J. B. Bury (New York, 1914), 4: 80. On Gibbon and Eastern monasticism, see Deno J. Geanako-

plos, 'Edward Gibbon and Byzantine Ecclesiastical History', *Church History*, 35 (1966): 1–16, esp. 7 and 13–16.

3. S. R. Maitland, *The Dark Ages*, ed. Frederick Stokes (London, 1889), p. 7. Maitland had in mind particularly the works of Robertson, Milner, Warton, and lesser eighteenth-century writers. On literary attitudes towards monasticism, see Rudolf Schneider, *Der Mönch in der englischen Dichtung bis auf Lewis's 'Monk' 1795* (Palaestra, 155; Leipzig, 1928).

4. David Knowles, 'Cardinal Gasquet as an Historian' (1957), reprinted in *The Historian and Character and Other Essays* (Cambridge, 1963), p. 258.

5. On the difficulty of approaching monasticism without prejudice, especially for Protestants, see R. Newton Flew, *The Idea of Perfection in Christian Theology* (Oxford, 1934), p. 160; cf. also Owen Chadwick, *John Cassian* (Cambridge, 1950), p. 163, citing Luther's condemnation of Jerome and the apparent tendency of early monastic writers 'to push the Gospel aside'.

6. *The Works of John Milton* (New York, 1931–40), 4: 311.

7. James Boswell, *Life of Samuel Johnson*, ed. G. B. Hill (New York, 1891–1904), 2: 498.

8. S. R. Maitland, *Dark Ages*, p. 208.

9. See Stephan Hilpisch, 'St. Benedikt in der neueren Hagiographie', *SMGBOZ*, 61 (1947–48): 115, and 'Benediktinerhistoriker der neueren Zeit', *Beten und Arbeiten*, ed. Theodor Bogler (Liturgie und Mönchtum, 28; Maria Laach, 1961), pp. 16–17.

10. W. E. H. Lecky, *History of European Morals from Augustus to Charlemagne* (London, 1930), 2: 79.

11. Adolf Harnack, *Monasticism: Its Ideals and History and the Confessions of St. Augustine*, trans. E. E. Kellett and F. H. Marseille (London, 1901); Herbert Workman, *The Evolution of the Monastic Ideal* (London, 1913; reprinted with Introduction by David Knowles, Boston, 1962).

12. Georg Schreiber, *Kurie und Kloster im 12. Jahrhundert* (Kirchenrechtliche Abhandlungen, 65–68; Stuttgart, 1910); E. E. Stengel, *Die Immunität in Deutschland bis zum Ende des 11. Jahrhunderts*, vol. 1: *Diplomatik der deutschen Immunitäts-Privilegien vom 9. bis zum Ende des 11. Jahrhunderts* (Innsbruck, 1911); Albert Brackmann, *Die Kurie und die Salzburger Kirchenprovinz* (Studien und Vorarbeiten zur Germania Pontificia, 1; Berlin, 1912); Hans Hirsch, *Die Klosterimmunität seit dem Investiturstreit* (Weimar, 1913).

13. Hans Hirsch, *Die hohe Gerichtsbarkeit im deutschen Mittelalter* (Reichenberg, 1922; reprinted with Epilogue by Theodor Mayer, Graz-Cologne, 1958); Theodor Mayer, *Fürsten und Staat* (Weimar, 1950).

14. Cf. Gerd Tellenbach, *Church, State and Christian Society at the Time of the Investiture Contest*, trans. R. F. Bennett (Studies in Mediaeval History, 3; Oxford, 1940): p. 55; David Knowles, *The Monastic Order in England*, 2nd ed. (Cambridge, 1963), p. 4: 'No work done within it [the Benedictine abbey], whether manual, intellectual or charitable, is directed to an end outside its walls.'

15. David Knowles, in a short notice in *English Historical Review*, 79 (1964): 822.

16. Cf. Romuald Bauerreiss, 'Bibliographie der benediktinischen Zeitschriften und Schriftenreihen II (1949)', *SMGBOZ*, 62 (1950): 48–55.

17. They have been published separately under the title *Two Saints: St Bernard and St Francis* (The Cambridge Miscellany, 4; Cambridge, 1932).

18. In *The New Statesman and Nation* (Aug. 24, 1940), p. 190.

19. See the remarks on this topic (one of his favourites) by G. G. Coulton, *Five Centuries* (cited n. 1 above), 1: 2–3, 318, 439–41, etc.

20. Cf. René Hesbert in *Théologie de la vie monastique d'après quelques grands moines des*

époques moderne et contemporaine (Archives de la France monastique, 50 [= *Rev. Mab.*, 51: 2–3], Ligugé–Paris, 1961, cited hereafter as *Théologie*, II), pp. 109–56.

21. H. R. Philippeau, 'A propos du coutumier de Norwich', *Scriptorium*, 3 (1949): 295, who pointed out that the editors of many monastic customaries were inspired by ascetic rather than documentary purposes.

22. A good general account will be found in vol. 5 of Philibert Schmitz, *Histoire de l'Ordre de Saint Benoît* (Maredsous, 1948–56).

23. David Knowles and R. Neville Hadcock, *Medieval Religious Houses: England and Wales* (London–New York–Toronto, 1953), p. 364. This rate of increase of approximately tenfold has been accepted by subsequent scholars. Cf. also J. C. Russell, 'The Clerical Population of Medieval England', *Traditio*, 2 (1944): 177–212, who said that 'A wave of enthusiasm for monasticism followed the Conquest and set up a system which included probably twenty times as many members by 1300 as in 1066' (p. 212).

24. See in particular F. A. Gasquet's introduction to C. R. F. de Montalembert, *The Monks of the West from St. Benedict to St. Bernard* (London–New York, 1896), 1: xi–xiv. (This introduction, which is said to have been written for Gasquet by Edmund Bishop and Elphege Cody, had some influence on Leo XIII and others engaged in revising the English Benedictine constitutions: see Knowles, *Historian and Character*, p. 252.) Montalembert made the same point himself and stressed that the missionary and cultural work of monks was not part of their purpose or essence. Cf. *Moines d'Occident* (cited in text), 2: 70–71 and 6: 324.

25. Dom Cuthbert Butler, *Benedictine Monachism*, 2nd ed. (Cambridge, 1924), pp. 24–26.

26. Cf. the account and bibliography of the liturgical movement in F. L. Cross, ed., *The Oxford Dictionary of the Christian Church* (London–New York–Toronto, 1957), p. 815.

27. See Damasus Winzen, 'Guéranger and the Liturgical Movement—Comments on Bouyer's *Liturgical Piety*', *American Benedictine Review*, 6 (1955–56): 419–26. Eligius Dekkers, 'Were the Early Monks Liturgical?' *Coll. OCR*, 22 (1960): 120–37, argued that the early monks were not inclined towards the liturgy and showed 'no trace of that ritualistic mania which was so dear to certain monastic circles in the Middle Ages' (p. 137). In his article 'Moines et liturgie', *ibid.*, 329–40, Dekkers insisted that monastic liturgy should be sober, authentic, and 'interior'.

28. Prosper Guéranger, *Institutions liturgiques*, 2nd ed. (Paris–Brussels, 1878–85), 1: 246.

29. See Jacques Winandy, 'Les moines et le sacerdoce', *La vie spirituelle*, 80 (1949): 23–36; O. Rousseau, 'Sacerdoce et monachisme', *Études sur le sacrement de l'ordre* (Lex Orandi, 22; Paris, 1957), pp. 216–31; and Jean Leclercq, 'Le sacerdoce des moines', *Irénikon*, 36 (1963): 5–40, who urged that the priesthood of monks should be justified only by the liturgical needs of the community. These three articles, all by eminent scholars, are good examples of the different lessons for monks today found by different historians of monasticism. On monastic performance of pastoral work, see also Philip Hofmeister, 'Mönchtum und Seelsorge bis zum 13. Jahrhundert', *SMGBOZ*, 65 (1955): 209–73, and the short and sensible article of Marjorie Chibnall, 'Monks and Pastoral Work: A Problem in Anglo-Norman History', *Journal of Ecclesiastical History*, 18 (1967): 165–72.

30. See Kassius Hallinger, 'Ausdrucksformen des Umkehr-Gedankens: Zu den geistigen Grundlagen und den Entwicklungsphasen der Instituta Conversorum', *SMGBOZ*, 70 (1959): 169–81.

31. J. H. Newman, *Historical Sketches*, 2 (London, 1881): 373. Later in the essay he said that 'Its spirit indeed is ever one, but not its outward circumstances' (p. 388).

32. Harnack, *Monasticism*, p. 10.

33. Introduction of Workman, *Mon Ideal* (cited n. 11 above), p. 4.

34. Harnack, *Monasticism*, p. 110. See also David Knowles, *From Pachomius to Ignatius: A Study in the Constitutional History of the Religious Orders* (The Sarum Lectures, 1964–65; Oxford, 1966).

35. Workman, *Mon. Ideal*, p. 340.

36. See *La séparation du monde* (Paris, 1961), with essays on the subject by various authors.

37. Alfred Adam, 'Grundbegriffe des Mönchtums in sprachlicher Sicht', *Zeitschrift für Kirchengeschichte*, 65 (4th S., IV; 1953–54): 209–39; cf. also Jean Leclercq, *Études sur le vocabulaire monastique du moyen âge* (Studia Anselmiana, 48; Rome, 1961), pp. 7–38.

38. Newman, *Historical Sketches*, 2: 374.

39. Gerhart Ladner, *The Idea of Reform* (Cambridge, Mass., 1959), p. 35.

40. Harnack, *Monasticism*, pp. 45–46; Workman, *Mon. Ideal*, pp. 10–11, and 85, citing with approval the view of E. G. Smith, *Christian Monasticism* (London, 1892), p. 3, that monasticism was 'the inheritance of the Church, not its invention; not the offspring, but the adopted child'.

41. Cf. Augustin Blazovich, *Soziologie des Mönchtums und der Benediktinerregel* (Vienna, 1954), pp. 112–14.

42. See Jacques Winandy, 'L'idée de fuite du monde dans la tradition monastique', *Le message des moines à notre temps* (Paris, 1958), pp. 102–4, citing Pius XII's encyclical of 11 April 1958.

43. François Vandenbroucke, 'Théologie de la vie monastique: A propos d'une publication récente', *Studia monastica*, 4 (1962): 373–76.

44. Giovanni Miccoli, in *Théologie de la vie monastique* (Théologie: Études publiées sous la direction de la Faculté de Théologie S. J. de Lyon-Fourvière, 49; Paris, 1961, cited hereafter as *Théologie*, I), p. 466.

45. Cited by Burkhard Neunheuser in *Théologie*, II (cited n. 20 above), p. 258. On Casel's study of St. Benedict as a pneumatic, see Stephan Hilpisch, in *SMGBOZ*, 61: 125.

46. Vandenbroucke, in *Studia monastica*, 4: 384–85.

47. Emmanuel de Severus, in *Théologie*, II, p. 251.

48. Blazovich, *Soziologie*, p. 116.

49. Cf. Karl Heussi, *Der Ursprung des Mönchtums* (Tübingen, 1936), pp. 280–304.

50. See L. T. Lefort, reviewing Heussi, *Ursprung*, in *Rev. d'hist. ecc.*, 33 (1937): 345–46; Heinrich Bacht, in *Théologie*, I, pp. 42–43; and M.-H. Vicaire, *L'imitation des apôtres: Moines, chanoines, mendiants (IVe–XIIIe siècles)* (Paris, 1963), pp. 25–27. This view applies particularly to Pachomius and the early cenobites.

51. Basilius Steidle, '"Homo Dei Antonius": Zum Bild des "Mannes Gottes" im alten Mönchtum', *Antonius Magnus eremita, 356–1956* (Studia Anselmiana, 38; Rome, 1956), pp. 182–83. According to Steidle, Athanasius presented Anthony as an ideal monastic type, a 'man of God', of this sort.

52. Roland Bainton, 'Changing Ideas and Ideals in the Sixteenth Century' (1936), reprinted in his *Collected Papers in Church History*, I: *Early and Medieval Christianity* (Boston, 1962), p. 166. M.-H. Vicaire, *Imitation*, p. 23, called it 'a powerful nostalgia for the primitive Church'.

53. Ernest McDonnell, 'The *Vita Apostolica*: Diversity or Dissent', *Church History*, 24 (1955): 15; cf. Vicaire, *Imitation*, pp. 17–23.

54. Adalbert de Vogüé, in *Théologie*, I, pp. 220–21.

55. See Eusebius, *Ecclesiastical History*, ii, 17, for excerpts from Philo's writings on the Therapeutae, whom Eusebius regards as primitive Christian ascetics. On the Qumran

community as a precursor of Christian monasticism, cf. the remarks of Bo Reicke, 'Die Verfassung der Urgemeinde im Lichte jüdischer Dokumente', *Theologische Zeitschrift*, 10 (1954); 106–7.

56. Henri de Lubac, *Exégèse médiévale* (Théologie, 41; Paris, 1959), p. 576.

57. Cited by Coulton, *Five Centuries* (n. 1 above), 2: 509. Coulton used some good metaphors himself in 1: 315, and 2: 18.

58. Newman, *Historical Sketches*, 2: 388; Workman, *Mon. Ideal*, p. 224; Butler, *Ben. Monachism*, p. 214 (the whole page displays a remarkable luxuriance of metaphors).

59. Jean Leclercq, 'Pour une histoire humaine du monachisme au moyen âge', *Analecta monastica*, 4 (Studia Anselmiana, 41; Rome, 1957): 1–7, stressing the importance of the spirituality and psychology of individual monks.

60. Paul Antin, 'Une question de vocabulaire: monachisme, "monachologie"', *Rev. d'hist. ecc.*, 59 (1964): 89–90.

61. Stephan Hilpisch, 'Das benediktinisch-monastische Ideal im Wandel der Zeiten', *SMGBOZ*, 68 (1957): 73–85. St. Benedict intended such adjustments to the *Zeitideal*, according to Hilpisch (pp. 75–76), who considered that contemporary monasticism is oriented predominantly towards prayer but shows signs of an increasing emphasis on solitude.

62. Leclercq, in *Irénikon*, 36: 33.

63. Blazovich, *Soziologie* (cited n. 41 above), p. 48: 'Die Trennung des wesentlichen von dem Zeitbedingten in der Regel ist eine Aufgabe, die jeder Generation, also auch der heutigen, aufgegeben ist.'

64. See especially the works cited nn. 12–13 above.

65. Christian Courtois, 'L'évolution du monachisme en Gaule de St Martin à St Columban', *Il monachesimo nell'Alto Medioevo e la formazione della civiltà occidentale* (Settimane di studio del Centro italiano di studi sull'Alto Medioevo, 4; Spoleto, 1957), pp. 47–72. 'The epidemic of vocations' at this time, according to Courtois, was 'a social phenomenon' (p. 52). Cf. Friedrich Prinz, *Frühes Mönchtum im Frankenreich: Kultur und Gesellschaft in Gallien, den Rheinlanden und Bayern am Beispiel der monastischen Entwicklung (4. bis 8. Jahrhundert)* (Munich-Vienna, 1965).

66. F. A. Gasquet, Introduction to Montalembert, *Monks of the West*, 1: xiv.

67. Cf. Butler, *Ben. Monachism*, pp. 301–3.

68. Montalembert, *Moines d'Occident*, 1: 139.

69. Harnack, *Monasticism*, pp. 62 and 114–15.

70. Workman, *Mon. Ideal*, p. 134. The words quoted apply to early monasticism in the East and 'even in the West'.

71. Heinrich Bacht, 'Antonius und Pachomius: Von der Anachorese zum Cönobitentum', in *Antonius Magnus* (cited n. 51 above), pp. 66–107, esp. 100, 101 and 104 on Anthony and 106–7 on the debt of Pachomius to eremitism; cf. also S. G. A. Luff, 'Transition from Solitary to Cenobitic Life (c.250 to 400)', *The Irish Ecclesiastical Record*, 84 (1955): 164–84, who pointed out that even hermits recognized the dangers of complete solitude and that there was 'a frame of common life' at Nitria (p. 171).

72. Arthur Vööbus, 'Sur le développement de la phase cénobitique et la réaction dans l'ancien monachisme syriaque', *Recherches de science religieuse*, 47 (1959): 406.

73. See especially Jean Leclercq, 'Pierre le Vénérable et l'érémitisme clunisien', *Petrus Venerabilis, 1156–1956* (Studia Anselmiana, 40; Rome, 1956), pp. 99–120, and, more generally, *L'eremitismo in Occidente nei secoli XI e XII* (Pubblicazioni dell'Università cattolica del Sacro Cuore, 3rd S., 4; Milan, 1965).

74. Cf. Louis Gougaud, 'Les critiques formulées contre les premiers moines d'Occident', *Rev. Mab.*, 24 (1934): 151–52.

44

75. See Adrian Hastings, 'St. Benedict and the Eremitical Life', *Downside Review*, 68 (1950): 191–211, who concluded that, 'It appears plain that St Benedict recognized the superiority of the eremitical life, and most likely made provision at Monte Cassino for elder monks, suitably inclined, to become hermits near the oratory of St John' (p. 211). Cf. Adalbert de Vogüé, *La communauté et l'abbé dans la Règle de Saint Benoît* (Paris, 1961), pp. 47–77, and for other works on this subject, Gregorio Penco's references in C. Vagaggini, *Problemi e orientamenti di spiritualità monastica, biblica e liturgica* (Rome, 1961), p. 218.

76. Jean Leclercq, *L'amour des lettres et le désir de Dieu* (Paris, 1957), p. 87; Rousseau, in *Études* (cited n. 29 above), p. 218; De Vogüé, Cf. *Communauté*, passim.

77. Emil Herman, 'La "stabilitas loci" nel monachismo Bizantino', *Orientalia christiana periodica*, 21 (1955): 115–42.

78. Cf. Kassius Hallinger, 'Progressi e problemi della ricerca sulla riforma pregregoriana', in *Monachesimo* (cited n. 65 above), p. 263, who mentioned the reduced importance given to Eastern influences on these movements as a result of recent research.

79. See, among others Jean-Marie Leroux, in *Théologie*, I (cited n. 44 above), p. 183, who said of Chrysostom that 'La distinction entre action et contemplation lui est totalement étrangère.'

80. This difference can be clearly seen in the exegesis of Luke 10:38–42, which is today almost universally interpreted as indicating the superiority of contemplation over action. The Church Fathers, however, believed that the *optima pars* chosen by Mary rather than her busy sister Martha showed the superiority of theory to practice, of complete (pneumatic) Christians to simple (fleshly) Christians, or of the Church to the Synagogue: see D. A. Csányi, 'Optima pars: die Auslegungsgeschichte von Lk 10, 38–42 bei den Kirchenvätern der ersten vier Jahrhunderte', *Studia monastica*, 2 (1960): 75. For Theodore the Studite, according to Julien Leroy in *Théologie*, I, p. 425, 'le rôle de Marie n'est pas seulement d'écouter la parole de Dieu, c'est aussi et surtout la mettre en pratique, et chercher à "plaire à Dieu".'

81. M. Olphe-Galliard, 'Vie contemplative et vie active d'après Cassien', *Revue d'ascétique et de mystique*, 16 (1935): 252–88; Chadwick, *Cassian* (cited n. 5 above), p. 83; D. A. Csányi, in *Studia monastica*, 2: 77–78; Adalbert de Vogüé, in *Théologie*, I, 230: 'Vie "active" culminant dans une vie "contemplative", voilà donc ce qu'est la vie monastique. Est-il besoin de préciser que ces termes ont un sens fort différent de celui que nous leur donnons couramment? Dire que la vie monastique est "active", ce n'est pas la faire consister dans des œuvres de bienfaisance ou d'apostolat; c'est au contraire la définir comme une ascèse visant à la purification du sujet, en vue de la contemplation.'

82. See the chapters on these two saints in Cuthbert Butler, *Western Mysticism*, 2nd ed. (London, 1926).

83. Aelred Squire, 'Aelred of Rievaulx and the Monastic Tradition Concerning Action and Contemplation', *Downside Review*, 72 (1954): 297.

84. Ibid., 290.

85. Gougaud, in *Rev. Mab.*, 24: 151–52.

86. Cf. Guéranger, cited by Gabriel Le Maître in *Théologie*, II, p. 171; Butler, *Ben Monachism*, pp. 123–34; Philibert Schmitz, *Ordre* (cited n. 22 above), 1: 32.

87. Cf. Herman, in *Orientalia christ. period.*, 21: 127–38.

88. Jean Leclercq, 'Mönchtum und Peregrinatio im Frühmittelalter', *Römische Quartalschrift für christliche Altertumskunde und Kirchengeschichte*, 55 (1960): 212–25, and 'Monachisme et pérégrination du IXe au XIIe siècle', *Studia monastica*, 3 (1961): 33–52; see also his article in *Séparation* (cited n. 36 above), pp. 81–82. Cf. Hans von Campenhausen, *Die asketische Heimatlosigkeit im altkirchlichen und frühmittelalterlichen Mönchtum* (Sammlung gemeinverständlicher Vorträge und Schriften aus dem Gebiet der Theologie und Reli-

gionsgeschichte, 149; Tübingen, 1930) and Gerhart B. Ladner, 'Homo Viator: Medieval Ideas on Alienation and Order', Speculum, 42 (1967): 233–59.

89. See on this topic Kurt Fina, 'Anselm von Havelberg [II]', Analecta Praemonstratensia, 32 (1956): 208–26, and ' "Ovem suam requirere": Eine Studie zur Geschichte des Ordenswechsels im 12. Jahrhundert', Augustiniana, 7 (1957): 33–56.

90. Cf. Augustin Blazovich, Soziologie (cited n. 41 above), pp. 66–67, referring to the works of Brechter and Rothenhäusler. In a parallel fashion, monastic separation from the world has shifted from a physical to a spiritual concept, a separation of intention rather than one in the desert or the monastery: see Leclercq, in Irénikon, 36: 20.

91. J. C. Dickinson, The Origins of the Austin Canons and their Introduction into England (London, 1950); Charles Dereine, Les chanoines réguliers au diocèse de Liège avant saint Norbert (Académie royale de Belgique: Classe des lettres . . ., Mémoires in-8°, 47.1; Brussels, 1952), an article under 'Chanoines' in Dictionnaire d'histoire et de géographie ecclésiastiques, 12 (1953): cols. 353–405, and a number of important articles, of which the early ones are analysed by J.-F. Lemarignier, 'Spiritualité grégorienne et chanoines réguliers', Revue de l'histoire de l'Église de France, 35 (1949): 36–38.

92. Charles Dereine, 'La "vita apostolica" dans l'ordre canonial du IXe au XIe siècle', Rev. Mab., 51 (1961): 47–53.

93. Josef Siegwart, Die Chorherren- und Chorfrauengemeinschaften in der deutschsprachigen Schweiz vom 6. Jahrhundert bis 1160 (Studia Friburgensia, N.F., 30; Fribourg, 1962), Chap. 4.

94. Ibid., pp. 159–60, 225.

95. Guy Oury, 'L'idéal monastique dans la vie canoniale: Le bienheureux Hervé de Tours († 1022)', Rev. Mab., 52 (1962): 1–29.

96. The author of the twelfth-century Liber de diversis ordinibus et professionibus quae sunt in ecclesia (in Patrologia cursus completus, series latina, ed. J. P. Migne [Paris, 1844–64], 213: 814 and 830–31) distinguished three types each of monks and canons and stressed the similarities between the more austere types of both groups, who lived in solitude and worked with their hands; cf. on this treatise and generally on this subject, Dickinson, Canons, pp. 198–208, who emphasized that the differences between the regular and secular canons in the twelfth century were in many ways more striking than those between the regular canons and monks. Some of the monks maintained that the strict regular canons really were monks: see Fina, in Anal. Praem., 32: 204–5.

97. This variation is clearly shown by the twenty-six chapters in Théologie, I (cited n. 44 above), in spite of the recurrent stress on the obvious monastic virtues of renunciation, humility, and poverty.

98. See the bibliography (down to 1957) of nine books and a hundred and thirteen articles, by a total of fifty-three authors, compiled by Odo Zimmermann, 'An Unsolved Problem: The Rule of Saint Benedict and the Rule of the Master', American Benedictine Review, 10 (1959): 86–106.

99. David Knowles, Hist. Enterprises (cited n. 1 above), p. 195 and cf. David Knowles, 'Some Recent Work on Early Benedictine History', Studies in Church History, 1 (1964): 35–46.

100. Acta sanctorum O.S.B. (Venice, 1738): 6: 150, cited by Robert Gillet in Théologie, 1, p. 323.

101. Cited by Gabriel Le Maître in Théologie, II, p.171. Work and obedience were the basic principles of Benedictinism for Guéranger's friend Montalembert, Moines d'Occident, 2: 49.

102. Blazovich, Soziologie (cited n. 41 above), pp. 108–9 (and 104–11 generally on the problem of the 'key' to Benedictinism).

103. Cf. the opposing views of Odon Lottin, 'Le vœu de "conversatio morum" dans la Règle de saint Benoît' (1957), reprinted with additions in his *Études de morale, histoire et doctrine* (Gembloux, 1961), pp. 309–28, and Jacques Winandy, 'Conversatio morum', *Coll. OCR*, 22 (1960): 378–86.

104. E. Manning, 'La signification de *militare-militia-miles* dans la Règle de saint Benoît', *Rev. bén.*, 72 (1962): 135–38.

105. Anscari Mundò, ' "Bibliotheca": Bible et lecture du Carême d'après saint Benoît', *Rev. bén.*, 60 (1950): 65–92. This article has profound implications for the accepted view of Benedictine literary culture.

106. Cf. Paul Volk, 'Das Abstinenzindult von 1523 für die Benediktinerklöster der Mainz-Bamberger Provinz', *Rev. bén.*, 40 (1928): 334–36; Sister M. Alfred Schroll, *Benedictine Monasticism as Reflected in the Warnefrid-Hildemar Commentaries on the Rule* (New York, 1941), pp. 174–76; and Josef Semmler, ' "Volatilia": Zu den benediktinischen Consuetudines des 9. Jahrhunderts', *SMGBOZ*, 69 (1958): 163–76.

107. Stephan Hilpisch, 'Der Rat der Brüder in den Benediktinerklöstern des Mittelalters', *SMGBOZ*, 67 (1956): 221–36, discusses the pre-Benedictine history of this regulation and its development in the later Middle Ages from a doctrine of counsel to one of consent.

108. Herbert Grundmann, 'Pars quamvis parva: Zur Abtwahl nach Benedikts Regel', *Festschrift Percy Ernst Schramm* (Wiesbaden, 1964), I, 237–51. Cf. the reply and counterreply by Hallinger and Grundmann in *Zeitschrift für Kirchengeschichte*, 76 (1965): 233–45, and 77 (1966): 217–23.

109. See the examples cited by Philibert Schmitz, 'L'influence de saint Benoît d'Aniane dans l'histoire de l'ordre de saint-Benoît', in *Monachesimo* (cited n. 65 above), pp. 401–2. Cf. Kassius Hallinger, *Gorze-Kluny: Studien zu den monastischen Lebensformen und Gegensätzen im Hochmittelalter* (2 vols; Rome, 1950), pp. 803–18.

110. Hilpisch, in *SMGBOZ*, 68: 77.

111. Introduction to Montalembert, *Monks of the West*, I: xxv, xxvii; cf. Workman, *Mon. Ideal*, p. 227; Schmitz, in *Monachesimo*, pp. 408–9; Blazovich, *Soziologie*, p. 157.

112. Eligius Dekkers, in *Coll. OCR*, 22: 336 (Cf. also his other article, ibid., 137: see n. 27 above); cf. Butler, *Ben. Monachism*, pp. 295–96.

113. Ibid., p. 357 ('He had even a contempt of St Benedict's Rule as fit only for tiros and weaklings, and his desire was to revert to the severer rules of Basil and Pachomius.'); Shmitz, *Ordre* (cited n. 22 above), I: 108–9.

114. See Schroll, *Ben. Monasticism*, pp. 114–15, 118 and 156–57 (on liturgical additions), and Mundò's comments during discussion of Schmitz's paper (cited n. 109), in *Monachesimo*, pp. 543–46 (on the eating place of the abbot, monastic prisons, etc.).

115. See Hallinger's own résumé, seven years after the appearance of *Gorze-Kluny*, in *Monachesimo*, pp. 257–61. There are useful surveys of the issues raised by Hallinger, with some reservations, by Theodor Schieffer, 'Cluniazensische oder Gorzische Reformbewegung?' *Archiv für mittelrheinische Kirchengeschichte*, 4 (1952): 24–44, and by Hubert Dauphin, 'Monastic Reforms from the Tenth Century to the Twelfth', *Downside Review*, 70 (1952): 62–74. The sharpest disagreements with Hallinger have been expressed by Gerd Tellenbach and his pupils in *Neue Forschungen über Cluny und die Cluniacenser* (Freiburg-im-Br., 1959). In the preface to this volume (p. 6) Tellenbach said, 'The question is whether the pendulum in the history of learning has not now swung too far and whether in place of too great unities, as previously, the divisions are being seen too sharply.'

116. See, for instance, the works of Schieffer's students: Josef Semmler, *Die Klosterreform von Siegburg* (Bonn, 1959), and Hermann Jakobs, *Die Hirsauer: ihre Ausbreitung und Rechtsstellung im Zeitalter des Investiturstreits* (Cologne, 1961).

117. Hilpisch, in *SMGBOZ*, 68: 83; cf. Kassius Hallinger, 'Le climat spirituel des premiers temps de Cluny', *Rev. Mab.*, 46 (1956): 117–40 (a revised version of part II of an article first published in the *Deutsches Archiv*, 10).

118. Jean Leclercq, 'Cluny fut-il ennemi de la culture?', *Rev. Mab.*, 47 (1957): 172–82 and, most recently, 'Pour une histoire de la vie à Cluny', *Rev. d'hist. ecc.*, 57 (1962): 385–408.

119. Cf. Ursmer Berlière, *L'ordre monastique des origines au XIIᵉ siècle*, 3rd ed. (Maredsous, 1924), p. 218 ('L'"ordre" clunisien offrait un reflect de la féodalité.'), Wollasch and Mager in *Neue Forschungen*, and Ernst Werner, *Die gesellschaftlichen Grundlagen der Klosterreform im 11. Jahrhundert* (Berlin, 1953), who stressed the alliance of Cluny with the feudal aristocracy and its opposition to the anti-feudal heresies of the eleventh century. (See also the refutation by Kassius Hallinger, and rebuttal by Ernst Werner, in *Monachesimo*, pp. 272–89 and 474–78.

120. In addition to Kassius Hallinger, who considered Cluniac exemption to be anti-feudal as well as anti-episcopal, see J.-F. Lemarignier, 'Hiérarchie monastique et hiérarchie féodale', *Revue historique de droit français et étranger*, 4th S., 31 (1953): 171–74 and 'Structures monastiques et structures politiques dans la France de la fin du Xᵉ et des debuts du XIᵉ siècle', in *Monachesimo*, pp. 357–400, esp. 393–94, where he argued that the monastic hierarchy had nothing to do with, and was indeed opposed to, the feudal hierarchy, and Hartmut Hoffman, 'Von Cluny zum Investiturstreit', *Archiv für Kulturgeschichte*, 45 (1963): 165–69.

121. This point of view is still held, for instance, by Eugen Rosenstock-Huessy, *The Driving Power of Western Civilization: The Christian Revolution of the Middle Ages* (Boston, 1950), pp. 64 ff.: 'The first revolution of the Christian era began in the loneliness of a monk's cell and a monk's heart . . . . Gregory fused the functions of Cluny and of the Apostolic Majesty . . . .' (p. 82).

122. Gerd Tellenbach, *Church* (cited n. 14 above), pp. 82–85 (and esp. R. F. Bennett's Appendix V on pp. 186–92) and 'Zum Wesen der Cluniacenser', *Saeculum*, 9 (1958): 370–78, where he summed up his previous points in the light of subsequent research.

123. Tellenbach, *Church*, p. 189.

124. Cf. Norman Cantor, 'The Crisis of Western Monasticism, 1050–1130', *American Historical Review*, 66 (1960): 47–67, who said that Cluny was 'inflexibly dedicated to the preservation of the prevailing system' (p. 57) and that 'the older view . . . that the Cluniac movement directly inspired the Gregorian reform was not only naïve but almost the complete opposite of the truth' (p. 61).

125. This important point was clearly made by Alfred Cauchie, *La querelle des investitures dans les diocèses de Liège et de Cambrai* (Louvain, 1890–91), 1: 18–62, and in several recent works (such as those of Josef Semmler), which show that many anti-Gregorians favoured monastic reform and that the attitude of an individual monastery in the Investiture Controversy often depended upon its relations with the local ecclesiastical and secular authorities.

126. The most recent discussion, citing Borino's articles, is by Alberic Stacpoole, 'Hildebrand, Cluny and the Papacy', *Downside Review*, 81 (1963): 142–64 and 254–72.

127. See the works cited n. 120 above, and Kassius Hallinger, *Gorze-Kluny*, pp. 582 and 584, where he said that Cluny's anti-feudal attitude (although essentially monastic in conception) helped prepare the way for Gregory VII; Cinzio Violante, 'Il monachesimo cluniacense di fronte al mondo politico ed ecclesiastico (Secoli X e XI)' *Spiritualità cluniacense* (Convegni del Centro di studi sulla spiritualità' medievale, 3; Todi, 1960), pp. 155–242; Theodor Schieffer, in *Archiv f. mittelrheinische Kirchengeschichte*, 4: 35–38, and 'Cluny

et la querelle des Investitures', *Revue historique*, 225 (1961): 47–72; and Hartmut Hoffman, in *Archiv f. Kulturgeschichte*, 45: 165–209. Cf. also the interesting discussion of Lemari‚ gnier's article in *Monachesimo*, pp. 522–43, and Tellenbach, in *Saeculum*, 9: 370–78, and in *Neue Forschungen*, pp. 3–16 (esp. 14–16). Tellenbach argued that Cluny, though not perhaps opposed to ecclesiastical reform, followed the lead of the papacy in this respect in the eleventh century (cf. Mager's article in *Neue Forschungen*). But he admitted that Cluniac stress on the sacraments and well‚organized Christian life may have helped prepare the way for the Investitute Controversy (*Saeculum*, 9: 376–77).

128. For two general studies, very different in point of view, of this crisis of cenobitism (a term which appears to have been used first by G. Morin, in *Rev. bén.*, 40 [1928]: 99–115), see Jean Leclercq, 'La crise du monachisme aux XIe et XIIe siècles', *Bulletino dell'Istituto storico italiano per il Medio Evo*, 70 (1958): 19–41, and the article by Cantor cited n. 124 above.

129. These interpretations, which all stress a difference in spirit between Cluny and Cîteaux, are found in the works of Berlière, Butler, Coulton, Schmitz, Bishop, Dekkers, and Knowles.

130. Leclercq, in *Bull. dell'Istituto storico it.*, 70: 24–25.

131. Cantor, in *American Hist. Rev.*, 66: 65.

132. Hallinger, *Gorze‚Kluny*, pp. 419–22: 'Die oben gezeichneten "psychologischen" Widerstände gegen Kluny wollen letztlich als Ausdruck darunterliegender *sachlicher* Spannungen verstanden werden' (p. 422).

133. Suitbert Gammersbach, 'Das Abtsbild in Cluny und bei Bernhard von Clair‚ vaux', *Cîteaux in de Nederlanden*, 7 (1956): 85–101.

134. See n. 119 above.

135. Herbert Grundmann, *Religiöse Bewegungen im Mittelalter* (Historische Studien, 267; Berlin, 1935; new ed. with additions, Hildesheim, 1961), pp. 29–38, and 'Eresie e nuovi ordini religiosi nel secolo XII', *Relazioni del X Congresso internazionale di scienze storiche*, III: *Storia del Medioevo* (Bibliotheca storica Sansoni, N.S., 24; Florence, 1955), p. 396.

136. Cited by Alexis Presse, 'Saint Étienne Harding', *Coll. OCR*, 1 (1934–35): 27 and Séraphin Lenssen, 'Saint Robert: Fondateur de Cîteaux', *Coll. OCR*, 4 (1937–38): 170, n. 2, who also cited Henriquez's comparison of Robert to Abraham (faith), Alberic to Isaac (victim), and Stephen to Jacob (fecundity). An impartial account of the roles of these three is given by J.‚M. Canivez, in *Dictionnaire d'histoire et de géographie ecclésiastiques*, 12 (1953), cols. 853–55.

137. Séraphin Lenssen, 'Saint Robert', *Coll. OCR*, 4: 2–16, 81–96, 161–77, 241–53 (also separately, Westmalle, 1937), and J.‚A. Lefèvre, 'S. Robert de Molesme dans l'opinion monastique du XIIe et du XIIIe siècle', *Analecta Bollandiana*, 74 (1956): 50–83, who concluded that Robert was 'le vrai chef de la réforme spirituelle qui vient de se concréter dans la fondation de Cîteaux (p. 83).

138. See esp. J. Othon [Ducourneau], 'Les origines cisterciennes', *Rev. Mab.*, 23 (1933): 153–63, who called Alberic 'Le véritable fondateur de l'ordre cistercien' (p. 162). For Séraphin Lenssen, in *Coll. OCR*, 4: 95–96, Alberic contributed persévérance but not initiative.

139. Roger Duvernay, 'Cîteaux, Vallombreuse et Étienne Harding', *Anal. SOC*, 8 (1952): 379–495, who argued that Cîteaux was the end of a development which began at Vallombrosa and that Stephen Harding visited Vallombrosa on his trip to Rome in 1080/90. For other opinions of Stephen, see the article by Presse cited n. 136 above and J. B. Van Damme, 'Saint Étienne Harding mieux connu', *Cîteaux*, 14 (1963): 307–13. Ducourneau, in *Rev. Mab.*, 23 (1933): 163–69, believed that under Stephen Harding

Cîteaux became increasingly ascetic and rigorous. For many Cistercian historians Stephen played the role of Brother Elias in Franciscan history.

140. See the bibliography and most recent survey of the issue by Polykarp Zakar, 'Die Anfänge des Zisterzienserordens: Kurze Bemerkungen zu den Studien der letzten zehn Jahre', *Anal. SOC,* 20 (1964): 103–38 and the reply by J. B. Van Damme, 'Autour des origines cisterciennes: Quelques à propos', *Anal. SOC,* 21 (1965): 128–37; also the account by David Knowles, 'The Primitive Cistercian Documents', in *Hist. Enterprises* (cited n. 1 above), pp. 197–222.

141. See the pre-Lefèvre survey, with references, by Ernst Werner, 'Neue Texte und Forschungen zur Charta Caritatis', *Forschungen und Fortschritte,* 29 (1955): 25–29, who stressed that the *Carta caritatis* is a document second only to the Rule of St. Benedict in importance in the history of Western monasticism.

142. See in particular Jean Lefèvre and Bernard Lucet, 'Les codifications cisterciennes aux XIIe et XIIIe siècles d'après les traditions manuscrits', *Anal. SOC,* 15 (1959): 3–22 and J. B. Van Damme, 'Formation de la constitution cistercienne', *Studia monastica,* 4 (1962): 111–37 and 'La constitution cistercienne de 1165', *Anal. SOC,* 19 (1963): 51–104. For later developments see the important work by Jean-Berthold Mahn, *L'ordre cistercien et son gouvernement des origines au milieu du XIIIe siècle (1098–1265)* (Bibliothèque des Écoles françaises d'Athènes et de Rome, 161; Paris, 1945). Mahn's untimely death in 1944 was a great loss to the study of monastic history.

143. Bruno Griesser, 'Die "Ecclesiastica officia Cisterciensis ordinis" des cod. 1711 von Trient', *Anal. SOC,* 12 (1956): 153–288, who remarked in his commentary on the close resemblance to Cluniac customs (pp. 171, 174); Bruno Schneider, 'Cîteaux und die benediktinische Tradition', *Anal. SOC,* 16 (1960): 169–254 and 17 (1961): 73–114, who showed that the majority of Cistercian usages derived from Cluny (see esp. 17: 97–98).

144. See the works cited in nn. 136 and 138 above. For a characteristic statement of the earlier view, which saw Cîteaux as a reaction to Cluny and the lax standards of contemporary monasticism, see Ursmer Berlière, 'Les origines de Cîteaux et l'ordre bénédictine au XIIe siècle', *Rev. d'hist. ecc.,* 2 (1901): 264, 267.

145. The attitudes of these writers are far from identical. For J.-M. Canivez see n. 136 above, and for J.-A. Lefèvre see the article cited n. 137 above and 'Que savons-nous du Cîteaux primitif?', *Rev. d'hist. ecc.,* 51 (1956): 5–41 (esp. 20, n. 1, on Ducourneau). M.-Anselme Dimier, 'Les concepts de moine et de vie monastique chez les premiers Cisterciens', *Studia monastica,* 1 (1959): 399–418, maintained that the Cistercians resembled other movements of monastic reform in their basic purpose, but not in their radical character or their later success. J. B. Van Damme, in *Studia monastica,* 4 (1962): 111–16 (see 116, n. 2, on Presse, Ducourneau, Laurent, and Lenssen), considered Cîteaux the natural outcome of the monastic work of Benedict of Aniane. Cf. Edith Pásztor, 'Le origini dell'ordine cisterciense e la riforma monastica', *Anal. SOC,* 21 (1965): 112–27.

146. For Herbert Grundmann, see n. 135 above; M.-D. Chenu, 'Moines, clercs, laïcs au carrefour de la vie évangélique', *Rev. d'hist. ecc.,* 49 (1954): 59–89, reprinted with other articles in *La théologie au douzième siècle* (Études de philosophie médiévale, 45; Paris, 1957); Étienne Delaruelle, 'La pietà popolare nel secolo XI', in *Relazioni* (cited n. 135 above), pp. 309–32 (and other articles by Delaruelle in the same volume).

147. See n. 50 above and the works by McDonnell, Dereine, Grundmann, and Chenu cited in nn. 53, 92, 135, and 146.

148. Historically, this view may not be altogether incorrect. See A. D. Nock, *Conversion* (Oxford, 1933), pp. 187–88: 'It is not likely that the Apostles in Jerusalem had a missionary aim in the full sense.' They were driven by opposition into a more active proselytizing role.

149. On the highly disputed question of the attitude of regular canons towards pastoral work, see my work *Monastic Tithes from their Origins to the Twelfth Century* (Cambridge Studies in Medieval Life and Thought, N.S., 10; Cambridge, 1964), pp. 154–57, with references to previous literature.

150. See M.-D. Chenu, in *Rev. d'hist. ecc.*, 49 (1954): 69–80, and M.-H. Vicaire, *Imitation*, pp. 59 ff., on this change in the ideal of the *vita apostolica*.

151. Giovanni Miccoli, 'Ecclesiae primitivae forma', *Studi medievali*, 3rd S., 1 (1960): 470–98, reprinted with additions in his *Chiesa Gregoriana* (Storici antichi e moderni, N.S., 17; Florence, 1966), pp. 225–99.

152. Ernst Werner, *Pauperes Christi* (Leipzig, 1956).

153. Matthäus Bernards, 'Nudus nudum Christum sequi', *Wissenschaft und Weisheit*, 14 (1951): 148–51, and Antin, in *Théologie*, I (cited n. 44 above), p. 195, n. 24.

154. On the beginnings of this shift, see Bernhard Schmeidler, 'Anti-asketische Äusserungen aus Deutschland im 11. und beginnenden 12. Jahrhundert', *Kultur und Universalgeschichte (Festschrift Walter Goetz)* (Leipzig–Berlin, 1927), pp. 35–52, who remarked on the great rarity in the eleventh century of any statement of the superiority of the secular clergy (bishops and priests) over monks (p. 49).

155. Cf. Philibert Schmitz, *Ordre* (cited n. 22 above), 3: 3–11.

he changing face
of medieval
literature

W. T. H. Jackson

We all remember—or perhaps I should say people of my generation all remember—certain courses in *Beowulf* or the *Chanson de Roland* or the *Nibelungenlied* which began with the first line of the poem and ended, ten weeks later, at the second. In the interim we had been conducted through a maze of verb-forms, historical grammar, Indo-European roots with asterisks on the front of them, and assorted noun and adjective declensions. Every word in these lines spouted forth a series of associate streams. If it was a verb, it must belong to some conjugation, and what could be more normal than to move from one conjugation to all conjugations, and to their origins in the remoter recesses of the south Russian steppe? (Remember, this was a long time ago.) The original verb was soon forgotten, swept away, so to speak, in a flood of its own making. If there was time, we might be introduced to the mysteries of Old English, Old French, or Middle High German prosody, but such instruction was usually rather mechanical and was regarded, perhaps, as slightly frivolous.

What did all this have to do with the study of literature? Very little that I can see, and yet for several generations it was the accepted method of reading the great works of the medieval period. No one, of course, would ever read Molière or Shakespeare or Goethe in this way, but for medieval works it was respectable.

Why? I think the principal reason was that medieval literature was very often taught by persons whose chief interest was in linguistics, and until relatively recently linguistics meant historical linguistics. Such teachers very naturally regarded the poems they were reading as a kind of mine of information about historical grammar, or, to change the metaphor, as a mosaic from which the individual stones could be taken out and examined under a microscope. The result, from the literary point of view, was just about the same as treating a Byzantine mosaic as a subject for mineralogical exploration.

We should not put all the blame on the students of historical grammar. Their colleagues in the classics had been doing something similar for much longer. The practice of reading one book of Vergil or Livy and subjecting every word to microscopic treatment was certainly normal procedure in my day. Epexegetic infinitives and mythological allusions were infinitely more important than poetical values, and I, for one, was compelled as a schoolboy to read two books of the *Aeneid* in this way without being told by anyone how the story began or ended. You will perhaps remember the famous story of Housman, who, on a lovely spring day, came into his lecture room and said,'Gentlemen [there were only gentlemen then], today I propose to talk about Horace as a poet.' It was revolutionary. Everyone gaped. He never did it again, of course. We must put it down to spring madness.

Curiously enough, it was not until people began to read the classics in translation that more attention was paid to their literary values by a broad public. I am, of course, well aware that there were always people who appreciated the poetic worth of the great classic authors. Dryden did not call the *Georgics* the greatest work of the greatest poet because he admired their grammar. What I do say is that the system of teaching the classics, with its insistence on grammatical and mythological minutiae usually stultified any literary interests the student might have had.

The study of medieval literature was deeply affected by that of the classics. All of the great scholars in the field of medieval literature had been trained in them. Some of them, like Karl Lachmann, deliberately applied to the study of medieval texts the techniques they had developed in their classical studies. Furthermore, the nineteenth century was largely a period of rediscovery of medieval works. The first and most urgent need was the publication of good texts, and here the experience of classical philology was invaluable. To produce such texts without accurate knowledge of grammatical forms and without accepted norms of orthography was clearly impossible, and it would be ungracious to fail to recognize the great services of earlier scholars in this field. We may perhaps add that many texts are still available—or unavailable—only in the editions which these nineteenth-century scholars produced. Yet without wishing to detract in the least from the services rendered, we must recognize a very important limitation. The text editors were professionals in a very strict sense of the term. They were interested in texts for their own sake, and the older and more complicated they were, the more fascination they had. It is characteristic, for example, that the *Hildebrandslied* has been edited scores of times; innumerable emendations, explanations, and even rewritings have been made. Yet the fragments of Béroul's *Tristram* were edited by Lichtenstein in 1876 and still await a much needed new edition. This fascination with early texts was also partly due to another reason, the nineteenth-century nationalism which sought to find in early fragments the characteristics of a particular culture. Thus, the text editors devoted almost as much attention to charms, fragments of prayers, and translations of the *Pater noster* and Creed as they did to *Widsith* and the *Hildebrandslied*. There was, in other words, little or no attempt made to separate works of literature from cultural historical material. The Strassburg oaths are a very interesting historical document and they are of great importance as evidence of the early forms of French and German, but they have no literary significance whatsoever. The same may be said of Ulfilas' Bible (we have the original), Alfred's translation of the *Pastoral Care*, and the Old High German version of Tatian's *Gospel Harmony*. Yet these works are always placed before students of early literature, and works of this kind make up a large proportion of the anthologies of early literature.

This failure to define what is meant by literature is clearly illustrated by the so-called histories of literature, which are mainly nothing of the kind. A glance at the standard works shows that in the earliest period everything goes in, even word lists and biblical commentaries. As the amount of available material grows larger, the purely theological works are often excluded, but a detailed work such as Gustav Ehrismann's *Geschichte der deutschen Literatur bis zum Ausgang des Mittelalters*[1] includes them all.

No true literary history could be written on this basis. The works included were often fragmentary and could be—and often were—interpreted in any fashion which suited the proponent of a particular theory. An obvious example is the 'Germanic hero', so much different from any other hero, who haunts the pages of so many literary histories of the late nineteenth and early twentieth century. Many fields which normally are the concern of the literary historian were clearly not available to the student of medieval literature. Literary biography is hardly feasible when a high percentage of the extant works are anonymous, and even known authors are little more than mere names. Even the dates of important works are often vague in the extreme and the criteria on which they are based often dubious. Under such circumstances it is hardly surprising that a great deal of attention should have been paid to 'origins'. Here at least was a topic which could exercise both the scholarly talents and the imaginations of the researchers. Historians, folklorists, anthropologists, and literary historians brought together a mass of motifs, analogues and cult practices which could be sifted and compared. Incidents in literary works could be shown to have connections not only with one another but with material recorded in non-literary productions. It was possible to show how a sophisticated literary work, such as a romance of Chrétien de Troyes, was connected with the mythology of the Celtic peoples, how Sigurd was a sun-god, and how Gawain and the Green Knight were natural forces in conflict. This study of origins became almost an obsession in regard to certain works. The *Nibelungenlied* was perhaps the chief victim, for almost all studies of the poem, until very recently, were concerned to show its connection with the historical event of the destruction of the Burgundians, with the Scandinavian poems on similar subjects, with Nordic mythology, and with its Germanic cultural background. Friedrich Panzer's *Das Nibelungenlied: Entstehung und Gestalt*[2] is devoted almost exclusively to the questions of text tradition and motif origins (where, in almost revolutionary fashion, he does recognize the existence of motifs originating in non-German countries). His chapters on the characters are so naïve as to be laughable, and it is quite clear that in a life largely devoted to the study of the *Nibelungenlied* he gave little thought to literary analysis, even though he was deeply moved by the poem as a work of art.

I suspect that one reason for the popularity of the 'origins' approach is its apparently scientific nature, the thorough analysis of works, the sorting out of motifs, the careful comparisons. Unfortunately the rational and scientific elements are more apparent than real. The amount of early material actually available for comparison is very small, and the researchers are compelled to project backwards from later material—a dangerous procedure. There is also a strongly subjective element, a tendency to emphasize those points where a resemblance is apparent and play down points of difference. Professor Loomis, one of the most distinguished of all students of sources and analogues, remarks in his latest book on the Grail, 'misunderstandings were inevitable in the transmission of stories from one language and cultural milieu to another and ... they were responsible for irrational and freakish features.'[3] I agree heartily—but we should be on our guard against thinking that such misunderstandings produce only the irrational and freakish features. In their desire to be scientific, the scholars make far too little allowance for the fact that most transmission in medieval times was oral, and that oral transmission means loss of detail, added detail, distortion, and misunderstanding. Far too little allowance is made in studies of sources for such things as human error, lapse of memory, and loss of important evidence.

But there is a more fundamental question yet. What does this eminently respectable study of origins contribute to the understanding of medieval literary works? Do we understand Arthurian romances better if we know that Arthur was a Romano-British chief of the early sixth century, or that the Loathly Damsel in *Perceval* is derived from Eriu, the Sovereignty of Ireland? In these instances the answer is a pretty firm 'No,' since the literary Arthur is a creation far removed from any historical individual or even from the heroic chieftain of Welsh and Breton folk tales. His literary *raison d'être* in the romances is as the head of a court of high chivalry, and as such he is the creation of writers of the twelfth century. Yet we could not say that knowledge of the historical and cultural background of *Beowulf* is irrelevant, or that our interpretation of the poem is unaffected by knowledge of similar motifs in other works. The *Chanson de Roland* is not the same poem if we think of it as a Christian work, composed by clerics on the pilgrimage route to the Shrine of St. James, as it would be if we follow Menéndez-Pidal[4] and think of a less deliberate composition springing largely from popular songs which preserved the memory of a spectacular defeat of the armies of Charlemagne, a defeat so humiliating that Charlemagne's biographer Einhard found it necessary to 'interpret' it and make it into a minor skirmish.

The greatest weakness of the studies of analogues and origins is, in my opinion, that most researchers have been content to stop at identification. They usually fail to ask the questions which are surely the most important ones: What use does this author make of the motif, historical event, or mythological figure that I am discussing? How aware is he of the fact that it is a common motif or is he merely accepting it because he found it in his source? What is his concept of history and does this concept affect his presentation of historical fact? Such questions are vital to the understanding of almost all the great medieval poems.

We have been discussing the principal characteristics of the study of medieval literature as it was a decade or two ago, but the title of this paper is 'The Changing Face of Medieval Literature'. It is time to ask in what ways it has changed, and to point out some significant trends in study. We may first express one of these changes in attitude in very general terms and then proceed to an analysis of individual characteristics. The shift of emphasis may be stated as a recognition of the need to understand the cultural milieu in which literary works were produced. This may sound like a blinding glimpse of the obvious. Yet a cursory examination of extant literary history and criticism of medieval works soon reveals how desperately little we know and how hard the knowledge is to acquire. Let us take a few examples. We have already noted that a large number of works are anonymous and that even named authors are little more than names. Even though we would not want to create a positivistic connection between the events of these men's lives and the works they wrote, it would be extremely helpful to know how they had been educated, what their religious views were, and even their social status. We know next to nothing about the way in which the vernacular poets learned their craft. How was the highly complex art of writing the *canzon* developed and passed on? There are scores of books and articles speculating on the origins of 'courtly love', but I know of none which tackles the problem of training. It is a hard task. Equally important and equally difficult is the question of the audience. Was there, shall we say, a different audience for the *Chanson de Roland* and the Tristan romances, for the *Nibelungenlied* and *Parzival*? Distinctions such as 'popular' and 'courtly' are virtually meaningless, since they refer rather to subject matter and style than to the audience. The author of the *Nibelungenlied* is clearly imitating courtly romances at times, the author of *Parzival* refers to the *Nibelungenlied*. How sophisticated were the audiences? Did they understand more or less about the poems than we do? Would they think our interpretations absurd or brilliant? Certainly the audience for Scandinavian poetry and the Provençal lyric must have had a great degree of sophistication in matters of imagery and prosody, or the works would have been completely wasted, but we cannot be absolutely sure what it was they appreciated and how far their knowledge went.

These are one or two questions of cultural milieu which need exploring but are hard to answer because of lack of evidence. There are many where there is an abundance of evidence available. One of the most important of these is the connection between literature and theology. We have long since abandoned the Romantic notion of a medieval world in which all men were obedient sons of the Church, where quiet monks copied manuscripts all day and the laity lived under a beneficent and uniform rule. We know a great deal of the turmoil, of the crosscurrents of thought, of shifts of emphasis. We realize that there can be no understanding even of secular works without a considerable knowledge of the religious background.

The Augustinian dichotomy of this world and the other world, of the two cities of man and God, was deeply impressed upon the medieval consciousness, and there can be no understanding of the great Arthurian romances without recognition of its role and of the oppositions and the compromises which developed in the twelfth and thirteenth centuries. It is naïve to think of the Arthurian romances as merely stories in which knights went on adventures and rescued damsels. The Arthurian ideal is not merely a fairy-story world of constant tournaments and lovemaking, nor is courtly love simply an adoring and occasionally adulterous relationship between a knight and his lady. In the great romances, at least, there is a serious question involved of the role of man in society and in the universe. There are no serious wars and matters of state in these romances. The pursuits are those of a nobleman's leisure. Yet they are far from being frivolous. Was there a serious alternative to the mere *vita activa,* which was inferior to the *vita contemplativa*? Was life on this earth nothing more than a preparation for the hereafter, its conduct governed by considerations of sin and penitence, grace and redemption? There seems to be considerable evidence that the authors of the Arthurian romances proposed a form of life which would be governed by its own code of manners and morals, whose requirements would be as rigid and whose practitioners would be as noble as those of the Christian life. Such a world was Christian, but its secular ambitions were an end in themselves. It drew much of its inspiration from Christian thinking and yet in some ways anticipated later developments in theology. German critics have taken the lead in showing how important are the intellectual and theological elements in the Arthurian romances. They have rightly pointed to the presence of mystical terminology and attitudes in both the lyric and the romance; they have pointed out the importance of the crusading spirit, of Bernardine conceptions of mystical love, of gradualistic ideas. It is not too much to say that our ideas on the romance have been utterly changed by this recognition of the importance of theological considerations.

Yet romances are not theological tracts, and there is a real danger of overinterpretation. The existence of a theological work, the fact that it was known to exist when the romances were composed does not, unfortunately, prove that the author had read it or even heard of it. Or he may have known generally of the ideas it contained without being aware of details. It is by no means certain that the authors of secular works were aware of a clear-cut body of theological beliefs to which they were supposed to subscribe and that they therefore were equally aware of deviations from these norms. If a generalization can be made on such a broad subject, it would surely be that observance rather than actual theological knowledge was characteristic of the layman and that there was greater flexibility of belief in the medieval church than in the period after the Council of Trent. Theologians do indeed dispute about minor points of doctrine, but can we honestly expect to find these disputes reflected in secular works and are we entitled to seize upon phrases or lines and regard them as evidence for a particular religious attitude?

It is equally misguided to smell heresy in a work because of a few expressions. We know that the Catharist or Albigensian heresy was widespread in southern France and even in some parts of Germany in the twelfth and early thirteenth centuries. It is certain that there were such heretics in the areas where many of the troubadours composed their songs. But careful research has failed to produce the slightest evidence that any known troubadour was a Catharist, or that any of the patrons were—although they may have tolerated heresy in their dominions. Are we justified then in interpreting, as some critics have done, the Provençal *canzon* as influenced by Catharist views of sterile love, even perhaps as disguised hymns to the Catharist church? Obviously not. Still less can I subscribe to the view which sees in Wolfram's *Parzival* evidence of Catharist ceremonies of the giving of the *consolamentum* by a lay priest. Wolfram's whole view of human existence is utterly alien to the Catharist idea of dualism, with its almost equally balanced forces of good and evil. To seize upon a scene such as that between Parzival and Trevrizent and interpret it virtually without reference to the spirit of the work in which it stands is to carry theological interpretation to absurd lengths.

The attempts to show that a poet's ideas of guilt, pride, ignorance, sloth, or other sin conform to a rigid theological specification are misguided. The mass of argument and counterargument proves this. What theological knowledge can do is to show us what may have influenced the poet's thinking. Further than that we should not go. The dangers of oversubtle theological speculations about secular works are evident in the criticism of the *Tristan* of Gottfried von Strassburg, which would attribute to the author a highly complex 'analogy of opposites', a love theme which uses the terminology of mystical love to describe an anti-spiritual love situation. No one would deny the play upon mystical love themes and terminology. But there is no evidence of a concerted scheme.

It would not be unfair to say that much of the interest in the theological influence on literature stems from a new awareness of one aspect of theological training in the Middle Ages—interpretation by allegorization. A great deal has been written on this subject recently, some of it strictly about theology, such as Henri de Lubac's *Exégèse médiévale,*[5] some more concerned with the history of the technique, such as Jean Pépin's *Mythe et allégorie.*[6] More important still, perhaps, is the growth of a tradition among scholars in the field to think allegorically. They are able to produce good evidence that medieval writers intended secular works to be interpreted. Dante says so in the often quoted letter to Can Grande della Scala. The *Gesta Romanorum* and similar works all show secular stories being interpreted in a religious sense. It is extremely tempting to take a poem like the *Pearl* or the *Owl and the Nightingale* and apply to it our knowledge of the techniques of allegorization. And it is hard to see what objection can be made to such a treatment where the poem belongs to a category in which such allegorization would have real value, the category of didactic poetry in a broad sense. But are we justified in using the same technique with other classes of poems? Is a secular love poem to be treated in this way, or an Arthurian romance? Were the authors, in fact, not writing secular works at all but allegories? This is the impression one would get from reading the interpretations by H. B. Willson of the German romances and by Sister Amelia Klenke of Chrétien's *Perceval.*[7] The actions of the principal participants are 'interpreted' in a Christian sense and the work proves to be religious in nature. I find it hard to agree with this kind of criticism. Certainly the great events in the Christian story are frequently reflected in secular works. The phenomenon of apparent death and rebirth is too common to be accidental. But we do not have to interpret this 'on a higher level' as the Death and Resurrection. It is Erec who is spiritually reborn,

not just a figure to be interpreted as Christ. There is no external evidence that
secular works were to be interpreted into being religious. Let us be satisfied with
the fact that we have a fuller knowledge of the secular work if we think of it against
its religious background.

It may be appropriate at this point to give some examples of what I consider to
be helpful and unhelpful use of theological considerations in interpreting secular
works. The German lyric poet Walther von der Vogelweide wrote a poem on the
marriage of the Emperor Philip, which took place at Christmas in 1199 at
Magdeburg. The poem is short enough to quote in full:

> In Magdeburg, the day our Lord was born,
> of a maid, his mother chosen,
> King Philip stepped before us like a lord,
> An emperor's brother and an emperor's child
> In the same dress, although the names are three.
> He bore the Empire's scepter and its crown;
> He walked in dignity, he did not haste.
> There followed him a queen of noble race,
> Rose without thorn, a dove that has no guile.
> Never had such nobility been seen.
> The Saxons and the Thüringer were there.
> The wise men see it and are duly pleased.

Walther is quite consciously playing on the holy events of the Christmas season in
this poem. Philip was a kind of Trinity—he was the son of Friedrich Barbarossa,
brother of Henry VI, and thus three emperors in one. The place was Magdeburg,
the city of the Maid, and the Byzantine princess whom he was marrying changed
her name at this time from Irene to Maria. Thus, she may be 'the lord's bride', and
the epithets 'rose without a thorn, dove without guile', usually associated with the
Virgin, may be applied to her. The poem imparts to the whole marriage ceremony
the atmosphere of an event far more significant than the mere joining of a royal
couple. Walther has made skilful use of the possibilities offered to him by the place
and the season to endow the marriage with a peculiar sanctity. Yet it would be
ridiculous to push the analogy any further, to see a close resemblance between the
individual emperors and the individual members of the Trinity. The hope for a
world reborn is implicit in what Walther writes, but further we need not go.

No critic, so far as I know, has attempted any 'theological-allegorical' interpretation of this poem. But in another poem of Walther's much more has been made of
the possibilities. In his famous 'I sat upon a stone', Walther discusses the difficulty
of reconciling three things: *varnde guot, ere,* and *gotes hulde.* We may describe
these as: 'this world's goods', 'honour', and 'the worship of God'. His general
meaning is clear enough—he is thinking of two aspects of worldly success,
the acquisition of material goods and the acquisition of the less tangible 'honour',
which means rather 'reputation for doing noble deeds' and which might with
justification be regarded as the ideal pursuit both for a great king and for an
Arthurian knight. These two are contrasted with the spiritual values, the worship
of God. Walther says categorically that this third quality is 'superior to the other
two', as the *vita contemplativa* is superior to the *vita activa.* But the whole point of his

poem is that the full possibilities of religious worship are unattainable without the establishment of a firm secular order. In other words, whatever the theory, in practice we must have effective secular government to ensure the maintenance of religion.

Anyone who knows Walther's poetry would recognize this as one of his basic themes. Yet knowledge of the triple values of Plato, conveyed to the Middle Ages by Cicero, the *utile, honestum,* and *summum bonum,* has led many critics to make a firm parallel between these and Walther's three qualities. At least one critic has gone a good deal further and sought to impose upon the poem a more rigid connec‚ tion with contemporary theological ideas. H. B. Willson, writing in *Germanic Review* in March 1964, stresses, quite rightly, the importance in the poem of the concept of *ordo,* of that idea which regarded all things visible and invisible as being subordinate to a divine principle of order. Willson then quotes from Hugh of St. Victor to the effect that material things are 'essentially symbols relating to spiritual truths; the visible world is symbolical of the invisible world.'[8] The assumption of flesh by God himself is the eternal illustration of this truth. Willson goes on to point out the affinity between the Church and the mystical body of Christ and the twofold nature of the Church—lay and cleric—which corresponds to the twofold nature of man himself. Here Willson comes against a problem—how can he equate the two natures which he has been discussing with the threefold nature of Walther's world? He rather lamely says that *varnde guot* and *ere* are really both secular and thus form one. He recognizes the difficulty but has no real solution to offer. The two natures, he adds, are unified by *caritas.* All this is very interesting, but it is hard to see what light it throws on Walther's poem. The poet does not seek for a means of reconciliation. His interest lies in the means by which suitable conditions for true religion can be assured by adequate secular government. Of course he is aware of the correspondence between the three goods and the threefold form of the Trinity, and of the ascending scale of values which he is describing. But his solution is not based on *caritas* or any theological consideration, but upon the setting up of an adequate secular government. There must be a secular *ordo* corres‚ ponding to the *ordo mundi.*

How dangerous it is to introduce extraneous considerations of this kind is shown by this quotation: 'The word "Tugendsystem" can, and perhaps should, be retained, but only with the important qualification that the system meant is that peculiar to medieval Christianity, the Divine *ordo,* in which all created things participate analogically, each in its own order and measure. At the head of this ordered hierarchy stands God, the supreme Ordinator, absolute Unity‚in‚ Plurality, the highest Measure, Justice, and Love, the Essence of Virtue. Neverthe‚ less, it cannot be denied that the indivisibility of ethics and politics is already prefigured in Plato's *Republic* and that Christian Universals owe much to Plato's Ideas, and the aim of this article will have been achieved if it has succeeded in demonstrating that the supreme integrating factor in Walther's three strophes is the universalism he shares with St. Augustine, Hugh of St. Victor, and ultimately with Plato.'[9] All this is very nice and very general. But note the next sentence. 'Through the analogical relationship between the individual human body and the Mystical Body the poet demonstrates the inseparability of morals, politics, and religion, of man and God in Three Persons, in medieval life and thought.'[10] This is a far cry from Walther's poem. As a result of some resemblances between Walther's work and that of Hugh of St. Victor, the whole basis of knightly morality is to be expressed in theological terms. I am unrepentant. I still think that *ere* is an important concept in courtly life and I refuse to lump it in with *varnde guot*. But the important consideration for medieval scholarship in general is the attempt, in my opinion misguided, to find reflections of theological thinking in even the most secular works.

Let us now glance at a recent book on the *Chanson de Roland* to see how an author examines a particular feature of the poem using a method very characteristic of present-day medieval scholarship. Karl-Josef Steinmeyer, in his *Untersuchungen zur allegorischen Bedeutung der Träume im altfranzösischen Rolandslied*,[11] decides that the well-known dream of Charlemagne in the poem must be interpreted in accordance with contemporary scholarly practice and in line with the view of patristic writers on the subject. We may note, parenthetically, that he assumes the authorship of 'Turoldus'. We have not yet reached the stage of collective-allegorical interpretations. His first chapter sets out the medieval concept of the dream, and he cites such authors as Rupertus of Deutz (first quarter of the twelfth century), Richard of St. Victor, Bernard of Clairvaux, and Honorius of Autun to support his views. The remainder of the work is an attempt to analyse the individual dreams in the light of the patristic material, and we shall select one example of his method. Steinmeyer has apparently decided that the second dream refers to the Battle of Roncesvalles, not to the trial of Ganelon, as many critics think. He rejects the emendation *urs* for *vers* in line 727 of the Oxford manuscript and decides that it is a wild boar which bites Charlemagne in the right arm and that this boar is Marsile. The attack on the right arm is the attack by Marsile's forces on Roland's rearguard. The leopard, according to Steinmeyer, is not Pinabel, as Bédier believed, but the Caliph.[12]

To support his view, the author produces several descriptions of the qualities of the wild boar and leopard from patristic and other sources and endeavours to show that they fit the characterizations of Marsile and the Caliph respectively. I must admit to being unimpressed. The wild boar is described as ferocious, wrathful, incapable of persuasion, and, allegorically, the person who rejects good teaching and Christian doctrine itself. These, we are told, are precisely the characteristics of Marsile. Why they should be more typical of him than of any other of the pagans, I find it hard to understand. And does the wretched, beaten Marsile of the second part really have anything in common with the wild boar who, in the words of one of Steinmeyer's own quotations, 'thrusts himself boldly against the hunter's steel and even when cut down gathers his strength against those who wound him and attacks them with his tusks'?[13] Hardly. He might also note that the boar attacks with its tusks. Who ever heard of a boar biting someone's right arm? Nor does the leopard fare much better. Steinmeyer stresses the hypocritical nature of the leopard, hence its similarity to the heretic. (He virtually ignores all the other, equally well-known characteristics of the beast.) But why should paganism be any more characteristic of the Caliph than of any other person opposed to Roland? I think Steinmeyer is probably right in his contention that the dream refers to the battle at

Roncesvalles rather than to the trial of Ganelon, but his dragging in of all the apparatus of allegorical interpretation is little more than cumbersome verbiage, and it proves absolutely nothing.

I hope the point has been made. Allegorical interpretation undoubtedly can be a help in the understanding of medieval works, but we should avoid the temptation to regard every work as an allegory and to force on secular works the technical interpretations of the theologians.

There was a time when it was customary to refer to 'loose structure' as a character-istic feature of romances, as if they were a series of episodes strung together with no informing purpose and no causal connection. No one would deny that such romances exist—and sloppily written epics and *chansons de geste* exist too. But fortunately great strides have been made in our knowledge of the structural principles of all forms of medieval poetry. The accusation of pointless digressions is rarely heard, since it is clear that these so-called digressions are often highly germane to the author's purpose. A good example is the 'Joie de la cort' episode in Chrétien's *Erec*. This episode, which seemed to earlier critics merely to be tacked on to the story, is now seen as a reflection of Erec's own situation, seen from a different view-point. Over and over again we find that medieval structure is designed to present a problem from many different points of view—the problem of leadership in *Beowulf* and the *Nibelungenlied,* the problem of individual realization in a particular social context in the romances. Even in the lyrics we are learning to expect not a logically developed sequence of thought but rather a series of illustrations of various facets of the love problem. In the lyrics, and perhaps in some narrative poetry, this type of structure is combined with syllable or line groupings which involve the use of specific numbers. This is not, of course, number symbolism but rather an attempt at symmetry by the use of groups of the same length. There is a great deal of work to be done on the subject of medieval 'literary symmetry'.

It is now time to turn to what is perhaps the best known of all the new approaches to medieval criticism—the study of *topoi*. It seems almost incredible now that before the publication of Curtius' *European Literature and the Latin Middle Ages* in 1948, so little attention should have been given to the importance of rhetoric in the study of medieval literature. The necessary material was available and Edmond Faral's *Les Arts poétiques du xiie et du xiiie siècle*[14] had not only provided the texts but shown their significance. Even so, Curtius' work had a great impact. It showed how many features of medieval literature which had been treated as the spontaneous produc-tions of their authors were far better understood as variants of a rhetorical tradition, of a method of treating a particular situation in a literary fashion. The most obvious example was the ideal landscape, which was seen to be not a piece of natural description but rather a device to show a particular emotional or spiritual situation.

Yet Curtius' method had its dangers. He was a pioneer in the field, concerned to point out the existence of the *topoi*. He often failed to make clear distinctions between motifs, commonplaces, and types of rhetorical description; and many subsequent writers have accepted his categorizations uncritically. There is a real danger of attempting to fit certain features of literary works into Curtius' categories as if those categories were somehow sacred. Nor is there any great advantage to be gained from a mere listing of *topoi* in a work. It is, to be sure, better to recognize the same *topos* in two works than to say that one influenced the other because of the similarities. But the real interest in *topos* research lies not in the recognition of the existence of a *topos* but in investigation of how that *topos* is used. Chaucer provides us with obvious examples. What for many years was regarded as 'realistic' description of medieval characters proves on closer examination to be brilliant variation of *topos* description. It is the very departures from the accepted delineations of such characters as the Prioress that Chaucer shows his genius for ironic characterization, whereas in the description of the squire the emphasis on the topical details produces the same ironic effect by making the young man an all too perfect exemplar of his type. The educated audience for medieval works was perfectly aware of the *topos* convention, for such training belonged to the most elementary forms of rhetorical education. It is therefore fair to assume that some part at least of the audience would be aware of the variations which were played on the topical themes.

Some of these variations are very subtle, and it is interesting to observe what we may call the progress of criticism of such a *topos* as the ideal landscape. The first stage was the recognition of the simple fact that we are discussing landscape not in terms of realistic description but as an idealized milieu in which the action of a poem is to take place. The landscape, if it represents any actual time and location, is that of the Mediterranean in spring, but this is due to its classical provenance and is in any case irrelevant. Typically enough, some efforts were made to find its 'origin' in Ovid or Horace, but these gave way to analysis of the individual elements of which the descriptions are composed. These elements are important not because of their significance as sense-phenomena and their allegorical value. It is the appeal to sight and sound, to light and shadow, and especially to the knowledge of the meaning of the *hortus conclusus*, the paradise garden, which is important. In the paradise garden the rules of secular life are suspended and existence is determined by eternal standards of beauty, of love, and of harmony. In the *Roman de la rose* and in the poem 'Phyllis and Flora' the existence of these eternal values is made clear by the setting in the ideal landscape. By this setting the author informs the reader that he is talking not of the world in which we live but of an ideal world.

But criticism must now go further and observe not only the general facts of the idealized landscape but also the variations on them. Perhaps the best example that I know of is in the *Tristan* of Gottfried von Strassburg. There is a long, elaborate description of the idealized spring landscape in the prologue which describes the tournament at which Tristan's father Riwalin meets Blancheflor. It is an appropriate setting for a typical knightly love-match, largely conventional and deriving its elements in great part from the descriptions of the ideal landscape found in lyric poetry. Later in the poem Tristan and Isolde withdraw to a grotto of love. To reach it they have to cross a belt of grim and inhospitable mountain country—the separation from the real world. The landscape in which they reach the highest attainable love possible in this world is described in terms very similar to those used in the earlier description. Several lines are actually repeated, but more often they are repeated with a change of one or two words, changes which make it clear that we are dealing with a passion much more refined and esoteric than that between Riwalin and Blancheflor and that all connection with the real chivalric world has been superseded by an artistic and intellectual milieu.

This need to observe the minutiae of the *topos* conventions is one of the real needs of criticism of rhetoric. If I may mention some of my own research in this regard, it has become clear to me that an actual emotional atmosphere can be established by the use of expressions which are associated with, say, courtliness, with the emotions of love, hate, or jealousy, and in particular with the juxtaposition of such expressions. In other words, the actual disposition of words and expressions can set up an emotional atmosphere which supplements, and occasionally even contrasts with, the sense of the narrative at the point where they occur. The recognition of the techniques of formal rhetoric thus requires to be supplemented by recognition of the variations on the techniques.

Which brings me to my last appeal—I use the word advisedly. Literature is in the end a matter of style, if we use 'style' in its broad sense. And yet the matter of style is probably the most neglected of all the disciplines in the study of medieval literature. How many of us can recall studies of medieval lyrics that are comparable in this respect to studies of modern poetry? We are only beginning to study lyric imagery in its relation to the subject matter of the lyrics, and in narrative poetry even less has been done. It is obvious that the style of the romances differs from one work to another, but that their style is generally very different from that of the *chansons de geste*. Yet the distinctions are still expressed in generalities, and, except for a few specialized studies of certain stylistic features of particular authors, no thorough studies of epic style exist. Problems which are commonplaces in the study of modern literature, such as epic time, the role of the narrator, methods of characterization, of plot development, of symbolic indication, have been raised only rarely, and there are few consistent studies of them. Prosody, too, needs a new approach. There have been some excellent examples recently of fruitful cooperation between specialists in metrics and music, and several studies have shown how much is to be gained by detailed studies of the numerical patterns in medieval metrics. Yet the relation between metre and subject matter remains largely unexplored. Let me make a plea, too, for more studies of some neglected types of medieval literature, for studies of the drama which are not concerned entirely with its staging, its origins, and its 'realism', for studies of the beast epic and *fabliau* which do not regard these genres as merely collections of motifs, for structural studies of the medieval Latin narrative-allegorical works and, on a wider front, of the relation between medieval Latin literature and its vernacular contemporaries. The long obsession of medieval scholarship with origins and relations has its advantages for students of literature in the field. It leaves them a great deal to do.

Notes

1. Gustav Ehrismann, *Geschichte der deutschen Literatur bis zum Ausgang des Mittelalters* 2 vols. (Munich, 1918–35).

2. Friedrich Panzer, *Das Nibelungenlied: Entstehung und Gestalt* (Stuttgart, 1955).

3. Roger S. Loomis, *The Grail: from Celtic Myth to Christian Symbol* (New York, 1963).

4. Ramón Menéndez-Pidal, *La Chanson de Roland y el neotradicionalismo* (Madrid, 1959).

5. Henri de Lubac, *Exégèse médiévale: les quatre sens de l'écriture,* 4 vols. (Paris, 1957–64).

6. Jean Pépin, *Mythe et allégorie: les origines grecques et les contestations judéo-chrétiennes* (Paris, 1958).

7. H. B. Willson, 'Sin and Redemption in Hartmann's *Erek*', *Germanic Review*, 33 (1958): 5–14; Urban T. Holmes and Sister Amelia Klenke, *Chrétien, Troyes and the Grail* (Chapel Hill, N.C., 1959).

8. H. B. Willson, 'Walther's "Erster Reichston" ', *Germanic Review,* 39 (1964): 86.

9. Ibid., 96.

10. Ibid.

11. Karl-Josef Steinmeyer, *Untersuchungen zur allegorischen Bedeutung der Träume im altfranzösischen Rolandslied* (Munich, 1963).

12. Ibid., pp. 34–54.

13. Quoting Johannes Gorus, Ibid., 46.

14. Edmond Faral, *Les Arts poétiques du xii*e *et du xiii*e *siècle* (Paris, 1924).

edieval
philosophy and
its historians

Armand Maurer, C.S.B.

We are witnessing today a growing interest in the historical study of the Middle Ages. Colleges and universities are opening new courses in the various facets of medieval culture, and in some these courses are being combined to form a medieval centre, where students can specialize in some area of medieval studies and at the same time obtain a well-rounded view of medieval civilization. Examples that readily come to mind are the recently opened medieval centres at the University of Western Michigan, the University of California in Los Angeles, and the University of Toronto. As early as the 1920's and 1930's Institutes of Medieval Studies were founded in Toronto and Ottawa (since moved to Montreal).[1] The present series of essays on the medieval world is another example of the educational trend to which I refer.

This developing concern for the study of the Middle Ages is due to an increased awareness of the riches of medieval literature, art, institutions, and ideas in the Christian, Islamic and Jewish worlds, and to their importance for an understanding of modern culture and history. An integral aspect of this awakening to the significance of medieval civilization is a greater appreciation of philosophy in the

Middle Ages. It is now generally acknowledged that there was a rich and varied philosophical speculation in the medieval period, and that this speculation had an important impact on the beginnings of modern philosophy. Few historians today would agree, without serious reservations, with Octave Hamelin's statement, written in 1905, that in philosophy Descartes came after the ancients almost as though there was nothing but a blank between.[2] Hamelin was expressing the view, widely held in his day, that the Middle Ages were philosophically sterile; that, having begun with the Greeks, philosophy suffered an eclipse during the night of the Middle Ages, only to revive again with Descartes. Through the patient research of many historians in the last hundred years, this view has been shown to be false. Gradually the blank between ancient and modern philosophy has been filled in, so that today it is generally accepted that without a knowledge of medieval philosophy one cannot see the continuity in the growth of philosophical ideas in the Western world.

This is not to say that all historians are in agreement as to the nature of philo-sophy in the Middle Ages.[3] While generally concurring on its cultural importance, they differ widely in their interpretations and evaluations of it. The historians of the nineteenth century were deeply divided on many aspects of medieval philosophy, and especially on the central problem of its status with regard to theology. These differences of opinion have by no means been completely removed today. This is not the place to recount the history of the notion of medieval philosophy in modern times, but I would like to trace some of the important steps in its development in the nineteenth and twentieth centuries.

The scientific study of the history of medieval philosophy began in the early nineteenth century, when the romantic movement was awakening curiosity in the Gothic culture of the Middle Ages. One of the first historians to give serious atten-tion to medieval thought was Victor Cousin. Besides editing the logical works of Abelard and his correspondence with Heloise, Cousin lectured for many years on medieval philosophy in his *Cours de philosophie* in the Faculté des Lettres at the University of Paris.

Cousin did not recognize the Middle Ages as a distinct period of history. For him there were but two, antiquity and modern times.[4] 'The Middle Ages', he wrote, 'are nothing more than the painful, slow, and bloody formation of modern civilization.'[5] In his view, the Middle Ages were the cradle of modern society, and medieval philosophy the cradle of modern philosophy. Modern philosophy emerged from medieval thought as Greek thought was born from the mythology that preceded it. As Greek thought lay in shadows in the mythology of Orpheus until it came to light with the Greek philosophers, beginning with Thales, so medieval philosophy was born under the aegis of the Church, developed little by little, and was finally emancipated in modern times.[6]

Victor Cousin acknowledged the beneficial role played by Christianity in the formation of our culture. For ten centuries, he wrote, Christianity laid a solid foundation for our civilization. It began industry, it formed the state to its own image, it produced art, and also philosophy: 'I mean that very famous philosophy, though badly known, that is called scholasticism.'[7] But Cousin denied that scholasticism was philosophy in the strict sense of the word. The philosophy of the Middle Ages, he wrote in his *Histoire générale de la philosophie*, is founded on the Bible, the Fathers of the Church, and the sovereign decisions of the Church. Living under the authority of the Church, it did not enjoy that absolute liberty of thought that characterizes philosophy properly so called. 'The Middle Ages', he continued, 'are nothing else in the order of the spirit than the absolute reign of the Christian religion and the Church. Philosophy in the Middle Ages could there⁄fore be nothing else than the work of the mind in the service of the ruling faith and under the surveillance of ecclesiastical authority.'⁸

Far from its being the last word in philosophy, then, Cousin said that scholasti⁄cism was not strictly speaking philosophy at all. Its proper name is theology. True philosophy, which to Cousin was purely rational, untainted by religion, could be found among the Greeks and the moderns, but not among the medieval school⁄men. Between antiquity and modern times, the light of Greek genius gradually faded away into the night of the Middle Ages, until it was reborn at the time of Descartes.⁹

The school of medieval historians that grew up under the influence of Victor Cousin advanced the study of philosophy in the medieval world. The most famous of the group was Barthélémy Hauréau, archivist at the Bibliothèque Nationale in Paris. Hauréau edited medieval texts and published two large studies of medieval philosophy, a two⁄volume *De la philosophie scolastique* in 1850 and a three⁄volume *Histoire de la philosophie scolastique* from 1872 to 1880. A rationalist and freethinker, Hauréau saw in medieval scholasticism 'the passionate work of minds who, too long enslaved to revealed dogma, were trying to merit and gain their emancipation.'¹⁰ Was not France the native soil of scholastic philosophy? And is not the French spirit one of bold curiosity and daring to overcome all obstacles in its path? Carried away by his patriotism, Hauréau proclaimed that the emancipa⁄tion that gave birth to medieval philosophy was the French Revolution in prepara⁄tion; and what is the Revolution but France itself? (Hauréau was forgetting that in the heyday of scholasticism at the University of Paris few of the great scholastics were French. Alexander of Hales was English, Bonaventure and Thomas Aquinas were Italian, Albertus Magnus was German, Henry of Ghent was Belgian, Duns Scotus was Scottish.)

Hauréau wanted to dispel the prejudices against scholasticism that dated back to the Renaissance. The most serious of these was that scholasticism was a false philosophy whose sole purpose was to serve papist theology. It was said that the scholastics did not search for truth for its own sake; their only purpose was to expound with a new and refined method the mysteries of the Christian faith. Hence philosophy in the Middle Ages was simply a form of theology—the disputatious form, very different from dogmatic and mystical theology.¹¹

Hauréau was willing to agree that the clerical and monkish philosophers of the Middle Ages had theological preoccupations, but he insisted that their philosophy did not lack independence. More than once theologians tried to put philosophy under their yoke, but the attempt was always in vain. Philosophy reduced to slavery would not merit the name of science nor would it have attracted the noble minds it

did in the Middle Ages unless it were free; it would have died of complete abandonment.[12]

Thus, contrary to Victor Cousin, Hauréau found philosophy worthy of the
name in the medieval world, a purely rational speculation separated from theology.
The medieval masters, he contended, did not confuse philosophy and theology;
they knew well enough how to distinguish between them. Philosophy occupies
the separate domain of this universe of ours and everything enclosed by it; theology
occupies the separate domain of the Christian mysteries and sacraments. These two
separate domains were confused only by those theologians whose names, obscure or
famous, do not belong to the history of philosophy.

As for the freedom of medieval philosophers, Hauréau continued, St. Thomas
expressed himself on the nature and operations of the soul as a philosopher and with
complete liberty. Indeed, this liberty went so far that some scrupulous thinkers
today, who want to bring religion into everything, openly reject the whole
Thomistic psychology in the interests of faith. Moreover, thirteenth-century
logicians always began their courses by declaring that they did not occupy a chair
of theology; they made no pretension to discuss the mysteries or sacraments, but
treated solely of questions within their competence. It is not only the moderns,
then, who know how to distinguish between the two domains of philosophy and
theology; the Middle Ages knew the distinction, professed it, and practised it more
or less scrupulously.[13]

Thus Hauréau found in the medieval world a philosophy with its own method
and genius. What gave this philosophy its particular character was its Aristotelianism. 'Whether we call our doctors in the Middle Ages theologians or philosophers', he wrote, 'Aristotle was their master.'[14] Scholasticism began in the Middle
Ages with the discovery of the works of Aristotle, not with the invention of a new
philosophical doctrine. The originality of the different scholastic systems produced
from the ninth to the fifteenth century consisted in their novel ways of interpreting,
adding to, and correcting the text of Aristotle.

From another point of view Hauréau defined scholasticism as the philosophy
taught in the medieval schools from their establishment in the Carolingian period
to their decline in the fifteenth century. This teaching, which was entirely oral, fell
into decadence at the beginning of the age of printed books. The invention of
printing brought philosophy out of the schools and gave it a new spirit of freedom.
Then philosophy was no longer under the control of the Sorbonne; it was in the
hands of free philosophers, such as Francis Bacon, Descartes, Hobbes, and Spinoza.
Thus with the passing of the medieval schools scholasticism came to an end; it
died with Gothic art, the monastic and feudal institutions, the ancient papacy and
royalty.[15]

The Catholic revival of interest in medieval philosophy began in the first half of
the nineteenth century. Several Italian theologians, disturbed by the inferior
quality of philosophical speculation and text books in Catholic circles, advocated
a return to the philosophy of Thomas Aquinas. They described his philosophical
doctrine as 'Christian philosophy'—a term indicating the Christian inspiration of
his doctrine.[16] The neo-Thomist movement begun by these theologians culminated

72

in the encyclical *Aeterni Patris,* published by Pope Leo XIII in 1879. The title of this encyclical is 'On the Restoration of Christian Philosophy in Schools'. In it the Pope asks his readers to 'open the history of philosophy' and to study the works of Christian thinkers from St. Justin Martyr to St. Thomas Aquinas.[17] For it is in history that his readers will find exemplified the notion of Christian philosophy. The Pope praises Thomas Aquinas as the model of the Christian way of philoso-phizing, but not to the exclusion of the other patristic and medieval theologians, such as Augustine, Anselm, Albert the Great, and Bonaventure.

The encyclical gave great impetus in Catholc circles to the historical study of philosophy in the Middle Ages. Of perhaps equal importance for the development of the neo-scholastic movement was the letter sent by Pope Leo XIII to the Univer-sity of Louvain in 1880, asking that a chair of Thomistic philosophy be established. In the letter the Pope wrote: 'We propose to restore the philosophy of St. Thomas Aquinas. We desire that Catholic schools go back to that doctrine, while at the same time proposing that it be brought into harmony with modern developments and discoveries duly and scientifically established.'[18]

The first occupant of the Thomistic chair at Louvain was a young priest named Désiré Mercier, later Cardinal Mercier. Mercier undertook to establish Thomism as a philosophy in the modern world, a philosophy in harmony with Christian faith and open to the discoveries of modern science. Thus modernized, he thought, Thomism could live in the modern world as a philosophy on an equal footing with other philosophies, and it would earn the respect of Catholics and non-Cath-olics alike.

Meanwhile historians continued their researches in the philosophy of the Middle Ages. The second half of the nineteenth century saw the work of many pioneers in this field. Besides Hauréau, there were Ehrle, Denifle, Baeumker, Erdmann, Ueberweg-Heinze, Picavet, Willmann, Mandonnet, and others. As a result of their discoveries, philosophy in the Middle Ages was seen to be much more complex than earlier historians imagined. At the turn of the century the time was ripe for a new synoptic view and assessment of medieval philosophy. Of the several that were produced, none was more important or influential than that of Maurice De Wulf.

De Wulf was one of the first pupils of Mercier at Louvain. One day about 1885, while Mercier was talking to De Wulf about his work, he asked his pupil, 'Why not study the philosophy of the Middle Ages from an historical point of view? What hidden riches it must contain! Go and find M. Hauréau in Paris, the octo-generian archivist who has examined so many manuscripts at the Bibliothèque Nationale. He will set you on the right path.'[19]

Thus began the long career of Maurice De Wulf dedicated to the study of medieval philosophy. The main fruit of this career was his *Histoire de la philosophie médiévale,* first published in one volume in 1900, and enlarged to three volumes in the sixth edition, which was completed in 1947, the year of his death. De Wulf has greatly influenced twentieth-century views on philosophy in the Middle Ages through this large history and also through his *Introduction to Scholastic Philosophy* (1907) and *Philosophy and Civilization in the Middle Ages* (1922). In 1922 De Wulf lectured at Harvard on *Medieval Philosophy Illustrated from the System of*

Thomas Aquinas. He was one of the first lecturers on medieval philosophy at the Institute of Mediaeval Studies in Toronto.

I do not know if De Wulf took Mercier's advice and consulted Hauréau in Paris, but he did read the French historian's *Histoire de la philosophie scolastique,* and he found in it a description of scholastic philosophy little to his liking. As we have seen, Hauréau described scholasticism as 'the philosophy taught in the schools of the Middle Ages'. To De Wulf this is a purely verbal definition devoid of meaning. It is like describing Greek philosophy as the philosophy taught at the Greek Agora, Lyceums, Academies, and so on. Such a definition tells us nothing of the content of the philosophy taught at these places. And according to De Wulf scholasticism does have a definable content. It is, he says, a clearly determined body of doctrine, an organism that slowly developed through the centuries. Beginning as a weak and loosely knit structure in the ninth century, it grew in the twelfth and reached the peak of its development in the thirteenth. It declined in the fourteenth and fifteenth centuries, only to be revived in the sixteenth. Each generation of philosophers added its own new ideas to the common scholastic synthesis, but they differed only in details. Consequently, the scholastics formed a school in the strict sense of the term.[20]

As for the doctrinal content of scholasticism, dominant in the Middle Ages, De Wulf, like Hauréau, thought it was Aristotelian in origin and vocabulary. Scholasticism is not a monist but a plurist philosophy. It is not a pantheism but a dualist system of God as pure act and creatures as composites of act and potency, matter and form, essence and existence. It is creationist, its God is a personal being, its interpretation of the material world is evolutionist and finalistic. Its psychology is spiritualistic, experimental, and objective.[21]

The formation of the scholastic system, according to De Wulf, began in the early Middle Ages, when the important doctrines were being formulated that would become 'the nucleus of the synthesis of the thirteenth century'. Hence the early medieval period can be called 'pre-scholastic', or the 'infancy of scholasticism'. In the thirteenth century scholasticism at first was rather loosely organized by the pre-Thomists such as Alexander of Hales and Bonaventure. Their thought was Augustinian and Neoplatonic, harking back to the early Middle Ages. Aristotelianism was superimposed on Augustinism, resulting in an eclecticism in which Aristotelian doctrines were compromised by alien views. In short, none of the pre-Thomists worked out a compact philosophical synthesis.

With Aquinas the scholastic synthesis appeared in all its fullness and power. It was he who 'set forth [this synthesis] as a grand and enduring system, while he at the same time dismantled many a theory that had previously loomed large in the schools.'[22]

Thus for De Wulf scholasticism was a truly organic system of doctrines. A product of medieval culture, it shared in that culture's unity. It was not, however, the whole of philosophy in the Middle Ages. There were other philosophical systems which denied one or more of the fundamental theses of scholasticism.[23] These were the work of what De Wulf called 'anti-scholastics', the chief of whom were John Scotus Erigena, the Cathars and Albigensians, pantheists of the twelfth-century school of Chartres, Amaury of Bènes and David of Dinant in the thirteenth century, Averroists like Siger of Brabant, heterodox mystics, Nicholas of Autrecourt, and John of Mirecourt. Other medieval philosophers, while not con-tradicting the essential doctrines of scholasticism, deviated from its spirit and hence were called 'dissident scholastics'. Among them De Wulf included Roger Bacon, Raymond Lull, John Baconthorpe, Meister Eckhart, and Nicholas of Cusa.

The main proponents of the scholastic system, according to De Wulf, were Thomas Aquinas and Duns Scotus, and to a lesser degree Alexander of Hales and Bonaventure. 'Their philosophy', he wrote, 'is an intellectual monument, and the sense of proportion which it reveals is the same as that of the Gothic cathedral to which it has so often been compared'.[24] There were different forms of this common philosophy, just as there were different forms of the Gothic cathedral, but they shared a common spirit and basic store of ideas. 'Its leading principles', De Wulf said, 'were accepted by all the scholastics. . . . The forms assumed by scholasticism were numerous and noteworthy, each of the great scholastics realizing in the concrete, according to the bent of his peculiar genius, the one dominant abstract synthesis.'[25]

De Wulf's notion of a common scholastic philosophy came under severe criticism as early as the first decades of the twentieth century. His critics pointed out that a close examination of the great medieval thinkers does not reveal a unitary philosophical teaching but a number of highly original and fundamentally diver-gent systems.[26] With progress in the knowledge of medieval thought it was becom-ing more difficult to maintain that the medieval scholastics taught a common doctrine with only incidental divergences. Taking this criticism into account, De Wulf somewhat modified his views on medieval philosophy after 1925. He dropped the term 'scholastic synthesis' and used the less rigid expression 'common intellectual patrimony' to designate the fund of ideas shared by the medieval philosophers. He also conformed to the more general practice of the time of identi-fying 'scholastic philosophy' with 'medieval philosophy'. After 1925 he used the term 'scholasticism' to designate any medieval philosophy; at the same time he dropped the terms 'anti-scholastics' and 'dissident scholastics'.[27] These changes in terminology indicate a more flexible and supple notion of medieval philosophy than before, but De Wulf never abandoned his thesis of a common body of philosophical ideas shared by the leading scholastics and expressed most system-atically by Thomas Aquinas.

The second important thesis defended by De Wulf was the independence of medieval philosophy from medieval theology. He insisted that these two were not to be confused. Theology is based on the revealed word of God and depends on authority; philosophy is based on the light of human reason and it proceeds by scientific proofs. All the scholastics of the thirteenth century knew this distinction and practised it.[28]

De Wulf was here taking sides with Hauréau against Victor Cousin. As we have seen, Cousin thought that what is generally called medieval philosophy was in reality theology; in the Middle Ages rational thought was trying to emerge from its bondage to religion but never adequately succeeded in doing so. Hauréau, on the other hand, insisted that philosophy was not enslaved to religion in the Middle Ages, especially in Thomas Aquinas.

In De Wulf's opinion, medieval philosophy had a long struggle to become independent of religion. In the ninth century John Scotus Erigena, faithful to the patristic tradition, made no distinction between revelation and philosophy. Like Augustine, he identified true religion and true philosophy. Gradually, however, philosophy became conscious of itself and its autonomy. The eleventh century broke with the past and achieved a practical distinction between philosophy and theology, and finally in the thirteenth these two sciences were clearly defined as distinct bodies of doctrine and their mutual relations were established.[29]

De Wulf did not deny that philosophy in the thirteenth century had close ties with theology. His Princeton lectures on *Philosophy and Civilization in the Middle Ages* emphasize the religious character of the medieval period and especially of the thirteenth century. Religious inspiration, he told his audience, affected all aspects of thirteenth-century civilization—politics, art, morals, family, work—and it likewise affected philosophy. In this century philosophy 'was bathed in a general atmosphere of religion which pervaded everything else.'[30] But he argued that this did not enslave philosophy to religion or destroy the autonomy of philosophy.

In defining the relation between scholastic philosophy and theology, De Wulf insisted on the subordination of the former to the latter. In the Middle Ages theology was the queen of the sciences, and philosophy was beneath it in dignity. Philosophical studies were rarely pursued for their own sake; for the most part they were a step to the higher science of theology. Theologians used philosophy in the work of apologetics. Thus we find in the theological *summae* genuine philosophical treatises; for example, in the *Summa* of theology of Thomas Aquinas there are integral philosophical treatises in psychology, ethics, and law. The scholastics, De Wulf says, had a passion 'for combining (but not confusing) philosophical and theological questions in the same work'.[31]

Not only did theology benefit from its contact with philosophy; philosophy was also assisted by the higher science of theology. Theology raised many problems for scholastic philosophers, and it gave them a negative guide by which to judge the correctness of their conclusions. They were convinced that the Catholic faith expresses the infallible word of God, and also that the truth cannot contradict itself. Consequently, when their conclusions in philosophy contradicted their faith, they knew these conclusions must be wrong. Thus faith prohibited scholastics from teaching certain doctrines, such as the eternity of the world, but this prohibition was purely negative; faith gave philosophy no positive proof for its own assertions. Philosophy had to furnish its proofs from its own resources. Moreover, the negative control of theology over philosophy applied only to matters which they shared in common. It had no force in many domains of philosophy where faith had no concern, for example in logic. Therefore scholasticism was affected only to a very limited extent by its subordination to theology. In its own domain it remained a distinct and independent science.

In brief, this was De Wulf's conception of medieval philosophy. He considered it to be a scholasticism held in common by all the leading medieval minds and expressed most clearly and in the most orderly fashion by Thomas Aquinas. This scholastic philosophy was made fruitful by the Christian religion, but its ties with religion were historical and sociological rather than doctrinal; they in no way deprived scholasticism of its autonomy. As for the location of this scholastic philosophy, it could be found incorporated in the vast theological works of the Middle Ages, such as the *summae* of theology and the quodlibetal and disputed questions.

Was it a mere coincidence that this description of scholastic philosophy fitted so neatly the needs of De Wulf's master, Monsignor Mercier? When Mercier directed De Wulf to the study of medieval philosophy, his interests were not primarily historical; he wanted to revive scholastic philosophy in the modern world. De Wulf found in the Middle Ages a scholasticism worthy of being revived: a common synthesis or partimony of ideas that could be disengaged from its theological setting and from the outmoded scientific notions of the Middle Ages. Moreover, since this scholastic philosophy was best exemplified by the thought of St. Thomas, Mercier's neo-scholasticism could be practically identified with neo-Thomism.

But we do not have to surmise that there was a connection between Mercier's project and the findings of his famous pupil, Maurice De Wulf. We have it from no less an authority on the subject than Monsignor Noël, the third president of the Institut Supérieur de Philosophie in Louvain. Writing on the occasion of the fortieth anniversary of De Wulf's teaching at the Institut, Noël had these illuminating remarks to make concerning the relation of De Wulf to Mercier:

'Nevertheless, in the mind of M. De Wulf, the point of his work has never been purely historical. From the very first it seems that the theses he defends are closely connected in his mind with the justification of the movement of the revival of scholasticism, of which his master, Monsignor Mercier, is one of the chief founders. How can scholasticism be revived if it has no systematic unity? How can we pretend to introduce it among contemporary philosophies if it is nothing but a theological doctrine? How can we make it live in the modern world if it is bound up with outmoded notions of pre-Copernican physics and astronomy? To these questions [De Wulf's] *Introduction to Neoscholastic Philosophy*, written in 1904, furnishes answers that can be drawn from [his] *History of Mediaeval Philosophy*. There is a doctrine common to the great scholastic doctors; this doctrine is a philosophy and above all a metaphysics; it is not necessarily tied up with the consequences that have been drawn from it by applying its principles to the data of brief experience or a naïve imagination. Moreover, the decline of scholasticism on the eve of the Renaissance was due to accidental circumstances: a barbarous language, the abuse of dialectics, the ignorance of its defenders. It collapsed "not from lack of ideas but from lack of men." Hence there is nothing to prevent its revival.'[32]

Let us grant at once that De Wulf's conclusions were well adapted to further Mercier's project of reviving scholasticism. But this is no criterion of their historical accuracy. The question remained whether the portrait of medieval philosophy drawn by De Wulf was true to historical reality. A number of critics in the 1920's thought it was not. Among them was a young man who was appointed Professor of the History of Medieval Philosophy at the Sorbonne in 1921, and who was destined to open a new phase in the understanding of medieval philosophy. His name was Etienne Gilson.

Gilson came to medieval philosophy by a most unlikely route—René Descartes.

While studying philosophy at the Sorbonne he sought the advice of Professor Lévy-Bruhl in choosing the subject of his doctoral thesis. Lévy-Bruhl suggested that he study the vocabulary and ideas borrowed from scholasticism by Descartes. At the time, Gilson says, neither he nor any of his professors knew anything about scholasticism. All the professors at the Sorbonne were convinced that since the time of Descartes scholasticism was 'a mere piece of mental archeology'.[33]

Gilson spent nine years preparing his thesis, which was printed in 1913 under the title: *La liberté chez Descartes et la théologie*. During these years he learned to read Thomas Aquinas and the other medieval schoolmen, and he also discovered, to his great surprise, that far from being dull and barren they were better metaphysicians than Descartes. 'As the work progressed', Gilson wrote in his recent philosophical memoirs, 'I experienced a growing feeling of intellectual dismay in seeing what impoverishment metaphysics had suffered at the hands of Descartes. Most of the philosophical positions he had retained had their proper justification, not in his own works, but in those of the scholastics. . . . From scholasticism to cartesianism the loss in metaphysical substance seemed to me frightening. Looking back across forty-five years I distinctly remember the feeling of fear I experienced on the day when, after holding back my pen for a long time, I finally wrote this simple sentence: "On all these points the thought of Descartes, in comparison with the sources from which it derives, marks much less a gain than a loss".'[34]

This simple sentence flatly contradicted the commonly accepted view of the historians of the day. And its consequence was immediately evident to Gilson. 'If it is possible to find in the middle ages', he continued, 'metaphysical conclusions better worked out technically and more completely justified than they are in Descartes, then it becomes difficult to maintain with Cousin that between the Greeks and Descartes there was nothing but a progressive dimming of the Greek light leading to a sort of intellectual night. If on certain points there is more in Saint Thomas than in Descartes, one can no longer say with Hamelin that "Descartes appears after the ancients as though there was nothing between the Greeks and himself".'[35]

The force of this conviction has sustained Gilson throughout his long career as an historian of medieval philosophy. His first work in the medieval field was a study of Thomistic philosophy entitled *Le Thomisme,* the first edition of which appeared in 1919. There followed in 1924 *La philosophie de saint Bonaventure.* The most remarkable conclusion of this work is that the thought of Bonaventure cannot be described as an inferior form of Thomism, a *thomisme manqué.* Like the philosophy of St. Thomas, that of St. Bonaventure is thoroughly Christian in inspiration and purpose, and yet it is a different philosophy, neither conflicting nor coinciding with Thomism. St. Bonaventure had no intention of imitating or following St. Thomas; he went his own way on the path to Christian wisdom, taking St. Augustine as his principal guide.

In 1922 Gilson wrote his first general survey of medieval philosophy, *La philosophie au moyen âge.* This appeared in a second, much expanded edition in 1944. In 1955 he published his monumental *History of Christian Philosophy in the Middle Ages.* These volumes, summarizing the results of his own research and that of many other historians, while putting the whole history of medieval philosophy in new perspective, made it abundantly clear that there was no common scholastic synthesis in the Middle Ages.

During these decades the philosophy of St. Thomas continued to be Gilson's main interest, and his deepening understanding of it, especially in its metaphysical aspect, is recorded in the successive editions of *Le Thomisme*. The fifth edition, published in 1944, contains a new chapter entitled 'Existence et réalité', which stresses the originality of St. Thomas' views on being and existence. Far from being a 'baptized Aristotelianism' or simple variant of a common scholasticism, Thomism in this perspective appears as a new metaphysical view of reality. Because it posits the act of existing as the keystone of metaphysics and as the very core of reality, Gilson calls it an, indeed the *only*, existential philosophy.[36]

Besides Thomism, other distinctive forms of medieval philosophy have emerged into clearer light in recent years. As far back as 1852 Ernest Renan did the pioneering work on the influence of the Arabian philosopher Averroës on the Christian West.[37] Since Renan's day more accurate and detailed information has been unearthed concerning the movement called Latin Averroism, or, as some historians prefer to call it, radical Aristotelianism. Siger of Brabant has been identified as its leader in the thirteenth century, and the history of the movement he initiated has been traced into the Renaissance. Siger's name was preserved in Dante's *Paradiso*, but after the Renaissance his identity and philosophy were lost to history. The discovery of his long lost manuscripts and the reconstruction of his thought and place in history are one of the significant achievements of historians of medieval philosophy in the past century.[38] More recently still, the works of Boethius of Dacia, an associate of Siger's in the Averroist movement, are beginning to come to light.[39]

The historical significance of radical Aristotelianism cannot be measured by its philosophical fecundity. It was singularly unproductive of new philosophical ideas, contenting itself with remaining as close as possible to the philosophy of Aristotle as interpreted by his commentator, Averroës. Radical Aristotelianism is important in the history of philosophy because it introduced into the medieval world the separation of philosophy from faith and theology that became the ideal of modern thought. As Professor Gilson says, Averroës and his followers were 'the representatives of philosophy *qua* pure philosophy in the middle ages, or, at least, of the purely philosophical spirit from the thirteenth century up to the beginning of modern times.'[40] Their effort to make philosophy as independent from theology as possible is at the origin of the opposition to the medieval notion of Christian philosophy. It is also the beginning of the elimination from theology of purely rationally demonstrable conclusions and its limitation to the explication of the dogmas of faith.

Another discovery of the last fifty years is the influence of the Arabian philosopher Avicenna on the Latin West. We now know that there was a Latin Avicennism in the Middle Ages as well as a Latin Averroism. One of Gilson's noteworthy discoveries is the combination of Augustinian and Avicennian doctrines in certain theologians of the Franciscan school, which he called by the rather cumbersome name of 'Avicennizing Augustinism.'[41] In 1938 Jean Paulus published an outstanding book on Henry of Ghent which showed the strong

Avicennian influence on his metaphysics.[42] Gilson's studies on Duns Scotus revealed that on more than one point the philosophy of Avicenna was the foundation of Scotism.[43]

More exact research has also clarified the role of Platonism in medieval philosophy. A continuous Platonic tradition has been traced from antiquity to the Renaissance.[44] Even the schoolmen of the later Middle Ages, when Aristotelianism held the dominant position in philosophy, show the influence of Platonism. St. Thomas Aquinas was no exception; his thought, like that of all his contemporaries, bears the impress of the Platonic current of philosophy.[45]

Through these and other important discoveries it has become clear how complex and diversified philosophical movements and syntheses were in the Middle Ages. All historians do not interpret them in the same way; but they no longer subscribe to De Wulf's notion of a common scholastic system or patrimony of ideas inspired mainly by Aristotle. As Anton Pegis recently wrote: 'Medieval philosophy, as we see it today, is a community of philosophizing theologians rather than a common synthesis.'[46]

While Gilson and others were laying the ghost of a common medieval scholasticism, they were also putting into better perspective the position of medieval philosophy in relation to Christian faith. As we have seen, De Wulf maintained the independence of medieval philosophy from theology. While recognizing the religious setting of philosophy in the medieval world and its negative subordination to theology, he insisted that as a body of doctrine it was autonomous, having its own formal object and methods of procedure. If this is true, it makes little sense to speak of a *Christian* philosophy in the Middle Ages, for this implies the direct and positive influence of Christianity on philosophy, and this is what De Wulf and his followers denied. Indeed, they thought that the notion of 'Christian philosophy' is a contradiction in terms. Is not philosophy, in the words of De Wulf, a *rational* study of the universal order of things by their ultimate causes and principles? How then can it be open to the positive influence of religious faith without ceasing to be philosophy?[47]

Gilson's study of the Middle Ages convinced him that it produced, besides a Christian literature and art, a Christian philosophy. This is the theme of his Gifford Lectures, published in 1932 under the title *The Spirit of Medieval Philosophy*. The reality of a Christian philosophy in the Middle Ages was forced upon Gilson by historical facts. Looking for the sources of philosophy in the Middle Ages, he discovered that there were in the main two: (1) the classical philosophy of the Greeks, and especially Aristotelianism, (2) Christian revelation. Under the influence of Christianity, philosophical ideas unknown to the ancient world were created in the Middle Ages, ideas which have become part and parcel of modern philosophy. Hence Christian revelation played a decisive and positive role in the formation of medieval philosophy, so that it merits the name of Christian.

If this is true, there is a kind of unity among the philosophies of the Middle Ages, since most of them were created under the influence of the same Christian revelation. Thus Gilson in effect substituted the notion of Christian philosophy for the outmoded concept of a common scholasticism. But Christian philosophy, in his view, had no doctrinal unity; it embraced a number of diverse and even mutually incompatible philosophical syntheses, the chief of which were Augustinism, Albertism, Bonaventurianism, Thomism, Scotism, and Ockhamism. Further, more, no one of these is a philosophy independent of theology. They were created not by pure philosophers but by theologians as rational tools for their theologies, and they were in the main expressed in their theological writings.

These were Gilson's views on medieval philosophy for many years. He is now in a new phase of his understanding of this philosophy, one that brings him closer to the reality of the medieval world. Like Cousin, Hauréau, and De Wulf, he approached medieval thought not as a theologian but as an historian of philosophy and as a philosopher. He found philosophy in the Middle Ages, not only in commentaries on Aristotle, logical treatises, and philosophical *opuscula,* but above all in theological writings. Paradoxically, he found the most original and important philosophical notions of the schoolmen in their works of theology. From these he extracted rationally demonstrable theses and presented them as the Christian philosophies of the Middle Ages. And he did not hesitate to call their authors philosophers. Did they not philosophize abundantly and wisely? Did they not create new philosophical notions that have entered into the heritage of Western philosophy?

With a deeper understanding of medieval theology, Gilson in recent years has come to see the work of the medieval schoolmen in a different light. He never doubted that schoolmen such as Thomas Aquinas were professionally theologians and that they philosophized within the context of their theologies and for the sake of their theologies. But as he studied more closely the Thomistic notion of theology he came to realize that what he presented as the Christian philosophy of St. Thomas is in reality a part of his theology—the part, namely, which St. Thomas considered to be demonstrable by reason. In short, what Gilson called medieval philosophies were in fact 'truncated theologies'.[48]

Thus, unexpectedly, medieval theology turned out to be the key to the understanding of medieval philosophy. Since the time of Descartes it has generally been thought that theology is separate from philosophy; that theologizing is something quite different from, and even incompatible with, philosophizing. This modern notion of theology was shared by the early historians of medieval philosophy and it intruded itself into their interpretation of this philosophy. De Wulf, while disclaiming any competence in the history of medieval theology, ascribed the Cartesian separation of theology from philosophy to the Middle Ages. He wrote that 'the distinction between philosophy where one proceeds according to *reason* and theology where one proceeds according to the data of *dogma* was already fully established at the time of Descartes. This distinction appeared already at the end of the twelfth century; the thirteenth century exposed it under its methodological form, and Descartes took it up in exactly the same terms that the scholastics had used.'[49] Under these conditions there is no room in theology for philosophical truths known by the light of human reason. But this is clearly not the case with the scholastic theology of St. Thomas. His summation of theology in his *Summa theologiae* is filled with philosophically demonstrated truths. As Gilson delved more deeply into the Thomistic notion of theology, he realized that in the intention of St. Thomas everything in the *Summa* is theological, even those parts that he had extracted and called Christian philosophy.

Thus Gilson proved that Victor Cousin was right: the philosophy of the Middle Ages was in fact theology.[50] But he also proved that Barthélémy Hauréau was right: schoolmen such as St. Thomas developed strictly rational philosophies worthy of the name.[51] This must be qualified, however, by adding that unlike modern philosophies those of the Middle Ages were created within theologies for theological purposes.

Looking back over the history of medieval philosophy in the last century and a half, we can see that the constant danger besetting historians was the interpretation of the Middle Ages through specifically modern concepts. The medieval world is so distant from our own; its life and spirit were so foreign to ours, that it is only through a persistent effort of intelligence and imagination that we can enter into it and see it as it really was. De Wulf himself was well aware of this. He warned students of the Middle Ages: 'To understand the medieval civilization—to penetrate into its very spirit—we must first of all avoid forcing parallels with the mentality and customs of our own age. Many a study has been marred because its author was unable to resist this temptation. Medieval civilization is not the same as that of our own age. Its factors have a different meaning; they were made for men of a different age. . . . Further, in order to understand the Middle Ages, we must think directly after their manner of thinking. . . . A right study of the civilization of the Middle Ages must take it in and for itself, in its internal elements and structure; it must be understood from within.'[52] If today we are closer than ever before to an understanding of the nature of philosophy in the Middle Ages, it is because historians have taken this lesson to heart.

Notes

1. See L. K. Shook, 'University Centers and Institutes of Medieval Studies', *Journal of Higher Education*, 38 (1967): 484–92.
2. O. Hamelin, *Le système de Descartes* (Paris, 1921), p. 15.
3. Examples of recent divergent interpretations of medieval philosophy are A. C. Pegis, *The Middle Ages and Philosophy* (Chicago, 1963), and F. Van Steenberghen, *Histoire de la*

philosophie: Période chrétienne (Louvain, 1964). The introduction and conclusion of the latter book were published under the title 'La philosophie en chrétienté', in *Revue philosophique de Louvain*, 61 (1963): 561–82.

4. V. Cousin, *Cours de philosophie* (Paris, 1836), p. 1.

5. V. Cousin, *Cours de l'histoire de la philosophie moderne* 2ème série [1828–30] (Paris, 1847), 1: 37.

6. V. Cousin, *Histoire générale de la philosophie*, 9th ed. (Paris, 1872), pp. 218–19.

7. V. Cousin, *Cours de l'histoire de la philosophie moderne*, p. 37.

8. V. Cousin, *Histoire générale de la philosophie*, p. 218.

9. V. Cousin, *Cours de philosophie*, p. 2.

10. B. Hauréau, *Histoire de la philosophie scolastique* (Paris, 1872), 1: 121.

11. Ibid., 29–30.

12. Ibid., 31.

13. Ibid.

14. Ibid., 33–34.

15. Ibid., 36.

16. See É. Gilson, 'What is Christian Philosophy?', in *A Gilson Reader*, ed. A. C. Pegis (Garden City, 1957) pp. 185–86. For a detailed account of the revival of Thomism in the nineteenth century, see É. Gilson, ed., *Recent Philosophy: Hegel to the Present* (New York, 1966), pp. 330–54.

17. *Aeterni Patris*, 10, trans. in *The Church Speaks to the Modern World*, ed. É. Gilson (Garden City, 1954), p. 39.

18. D. Mercier, 'La philosophie néoscolastique', *Revue néoscolastique*, 1 (1894):10.

19. This is De Wulf's own report of Mercier's words, cited by L. Noël, 'L'œuvre de Monsieur De Wulf', *Hommage à Maurice De Wulf: Revue néoscolastique de philosophie*, 36 (1934): 11. For De Wulf's work as an historian of medieval philosophy, see ibid., 11–38; F. Van Steenberghen, 'Maurice De Wulf, historien de la philosophie médiévale', *Revue philosophique de Louvain*, 46 (1948): 421–47; E. Bertola, *Saggi e studi di filosofia medioevale* (Padua, 1951), pp. 70–77.

20. M. De Wulf, *Histoire de la philosophie scolastique dans les Pays-Bas et la Principauté de Liége* (Louvain and Paris, 1895), pp. xi–xii.

21. M. De Wulf, *Histoire de la philosophie médiévale*, 1st ed. (Louvain, 1900), pp. 288–89.

22. M. De Wulf, *History of Medieval Philosophy*, 1st English ed. [3rd ed. of *Histoire de la philosophie médiévale*], trans. P. Coffey (London, 1909), p. 268.

23. M. De Wulf, *An Introduction to Scholastic Philosophy*, trans. P. Coffey (New York, 1956), pp. 37–53.

24. M. De Wulf, *Philosophy and Civilization in the Middle Ages* (Princeton, 1922, reprinted New York, 1953), p. 109.

25. M. De Wulf, *Histoire de la philosophie médiévale*, 2nd ed. (Louvain, 1905), p. 265.

26. De Wulf takes account of these criticisms in 'Notion de la scolastique médiévale', *Revue néoscolastique de philosophie*, 18 (1911): 177–96.

27. M. De Wulf, 'Y eut-il une philosophie scolastique au moyen âge?', *Revue néoscolastique de philosophie*, 29 (1927): 5–27.

28. M. De Wulf, *An Introduction to Scholastic Philosophy*, pp. 8–10.

29. M. De Wulf, *Histoire de la philosophie en Belgique* (Brussels, Paris, 1910), pp. 7–8.

30. M. De Wulf, *Philosophy and Civilization in the Middle Ages*, p. 167.

31. Ibid., 170.

32. In *Hommage à Maurice De Wulf*, pp. 25–26.

33. É. Gilson, *God and Philosophy* (New Haven, 1941), p. xii.

34. É. Gilson, *The Philosopher and Theology*, trans. Céale Gilson (New York, 1962), pp. 88–89.

35. Ibid., 89.

36. É. Gilson, *Le Thomisme* (Paris, 1944 and 1947), p. 511; 6th ed. (Paris, 1965), p. 448.

37. E. Renan, *Averroès et l'averroïsme* (Paris, 1852).

38. See A. Maurer, 'The State of Historical Research in Siger of Brabant', *Speculum*, 31 (1956): 49–56.

39. See G. Sajó, 'Boetius de Dacia und seine philosophische Bedeutung', *Miscellania mediaevalia*, vol. 2: *Die Metaphysik im Mittelalter*, ed. P. Wilpert (Berlin, 1963), pp. 454–63. Boetius de Dacia, *Tractatus de aeternitate mundi,* ed. G. Sajó, 2nd ed. (Quellen und Studien zur Geschichte der Philosophie, 4; Berlin, 1964).

40. É. Gilson, *History of Christian Philosophy in the Middle Ages* (New York, 1955), p. 542.

41. See É. Gilson, 'Pourquoi saint Thomas a critiqué saint Augustin', *Archives d'histoire doctrinale et littéraire du moyen âge*, 1 (1926): 5–127; 'Les sources gréco-arabes de l'augustinisme avicennisant', *Archives . . .*, 4 (1929): 5–149.

42. J. Paulus, *Henri de Gand: Essai sur les tendances de sa métaphysique* (Paris, 1938).

43. See É. Gilson, 'Avicenne et le point de départ de Duns Scot', *Archives . . .*, 2 (1927): 89–149; *Jean Duns Scot: Introduction à ses positions fondamentales* (Paris, 1952).

44. See R. Klibansky, *The Continuity of the Platonic Tradition during the Middle Ages* (London, 1939).

45. See R. J. Henle, *Saint Thomas and Platonism* (The Hague, 1956); C. Fabro, *La nozione metafisica di partecipazione secondo S. Tommaso d'Aquino*, 3rd ed. (Turin, 1963); L. B. Geiger, *La participation dans la philosophie de S. Thomas d'Aquin*, 2nd ed. (Paris, 1953); P. O. Kristeller, *Le thomisme et la pensée italienne de la Renaissance* (Montreal, 1967).

46. A. C. Pegis, *The Middle Ages and Philosophy*, pp. 50–51.

47. M. De Wulf, *An Introduction to Scholastic Philosophy*, p. 7; *Histoire de la philosophie médiévale*, 6th ed. (Louvain, 1934), I: 19, 285. See also F. Van Steenberghen, *Histoire de la philosophie: Période chrétienne*, p. 174.

48. See É. Gilson, *The Philosopher and Theology*, p. 94. In his *History of Christian Philosophy in the Middle Ages*, p. 543, Gilson concluded that on historical grounds one is forced to recognize the presence of purely rational speculation in medieval theology.

49. These words were spoken by M. De Wulf in criticism of Gilson's broad use of the word 'theology' in his thesis *La liberté chez Descartes et la théologie*. See *Bulletin de la société française de philosophie*, 14 (1914): 220–21. For De Wulf's avowal of 'incompetence in the domain of the history of dogmatic and mystic theology', see his *Introduction to Scholastic Philosophy*, p. 10.

50. See É. Gilson, *The Philosopher and Theology*, p. 95.

51. See É. Gilson, *Le thomisme*, 6th ed., p. 7.

52. M. De Wulf, *Philosophy and Civilization in the Middle Ages*, pp. 4–5.

harlemagne
and
his empire

Robert Folz

This article is an attempt to take account, briefly, of a few of the many problems presented by the reign of Charlemagne. They have been ranged under four head-ings: the economy, the society, the Empire, and the imperial administration. This method was the only practical one in view of the complexity and the richness of the subject. Perhaps, in spite of this fragmentation, there will emerge a general idea of the vast amount of historical material that the subject entails.

The problems which are commonly associated with the Carolingian economy have been reopened in the last thirty years by the great work of Henri Pirenne, *Mahomet et Charlemagne* (1936). Without recapitulating the theses of the celebrated historian, or following the controversies to which they have given rise since their appearance,[1] it may be taken as an established fact that the economic life of the Carolingian Empire was based on land, within a society which was essentially rural and in which the towns played but a secondary role. The question of the prevailing size of agricultural units has been equally controversial. More than half a century ago Alfons Dopsch, raising his voice against the traditional view that the great estate was predominant, attempted to demonstrate that large holdings of land were much less extensive and numerous than had been supposed and that the greater part of the cultivated land was covered with small estates.[2] Even though the views of the Austrian historian met with little acceptance, they had at least the merit of drawing attention to the small estate and to the untenability of the notion that a uniform agrarian system prevailed thoughout the Empire.[3] The fact remains, nevertheless, that in the heart of the Carolingian state, between the rivers Loire and Rhine, the great estate generally prevailed; it was equally common in central and southern Germany (Franconia, Swabia, and Bavaria). It is in these regions that the relatively numerous and detailed sources[4] allow us to see most clearly the characteristics of this system: an unequal distribution of acreage among the great domains; a bipartite land structure consisting of the *indominicatum* and the *mansus*; the hereditary tenants of the latter being under an obligation to render dues both in money and in kind to their masters and, above all, labour services on seigniorial lands, because of the lack of manpower directly attached to these estates.[5] The problem most discussed nowadays is that of the *mansus*, as it appears in the sources. In particular it seems impossible to consider it as being, at the outset of the ninth century, a family holding of more or less constant area or to surmise that it originated in a general distribution of lands put into effect at a very early date. Nor does it seem possible simply to identify the *mansus* with the *hoba* (*Hufe*) which one encounters on Germanic estates.[6] The works of Charles E. Perrin on the *mansus* in the Parisian region have emphasized the inequality of the tenures in the west of the Empire, their overpopulation and their fragmentation into half- and quarter-*mansi*.[7] One should not conclude, however, that the above-mentioned overpopulation was general; it appeared only in certain districts and on particular estates. The density of the rural population remained low. At the same time assarts existed both within existing estates and in certain regions such as Septimania, Franconia, and Carinthia, where they were far from negligible.[8] As for the economic role of the domain, it was above all to assure the sustenance of the owner; on a secondary level of importance, it took part in the existing barter economy.

As for the barter economy, various signs bear witness to the occurrence, from the middle of the eighth century, of a certain economic expansion. Even though the towns kept the characteristics which they had assumed during the preceding period,[9] there appeared—above all in Northern Gaul, in the very area where the domanial system had experienced its greatest expansion—new agglomerations of population which were closely linked to the river network of the region. These were the *portus*, small settlements on the rivers, with wharfs and warehouses, where the inhabitants busied themselves with inland transportation and commerce. They could be found either under the ramparts of old episcopal cities (Mainz, Cologne) or consisting of entirely new foundations, as on the Meuse (Huy and Namur) or the Scheldt (Valenciennes and Ghent). The most important of them were located on the water front of the Channel (Quentovic) and of the North Sea (Duurstede on the Lek).[10] To this first sign of economic awakening must be added the activities of the *negotiatores*, that is to say, the merchants.[11] Among them there were numerous pedlars, who were far from prosperous. Side by side with these there were Jews, who continued the activity of the Syrian traders of the Merovingian epoch by supplying Oriental products and trading in slaves. Finally there were professional merchants, such as those from Mainz and Verdun, and especially the Frisians, who imported Oriental products and English cloth and exported cloth woven in the domanial workshops of Northern Gaul. Thus the activities of the barter market varied considerably in nature and volume. The local markets had multiplied during the eighth century, encouraged as they were by the local lord who aimed at levying lucrative taxes as commerce developed. The transactions, however, involved only retail trade on a small scale. More considerable seems to have been the interregional trade in foodstuffs or certain raw materials: grain, for which Mainz was an important market place; wine from the Rhine valley and the hills bordering the Seine, Oise, and Aisne: finally salt, and metals such as iron and lead.[12] There existed also a *grand commerce* in products which were less bulky but fetched a high price. They were reserved to a wealthy clientèle provided by the court, by cathedrals and monasteries, and by lay *proceres*. Among these products figured spices, perfumes and silks,[13] which came from the Byzantine and Moslem East and were transported, always in small quantities, by the northern route through Russia and Belgium; or on highways passing through the Slavonic countries and the Danube plain; or by way of the eastern Mediterranean, southern Italy, or Venice; or, lastly, across the western Mediterranean, where navigation, though hampered by Arab piracy, was carried on by one means or another.[14] But on the whole, although these few facts allow us to qualify Pirenne's thesis, it must not be forgotten that such commercial transactions were 'precarious, irregular, and spontaneously organized in frail networks'.[15]

However diminished this commercial movement had been, it presupposed, in order to maintain itself, some means of payment, without which it would soon have collapsed. What were these means of payment? During the centuries which preceded the rise of the Carolingians, the monetary standard in the West had remained the gold currency of Byzantium, the *solidus* of gold with its subdivisions (such as the *triens*). It was in imitation of this currency that the Germanic kings had minted gold coins intended to cover the purchases made by Westerners in the East. As a result of the progressive exhaustion of the supply of gold, which the West did not produce for itself, this monetary system weakened rapidly in the course of the seventh century, to disappear completely at the beginning of the eighth. At the same time, silver money had continued to deteriorate; it became a 'black' currency of almost no intrinsic value.[16] The work of the first two Carolingian rulers was to restore the silver currency, to strengthen it, and to transform it into the only medium of exchange on the internal Frankish market. It is true that Charlemagne had a few pieces of gold struck when he became king of the Lombards. The rarity of these coins, however, shows that their issue was not regular. The Carolingian system was monometallic and was based on silver. The restoration which had begun under Pepin the Short was continued and completed by Charlemagne.[17] To begin with, the latter decided to cut only 240 pennies to the pound of silver, not 264 as his predecessor had decreed about A.D. 760, thus raising the content of silver in a penny to 1.36 gm. The gold *solidus*, having disappeared, was replaced by a silver *solidus*, a money of account whose value was fixed at twelve pennies. This proportion of one to twelve corresponded roughly to that of the value of silver to gold. Then, at the end of the eighth century, Charlemagne considerably reinforced the weight of the pound, raising it to 491 gm, and, as 240 pennies continued to be cut to a pound, the content of silver in a penny amounted to 2.04 gm. These measures represented considerable progress in relation to the previous period; the strengthening of silver gave some vigour to local and regional exchanges of goods, which previously had been reduced to barter. But the fact remains that white metal was rare and the circulation of money was reduced; prices continued to go down.[18] In short, even though there had been genuine trading activities, they had only a limited effect; they did not create productive personal fortunes. There was only one possible form of wealth—land. The society of the Carolingian empire was essentially a land-holding society.

The principal fact to be emphasized in this social structure is the existence of a strong landed aristocracy which no other class could properly counter-balance— neither the merchants, who were too few in number, nor the free small peasants, who, because of unfavourable economic circumstances, were exposed to contin-uous pressure exerted by the *proceres*. The aristocracy was composed of two amalgamated elements: first, a Frankish element, which consisted of families either noble by birth or elevated by their service to the king, both endowed with consider-able estates; second, a Gallo-Roman element, which included families of the old senatorial class who had 'ruled' over the countryside since the decline of the Empire. The fusion of these aristocratic elements had come about since the middle of the eighth century.[19] The material strength of this land- and power-hungry class brought ruin to the Merovingian royalty. The accession of the Austrasian mayors of the palace to royal status signifies the seizure of political power by the aristocracy of the kingdom.

The great problem that the Carolingians had to face was to maintain in their service a rapacious and turbulent social class of doubtful fidelity. At a time when the stock of gold had been exhausted and the monetary circulation had slowed down, the rewards for services and fidelity could be bestowed only in land. Two solutions could then be envisaged. One might grant lands in perpetuity to powerful individuals, a method which had been practised on a large scale by the Merovin-gians and had brought about the depletion of their land capital. The other solution was to reward a faithful retainer with a short-term concession of land, as long as his services were needed (the precarial system).[20] Although the latter solution apparently allowed the king to keep an overriding property right in the land conferred and thus to reacquire it in order to reward another for faithful service, in practice, because of the absence of land registers and domanial archives, this possibility remained illusory; the beneficiary always strove to incorporate his holding, to-gether with all the powers of command which were attached to it, into his familial lands. On the whole, this way of rewarding services only increased the material power of that class which the king had intended to subject. In order to mitigate the inconveniences of the system, the first Carolingians resorted to three measures: they secularized the estates of the Church, an operation which helped them to satisfy the appetite of the great nobles; they engaged in wars of conquest, eventuating in confiscations on a large scale, which they partially redistributed among their followers; above all, they attempted to impose a hierarchical structure on society by chains of oaths which bound individuals among themselves and culminated in the king. These relationships constituted the system of vassalage.[21]

The basic elements of vassalage were derived from both the Roman *commendatio* and the German *comitatus* (*Gefolge*). One can recognize in the Merovingian epoch the general practice of commendation, which led to the formation around the king and each of the great nobles of a numerous following. In general these clients, the *ingenui in obsequio*—called *vassi* or *vasalli* from the eighth century—were rewarded by their protectors with estates which were ceded to them with full proprietorial right. Besides these grants 'in benefice' (*ad beneficium*), there were 'precarial' tenures (*precaria*), under which the occupant of the land held it in usufruct for life and subject to certain obligations. What remained to do was to co-ordinate these elements, to turn the 'good deed', or benefice, into a normal consequence of vassalage and to bind the possessor of the now precarial benefice to the fulfilment of the service of a vassal.

Such was the work of the first Carolingians. The important stages of the process seem to have been the following. The conditions surrounding the assumption of power by the Austrasian mayors of the palace from the end of the seventh century—civil wars and military campaigns (Poitiers, 732)—had obliged even Pepin II and above all Charles Martel to maintain a numerous, well-equipped (especially for cavalry) and fully dedicated army. This army was made up of the *clientes* of the house of Pepin, and its service was rewarded by grants of land given in full owner-ship. Most of these lands were taken from the estates of the Church, which had already been used for a similar purpose by the Merovingian kings. However, the extent of the secularization which Charles Martel carried out was without previous parallel. This massive transfer of lands aggravated the already tragic situation of the Church at that time. A reform was unavoidable; the councils in Austrasia and Neustria, in 742, 743, and 744, which brought together the sons of Charles Martel, Carloman and Pepin for this purpose, dealt, among other things, with confiscated properties. It was decided that these properties would return to their original owners. In practice, however, the latter failed to recover them; the prince—that is to say, one mayor or the other—kept them and granted them in the form of a benefice for life to those of his vassals who already occupied them. In recognition of the Church's rightful ownership of the land, the vassals would pay the Church a token sum, thereby placing themselves in the position of precarial holders. Such military service as they were responsible for they owed to the prince alone, so that later the benefices they held were called *precariae verbo regis* (precarial grants by the king's command). After that the practice of granting life benefices to vassals became common. The properties involved could either be those of the Church (the secularizations continued in the eighth century) or be owned directly by the mayor or, from 751 on, the king. The union of the benefice with vassalage thus became a reality.[22]

Vassalage, which previously had been a private institution, became from the middle of the eighth century, and above all from the reign of Charlemagne, a public institution. Precise vocabulary and rites of entry developed (commendation by the hands, oath of fealty, tradition of the benefice). Charlemagne incorporated it into the structure of the state, in order to reinforce the monarchical authority over the mass of the landowners and to make of it the solid framework of the kingdom. The king increased the number of his own vassals (*vassi dominici*) and he required the representatives of public authority, recruited mainly from among the Austrasian, Neustrian and Alamannian aristocracy, together with a number of bishops and abbots to become vassals to himself. Thus the service which these magnates owed to the sovereign in virtue of their function was reinforced by the allegiance which as vassals they owed to their lord. Finally, Charlemagne at the same time encouraged his personal vassals to imitate his example and attach to themselves as many men as possible by ties of homage and fealty. With the extension of this procedure, the land-holding society would find itself strictly hierarchized; each level would be bound to the others by chains of oaths, with the king holding one end. By this means he would hope to increase his control over his subjects.

Vassalage, however, was not intended solely as a means of marshalling men. As conceived by Pepin and Charlemagne, it represented a considerable state saving. The first two Carolingians, who had managed to restore the fisc by means of repossessions, assarts, and conquests, disposed of their lands very sparingly. By encouraging the freemen—in this case owners of small and medium-sized holdings —to enter into the vassalage of magnates 'for our aid', Charlemagne mobilized the wealth of the landed aristocracy. It was from their estates that the magnates had to establish the benefices with which they remunerated the vassals whom they had to retain for the service of the king. The monarch was thereby relieved of the expense of maintaining an army: the vassals thus became the nucleus of the Frankish army before they formed it in its entirety.

It remained to be seen whether the system of vassalage would remain the same as the first Carolingians had intended it to be. When the inherent vices of the system began to appear immediately after Charlemagne's reign, the lands, even those which had been granted for a term of years, were practically withdrawn from free royal disposition. The vassals tended towards the appropriation of these lands and the incorporation of them into their family estates; the fidelity of the vassals in rendering their services could not always be relied upon. These were signs fore-shadowing the very serious crisis of the ninth century during which vassalage, an institution which Charlemagne had wanted to keep centripetal, was completely transformed.

If, after considering the leaders of Carolingian society, we turn our attention to the lesser classes, we must distinguish the free peasants, who were complete masters of their lands, from those who lived under the domanial regime.

The existence of the first group, already difficult before the Carolingian era, seems to have been seriously jeopardized at the time in question and especially after A.D. 800, if we are to believe the capitularies which were promulgated in the years following the imperial coronation. They are full of alarming details as well as of measures taken to save the *pagenses*.[23] The causes of the crisis were diverse. Some derived from the obligations associated with their free status: both military service and the duty to attend the mall of the county constituted very onerous burdens. Other causes were inherent in the tyranny exercised over their people by the local notables, the great proprietors and representatives of public power, who were always ready to impose heavy fines on those who had not fulfilled their obligations; the *pagenses,* in their efforts to acquit themselves of these penalties, fell inevitably into debt. Let us add to these causes the occurrence of such unpredict able catastrophes as famine and pestilence, the practice of speculation in wheat, and the permanent pressure exerted on the peasants by the magnates, both lay and ecclesiastical, to force them to hand over their lands. In consequence, there was considerable disruption within the mass of free peasants: lands were abandoned; brigandage and spoliation prevailed. Even worse, in order to free themselves of debts, proprietors were forced to alienate their persons or their possessions. If the first of these alienations tended to be but temporary, an extreme danger lay hidden in the second, since the land recovered by a *pagensis* from his creditor was no longer held in full property but only as a *tenure*; the former freeman thus became a colon.

The colons, who represented the majority of the domanial tenants, came from various sections of society.[24] There were among them the descendants of Roman colons and of enfranchised slaves, but there were also former freemen who had been compelled to enter into the framework of domanial administration. Among them could probably be found as well peasants who were settled on lands of the fisc which, since the seventh century, had been given by the kings to churches.[25] Free in theory, the colons were not proprietors but usufructuary possessors of their holding. They ceased to be linked to the state, which indeed did nothing to retain them: incapable of maintaining control over all its subjects, it sought to hold the rural populace by subjecting it to the landed aristrocracy, which itself was bound by ties of vassalage. Thus the colons passed into dependence on their masters, who then overburdened them with dues, corvées, and services and exercised over them a coercive jurisdiction which soon developed into the power to judge them. The original military obligation of the colons was then replaced by menial obligations— a series of cartage corvées and food requisitions (*hostilicium*), which the landlords transformed into dues wrung from the colons in money or in kind. This debased status of the colons increasingly resembled that of the unfree peasants.

The latter, who were descendants of slaves,[26] could be divided into two principal categories. There were domestic serfs who lived in the centre of the domain and were obliged to devote all their time to such work as they had been ordered to perform; often they were specialized artisans who were in charge of the crafts (*ministeria*) attached to the seigniorial house (*curtis*). The great majority of the unfree peasants were serfs who lived in separate dwellings and occupied land holdings; they were less numerous than the colons, from whom they always remained juridically distinct because of the 'servile stain', which was hereditary.[27] Their condition, however, was eased by the fact that as tenants they escaped from the immediate authority of their masters.

Close as the colons and serfs were to each other by virtue of their material condi tion, their respective lots were never confused in law. It is no longer presumed that they merged into one and the same servile class.[28] The line of division between liberty and servitude did not shift, because it was founded exclusively on birth and not on the characteristic duties of a juridical status. The payment of *chevage* and the lord's rights of *formariage* and *mainmorte* weighed on the colons as much as they did on the serfs, and they were both subject to exactions on the part of their masters. Though both were closely dependent on the latter, the colons and the serfs nevertheless differed significantly, the persons of the colons being free whereas the serfs were deprived of liberty. The former represented the majority of the rural population, the latter the minority; the same proportion reappears without significant change at the outset of the eleventh century.[29]

In 768 the kingdom of the Franks included Gaul, from the Pyrenees to the Rhine and western Friesland; Septimania and Aquitaine had just been reoccupied by Pepin, and since 753 Armorica had been placed under the surveillance of a Frankish count. Beyond the Rhine the kingdom encompassed Alamannia, Franconia, Hesse, and Thuringia; to the southeast, Bavaria, whose duke Tassilo III had rendered homage to Pepin, was slowly coming under Frankish influence.

It was from 771 that Charlemagne, the death of his brother and associate Carloman having left him sole master of the Franks, engaged in the ventures that led to a striking expansion of the kingdom. This expansion of the Frankish state was achieved without a preconceived plan, the king taking what advantage he could of circumstances that confronted him. He was never able to concentrate on a single task and bring it immediately to a suitable conclusion, obliged as he was to conduct several operations simultaneously. When he found it necessary to abandon an operation because his presence was required elsewhere, he took it up again later, at the point where he had left it, and continued it as far as was then possible. He knew what his means were and advanced step by step. If his activity until 779 seems to have been inspired by his father's example, it assumes in that year a much more personal character; it also allows us to discern the progress of the edifice still in construction.

The best method of depicting the territorial expansion of the Frankish state would therefore be to follow the king's itinerary throughout his long reign. Not being in a position to do so here, we shall attempt merely to present a summary account of the growth of the monarchy by considering in turn the *Regnum Francorum* in the proper sense of the term, then Italy, and finally the accession of Charlemagne to the Empire.[30]

The territorial formation of the Frankish kingdom. In the south, where Charlemagne had been obliged soon after his accession to suppress the revolt of the Aquitanian lord Hunaud, the policy of expansion began inauspiciously. Appealed to in 777 by the governor of Zaragoza for aid against the emir of Cordova, Charlemagne believed that he could wrest a part of Spain from its Islamic lords. The campaign that he led beyond the Pyrenees in 778 was unsuccessful and it came to an end at Roncesvalles, where his rearguard suffered a defeat at the hands of the Basque mountaineers. The commotion that this news created in Aquitaine convinced Charlemagne of the necessity of establishing in this region a strong base for future expeditions. Being aware also of local particularism, he made of Aquitaine a dependent kingdom in the form of a benefice held by his third son, Louis (781).

This measure consolidated Frankish power, which was able from this time on to make itself felt beyond the mountains: Gerona submitted as early as 785 and other localities followed its example. An Arab counter-offensive, which reached Narbonne in 793, induced Charlemagne to conquer an important territory south of the Pyrenees with the object of providing protection for Aquitaine against future invasions. This was the Spanish March, which, following the capture of Barcelona in 801, was extended to the Ebro in 811.[31]

In the direction of Brittany, the king at first limited his actions to organizing solidly the *limes britannicus* between the lower Seine and the lower Loire, a first step toward a methodical conquest of the whole territory. In 799 several campaigns brought about the submission of Armorica, a submission which struck contem-poraries as final, since it was followed by an attempt to assimilate the region into the rest of the kingdom, especially in ecclesiastical matters. The results of this victory, however, were to be put in jeopardy even before the end of Charlemagne's reign.[32]

On the right bank of the Rhine, the conquest of Saxony took no less than thirty-three years; *quo nullum neque prolixius neque atrocius Francorum populo laboriosius susceptum est* (Einhard, *Vita*, c.7). It was a long series of advances and retreats, of offensives and rebellions.[33] The basic cause of the long campaign seems to have been that Charlemagne always found himself faced with one group or another of the Saxon people (Westphalians, Angrarians, Ostphalians, Nordalbingians) but never with the whole *Stamm*, as it lacked a common leadership.[34] In these circum-stances a victory over one section of the population could always be challenged by another. On the other hand, the objective sought by Charlemagne varied as time passed. The expeditions, begun in 772, were at first merely actions of reprisal against Saxon raids and were only partially successful: fortified Saxon camps were seized and a march was established between the rivers Lippe and Diemel. In 777, however, the Frankish general assembly was held for the first time in Westphalia, at Paderborn. The Saxon leaders were summoned there, being thus treated as subjects; many of them attended and thereby made their submission to Charles. Mass baptism of the Saxon population began at about the same time, and one might conclude that the king of the Franks had decided to evangelize as well as conquer the whole country.[35] Saxon resistance gathered around the Angrarian nobleman Widukind, who organized tactics of harassment against the Franks and evaded capture for a long time. Thereupon the expeditions followed one another without respite and were conducted with implacable cruelty. At the same time, the rallying of the major part of the Saxon aristocracy proceeded. An army of the Franks having been defeated in 782, Charlemagne wreaked terrible vengeance the following year at Verden by ordering the massacre of 4,500 men who had fallen into his hands. A number of Frankish successes compelled Widukind to lay down his arms in 785. He was then baptized at Attigny and his submission was followed by that of his people west of the Elbe. Saxony was incorporated into the kingdom; the Church was organized there in an atmosphere of terror, as we can see from the capitulary *De partibus Saxoniae*. Eastern Friesland suffered the same fate. The severity of Frankish administration gave rise to another rebellion in 792. Beginning in Nordalbingia, it spread rapidly to the region of Wihmode (between the lower Elbe and the lower Weser) and to adjoining regions. Charlemagne was able to pacify it only by massive deportations and by transforming little by little the status of Saxony. The regime of terror inaugurated by the capitulary *De partibus* was revoked, and progressively from 797 to 803 the Saxons attained full equality with the Franks. The resistance of Nordalbingia continued, however, until 804, when this territory, almost completely emptied of its inhabitants, was assigned to a Slavic people, the Abotrites. In the same way, after A.D. 800 the Wiltzes, the Sorbs, and the Czechs entered the Frankish sphere of influence.[36]

In Bavaria, Tassilo III for a long time pursued a very ambiguous policy. Although he was a vassal of Pepin III, he deserted the royal army in 763 and soon reassumed his freedom of action. Allied as he was to the Lombard king Desiderius, whose daughter he had married, he nevertheless avoided provoking Charlemagne and gradually imposed his domination over Carinthia. Called upon by the king of the Franks to respect his obligations in their entirety, he submitted himself for the first time in 781 but did not hesitate to renew his intrigues with the enemies of Charlemagne, in particular with Arichis of Benevento. Threatened by three Frankish armies in 787, he yielded again and renewed his oath of vassality. That did not prevent him, however, from entering into negotiations with the Avars. He was summoned to the diet of Ingelheim the following year, was accused of false oaths, perjury, and desertion, and was deprived of his duchy. Bavaria was not purely and simply incorporated in the kingdom; it retained provisionally its distinct organization and was placed under the command of a prefect, Gerold of Swabia, who was Charlemagne's son-in-law.

The immediate consequence of the annexation of Bavaria was the opening of hostilities against the last allies of Tassilo, namely the Avars, who were settled in the middle of the Danubian basin from the Tisza to Carinthia; they had launched raids in 788 against Bavaria and Friuli. The first expedition, led by Charlemagne himself, penetrated into western Hungary in 791, but the king was forced to retreat because of an epidemic which had broken out in the army. Postponed for a few years, the conquest was resumed in 795 and 796 and it culminated in the seizure of the fabulous treasure which the Avars had accumulated within the entrenchments of the Ring. As for the Avar kingdom, it must have seemed weak enough to Charlemagne for him to allow it to remain in existence just as it was. He annexed only the territory between the Enns and the Vienna Forest—the future Austria—which became a march whose counts were responsible for the surveillance of Pannonia (western Hungary).[37]

Thus Charlemagne was successful in adding to Gaul all of Germany as far as the Elbe and, beyond Bavaria, a territory which encompassed the eastern Alps and the Hungarian plain from its western extremity to the Danube. In this immense space, from the Spanish March to Pannonia, there lived people of various nationalities who preserved their own laws but were integrated into the Frankish kingdom. They were united not only by allegiance to the person of the sovereign but also by the very strong spiritual and religious bond that Christianity provided.

The annexation of the Lombard kingdom and its consequences. Under the influence of his mother Bertha, Charlemagne had at first maintained peaceful relations with the kingdom of the Lombards, and at the very outset of his reign he had married a daughter of King Desiderius.[38] However, the intrigues of the latter at Rome, where he led an active party,[39] rapidly gave rise to tension between the two kings, a tension which became more pronounced when Charlemagne repudiated his wife and when Desiderius received at his court the widow of Carloman and her two sons, who had been excluded in 771 from the line of succession descending from their father. Directly threatened with a renewal of the march of the Lombards on Rome, Pope Hadrian I appealed to Charlemagne for help.

In the autumn of 773, while he was blockading Pavia, where Desiderius had taken refuge, the king of the Franks advanced as far as Verona. There he seized his sister-in-law and his nephews, and nothing was heard of them thereafter. At the time of the Easter festival of April 2, 774, he made his first visit to Rome. Received with the same honours as the Byzantine exarch had once enjoyed, Charlemagne confirmed to Hadrian the donation that Pepin had recently granted to Stephen II,[40] and he renewed the treaty of alliance of Ponthion, thus assuming in effect the protection of the pope and of the city of Rome. This reality was expressed by the title of patrician of the Romans, a title which he bore in the acts of the chancery until A.D. 800. In June of the year 774 Pavia fell and Desiderius was made prisoner. Charles, who had received the submission of all the regions of the kingdom, proclaimed himself king of the Lombards. A personal union was thus created between the two kingdoms.

The Lombard state at first retained its own institutions and its own administrative personnel. It was only in 776, following the insurrection raised by the duke of Friuli, Hruodgaud, that the Frankish institutions were introduced south of the Alps and together with them a new personnel from beyond the mountains which was mostly Frankish and Alamannian. Counts, marquises, *missi*, and even some bishops of Frankish origin were placed alongside of Lombards in governing posts. Royal vassals were provided with fiefs; Frankish monasteries (Saint-Denis, Saint-Martin de Tours) were endowed with lands there; and colons were settled in ancient Lombard *arimanniae*. All this led to close relations between the two juxtaposed kingdoms.[41] The rallying of the Lombards to the new regime was also facilitated when Charlemagne gave them as their particular king his second son Pepin, whom he arranged to have crowned at Rome in 781. As he had done at the same stage in Aquitaine, Charles respected the conquered country's sense of distinctness, while reserving the ultimate direction of affairs for himself. The same year he concluded an agreement with the pope which put an end to the territorial claims which the latter had kept on raising since 774, that is to say since the time he had been promised the donation which we have mentioned previously. He acknowledged the pope's possession of the duchy of Rome, of the Exarchate, of Pentapolis and of Sabina; a few years later he also ceded Roman Tuscany to the pope. In return Hadrian gave up his other demands and ceased to assert his rights to the duchy of Spoleto, which had placed itself in dependence upon him in 773 and which now became a part of the kingdom of Italy.

Now that he was master of northern and central Italy, Charlemagne came into contact with the Byzantine Empire, which still possessed some territories in the peninsula (Venetia and Istria; the regions of Naples, Apulia, and Calabria) and which still claimed the duchy of Rome. Even though the motives for a conflict were not lacking, it seems that at first both parties tried to maintain peace: in 781 the young emperor Constantine VI, for whom his mother, the Empress Irene, exercised the regency, was betrothed to Rothrude, one of Charles's daughters. These friendly relations came to an end when Irene, eager to recover some authority in Italy, not only concluded an alliance with the Lombard duke Arichis of Benevento,[42] whom Charlemagne was in the course of subjecting to his rule, but also prepared and assisted the landing of Desiderius' son Adalgise in the south of Italy (787). Under the circumstances, the proposed engagement was broken off, although we cannot determine who took the initiative therein. The new duke of Benevento was obliged to recognize the Frankish supremacy. The Byzantine troops which had set foot in southern Italy were crushed, while the Franks proceeded to occupy Istria. The Frankish-Byzantine tension continued until 797 when Irene, who had deposed her son and assumed authority over the Empire, asked for and obtained peace. Istria, however, remained a part of the kingdom of Italy.

The elevation of Charlemagne to the office of emperor. Charlemagne's assumption of imperial status had been slowly prepared during the last quarter of the eighth century. Besides the formation of a large territorial unit under the sceptre of the king of the Franks, several other circumstances entered into the process. We shall examine them in turn.[43]

First of all, the prestige which the Frankish royalty had acquired during the reign of Charlemagne conferred on him an authority similar to that of the emperor within the Byzantine Empire. For the popes, since the pontificate of Stephen II, and for the Franks themselves this royalty was founded on God and inspired by Him: the king of the Franks was the guarantor of the peace of the Christian people. Herein the ideas of divine service and royal service were conjoined in an indissoluble manner. The king of the Franks was in addition the defender of the Church. He strengthened its organization and awakened it to a cultural renaissance.[44] Anxious not to appropriate any spiritual authority, Charlemagne only wanted to be the very devoted son of the Church and not its rector; yet it must be acknowledged that the protection that he exercised over the ecclesiastical world was basically authoritarian.

Charlemagne asserted his position as the protector of the Church and of the western Christian peoples especially in his relations with the Byzantine Empire in the years following 787. In that year, at the height of her conflict with the king of the Franks in Italy, the Empress Irene summoned the seventh oecumenical council at Nicaea, a council which re-established the cult of sacred images which her predecessors had condemned since 726. We know how Charlemagne, excluded from the assembly, resorted to anticonciliar action and promulgated the famous Capitulary on Images, the *Caroline Books*, written about 791–92. Leaving aside the dogmatic problems with which the document dealt, we shall concern ourselves only with a few leading ideas which throw light on the political and religious thought of the Frankish court as it relates to the Empire. In this capitulary Charlemagne represented himself as 'king of the Franks, governing the Gauls, Germany and Italy, and the adjacent regions as well', that is to say, the provinces of the former Roman Empire in the West. We can infer, then, that Charlemagne presumed to take the place of the Roman emperors in this part of the Roman world. It is noteworthy, however, that he did not claim succession to them. The king of the Franks contested neither the existence nor the legitimacy of the Empire in the East, but he denied that it had the universal character which it still claimed, and he condemned the arrogance of its princes in pretending to be similar to Christ and the apostles and making themselves the object of a cult which was strongly marked by paganism. The pride of the *basileus* is contrasted to the humility of the king of the Franks, possessor of an office which has been entrusted to him by God: he is the minister of the Most High and is personally responsible for the union of the Frankish church with Rome. The West was thus finding a spiritual unity under Charlemagne's leadership, a unity which did not cease to affirm itself against the Byzantine Empire and its church (Council of Frankfurt, 794). This awareness went hand in hand with the growth in prestige of the king of the Franks, who in his own sphere tended to place himself on a level similar to that of the emperor. Numerous signs bore witness of his aspiration. It found expression in the usages of the chancery (the resort to bulls of lead and, later on, to golden bulls); in the Davidic appellation of Charlemagne (David, the king inspired by God, leader of the new, elect people, whose name the Byzantine emperor himself sometimes used); in the titles of *serenissimus* and *orthodoxus*; in the palace and chapel at Aix-la-Chapelle, which were built in the last years of the eighth century and which, in the eyes of contemporaries, duplicated imperial splendours. Everything pointed toward Charlemagne's becoming in his territory the *rex imperatori similis*.

Finally, at Rome, Charlemagne was unobtrusively assuming the place of the emperor and was actively intervening in the affairs of the pontifical state. In the lifetime of Hadrian the interventions of the king of the Franks were always tempered by the friendly relations which bound him to the pope, but the relationship changed abruptly with the accession of Leo III (795). The latter, being a mediocre personality and also encountering serious difficulties at Rome, cultivated close relations with the king in order to render even more efficacious the protection which he so much needed. The delivery to Charlemagne of the keys of the Confession of St. Peter and of the standard of the city of Rome; the famous fresco decorating the Lateran reception hall in which Charlemagne occupied a position of honour similar to that of Constantine; the dating of pontifical acts according to the regnal years of the king-patrician—all these were signs of Leo III's desire to invest Charlemagne with a superior authority which he would exercise in the pope's name, by right of delegation. The superimposition of the image of Constantine—the 'good emperor' in the eyes of the curia—upon the king of the Franks was certainly the most significant of all the pope's initiatives. There is nothing to suggest, however, that Charlemagne had decided to fall in with the views of Leo III.

The three facts that we have recalled account for the movement which carried Charlemagne to the Empire. They explain also how a minor occurrence, the attack against the person of the pope, could have brought about the imperial coronation.

We shall not touch on the incidents in Rome of April 25, 799, nor on the stay of Leo III at Paderborn near his protector, nor on the conflict of opinions that prevailed then at the Frankish court. Let us say only that there is a certain discordance between the famous letter of Alcuin on the three powers which guaranteed the order of the world, a letter which manifests a Roman and Christian perspective, and the anonymous poem *Charlemagne and Leo III*, in which is adumbrated the picture of a Frankish empire with Aix-la-Chapelle as its capital.[45]

However, the logic of the situation and above all the weight of tradition dictated that the Empire, if it was to live again, must be reborn at Rome. It was reborn actually in two stages. The first occurred on December 23 in the form of a wish expressed by a mixed assembly of Romans and Franks in the presence of the pope himself, who had come to the assembly to clear himself by oath of accusations which had been levelled against him. This affirmation was the basis on which the *nomen imperatoris* was to be conferred on Charlemagne. The latter, yielding to a unanimous entreaty, accepted the title which had been proposed to him. He was therefore emperor. It remained to seal his elevation by an official ceremony, which took place two days later on December 25 in the basilica of St. Peter. The pope, who had until then played a passive role, reassumed the initiative and crowned Charlemagne emperor 'with his own hands', as the *Liber pontificalis* significantly notes. The imperial acclamation—the act which brought the Empire into being—played but a secondary role, that of expressing the adherence of all those present to the creation of the emperor. According to the Roman-Byzantine tradition, it should have preceded the coronation; in fact, it followed the coronation. We can assume that this inversion of the coronation rites was the result of careful premeditation by Leo III, to whom it was most probably repugnant to appear to act as a mandatory of the Roman population or, perhaps better, as that of the assembly which two days previously had brought Charlemagne to the Empire; Leo III himself wished to be considered creator of the emperor. It is also certain that the form under which the prestigious institution was reborn was not entirely satisfactory to its beneficiary. Einhard assures us of that. And we realize it all the more when we consider how the thirteen years which followed the imperial coronation were marked by Charlemagne's efforts to clarify, and indeed to correct, the situation that arose from the rebirth of the Empire in the West.

Let us note first in this readjustment the adoption of an imperial title binding together the two royal titles (king of the Franks and of the Lombards) with that of *Romanum gubernans Imperium*. This union well expressed the rebirth of the Roman *imperium* as an office superior to the idea of personal royalty, but it denied the Romans a predominant position in the new Empire. Then there were the considerable efforts, as manifested by the capitularies promulgated after 802, to give an ethical and religious content to the notion of the Empire. These capitularies bound together both clerics and lay persons, inviting them in 802 to swear fealty to their sovereign as emperor; this innovation of a general swearing of fealty appears to have been a kind of ratification by the Franks of the Roman act of December 25, 800. Finally, there were the steps taken by Charlemagne to be recognized by Byzantium. This was of course a difficult undertaking, because in the eyes of the imperial court Charles's coronation was a manifest usurpation. It took twelve years to arrive at a compromise in which the Emperor Michael I agreed to recognize the imperial title of his rival, but without defining its geographical scope and excluding connections, in particular, with Rome: only the *basileus* could be emperor of the Romans, and that usage was definitively established in the acts of the chancery. Charlemagne easily reconciled himself to this situation; the essential consideration for him was to have Byzantium accept the principle of the co-existence of two juridically equal empires. He was thus able to pass on his empire—Roman in origin, Frankish in substance, Christian in vocation—to Louis of Aquitaine, the last of his living sons. The coronation of the latter at Aix-la-Chapelle in 813 in the presence of the Frankish *proceres*, but without the intervention of the pope, corrected whatever had been excessively 'papal' and excessively 'Roman' about the rites of December 25, 800.

The building of the Empire was accompanied by a great effort, begun by Pepin and continued by Charlemagne, to free the Frankish state from the anarchy that afflicted it about the middle of the eighth century, to establish internal order and assure obedience to the commands of the sovereign. The Carolingian Empire, however, was far from possessing the framework of a state in the sense in which this term is now understood. The immense aggregate of peoples which it consisted of could in reality maintain its unity only by the good will of an aristocracy more concerned with its own interests than with service to the king. Because of the lack of a body of officials who were trained specifically for the task and who were salaried like those of the Byzantine and Abbasid Empires, where an economy based on money prevailed, the administration was rudimentary, overstretched, and practically ineffectual. The institutions were still those of the Merovingian epoch;[46] the most one can say is that they were 'reactivated' and elaborated according to Charlemagne's personal ideas or as a result of new needs arising out of the circumstances.

Charlemagne conceived of government, in the first place, as exercising its power much more over men than over the land, as the royal title itself clearly indicates (*rex Francorum*). He insisted on attaching men to himself by the oath of fealty, thus reviving an institution which had already existed under the Merovingians but which had fallen into disuse in the course of the eighth century. The oath guaranteed for him the fidelity of the various populations, and its moral force supported the royal power. At three successive times—in 789, 793, and 802—Charlemagne had the oath sworn to him, on the first two occasions in consequence of conspiracies directed against him, on the third occasion when he had become emperor.[47] This last oath was especially solemn; its religious nature was more accentuated; its form was modelled on that of the vassals. The *missi* were to make it understood to those who swore that in the future each infraction of civil and of moral law would be treated as tantamount to perjury. That this extended conception of the oath had, however, no practical effect is shown by the heavy malaise which weighed upon the Empire during the last years of the reign.[48] Even more, the multiplied offering of the oath gradually gave credence to the idea that obedience was due to the prince not because of the subject's duty but on account of an explicitly formulated promise. The notion of contractual fidelity, reinforced by the extension of vassality, profoundly transformed the very conception of royalty in the course of the ninth century. If, however, we consider only 802 and the following years, we shall not have reason to discount the effort of the imperial government to revive in a new form the idea of the state, which men had altogether ceased to entertain.[49] Born in the circle of clerics who were associated with Charlemagne, sustained by a profoundly religious atmosphere, the theory in question emphasized not only the

collective duties of the subjects to the emperor but also those of the emperor to his
subjects. There were therefore between the emperor, who held his power from God,
and the Christian people, whom he was entrusted to keep in peace and to guide
towards salvation, reciprocal obligations which bound them together in the
service of their 'common welfare' and their 'common salvation'. By virtue of this
interpretation of the common good, it was possible for the idea of the *respublica* to
revive: the term itself reappeared under Louis the Pious, accompanied by the
epithet '*christiana*'. The proclamation of the Empire contributed to the rediscovery
of the idea. Unfortunately for the cause of the monarchy, the new conception
commanded enthusiasm only among the clerics who had inspired it. There was
scarcely any place for it in a rural and warlike society, cemented by a multitude of
oaths creating personal relations and absolutely incapable of understanding the
abstract idea of the common good even when it was supported by Christianity.
The emperor, on the other hand, had neither the means nor the supporting personnel that were necessary to impose it. A summary review of the imperial institutions
will suffice to demonstrate the point.

The centre of the government remained the palace, consisting of the reigning
family and the lay and ecclesiastical *proceres* whom Charlemagne called to his side.
These members of the palace formed the council, which met when the ruler
considered it useful to convoke it. Certain departments of the palace had been
improved and supplemented by Charlemagne. One was the chapel, under the
direction of the *summus capellanus*, who, being always of high rank, either abbot or
bishop, was the emperor's chief ecclesiastical counsellor.[50] To him also was
attached the chancery, staffed by notaries recruited mainly from the ranks of the
clerics of the chapel. Their head, the prothonotary, gradually acquired the title of
cancellarius. He, like the personnel he supervised, had only limited authority: he
drew up neither the judicial sentences nor the capitularies; his role was confined to
drafting and authenticating diplomas, which were solemn statements of grants. It
is therefore scarcely possible to consider the chancery as a sort of 'central secretariat'
of the monarchy. We must not forget either that, despite a certain revival of its use,
the written legal document had only a restricted value at this time.[51] In addition to
the counsellor-clerks, there were lay participants, such as the holders of the private
offices of the court, who might be called upon to act as *missi*: the seneschal, the
butler, the constable, and above all the chamberlain, who was responsible for
watching over the private treasury of the sovereign. The most important lay
auxiliary was the count of the palace, who dispensed royal justice by right of
delegation; around him, as well as around the chamberlain no doubt, there
existed some rudimentary offices which were occupied by subordinate employees.

The regional units of the Carolingian administration were scarcely more solid
or better equipped than the departments of the palace. The territory was everywhere
divided into counties (*pagi*) of extremely varied extent. In Gaul as in Italy they
corresponded in general to the ancient cities or to their subdivisions. In Germany
the county usually comprised a *Gau* (synonymous with *Bar, Feld, Land*) and bore
the name of a people (Bardengau—the county of the Lombards; Hamaland—the
county of the Chamavi), or a geographical name (Eifelgau, Thurgau), or the name
of a town (Wormsgau). County and *Gau*, however, did not always coincide; when

the counties were introduced, *Gaue* were occasionally merged; later there were revisions of county boundaries both in Germany and Gaul. It is therefore difficult to establish the exact number of these districts; it is believed that at the time of Charlemagne there were about 250. It must also be noted that, while in Gaul and Italy there was a continuous network of counties, it was not so in Germany. Even though the county structure was introduced in Alamannia, in Rhaetia, in Bavaria (where it was possibly based on fiscal districts created by the dukes), and in Saxony, it should not be assumed that the county was everywhere a territory with well-defined limits; it is appropriate to see it rather as an area placed under the supervision of a royal 'commissary', who had judicial and military competence and to whom particular tasks might fall, such as, in Franconia, the control of the peasants, colons, and soldiers, settled by the Carolingians on royal lands.[52]

Let us now return to the west of the Empire. In his *pagus* the count was assisted by certain subordinates. The viscount, who is not encountered outside Gaul, was a kind of deputy appointed by the count himself. Under the command of the count there were the vicars (*viguiers*) or hundredmen, who were in charge of the subdivisions of the county—the vicariates or hundreds (*vicariae, centenae*).[53] It seems that they were also appointed by the count.

Although inadequately supported, the count exercised substantial powers. As a representative of the king, and appointed by him, he published and applied all the orders of the sovereign; he was responsible for the maintenance of public order; he conducted the levy of the freemen whom he led to the host; he supervised the collection of the dues and fines owed to the king. He was above all charged with the administration of justice: the title of *judex* which the count bears in numerous documents defines the essential part of his responsibility. He did not render this justice himself but dispensed it always in the presence of the assembly of freemen, the *placitum* or the *mallus*, which met at the central place of the various subdivisions of the county. About 780 a very important judicial reform reduced to three the maximum number of sessions that the count could hold each year in a hundred or vicariate without previous convocation of assistants. These were general sessions, in addition to which others were also held at the rate of one every fortnight in any hundred and at which only the judges, the witnesses and the parties were called together. From then on the hitherto undefined competence of the two categories of courts became clear: major causes were presented to the court of the count while all others were presented to the courts presided over by the hundredman or the vicar. On the other hand the reduction of the number of general sessions brought about the creation of a body of judges who were specialists and versed in law. These were the *échevins* (*scabini*), nominated by the *missi* in agreement with the count and appointed for life; they probably numbered twelve in each county. They had the power to create law through the non-general sessions, in that they were the sole judges there. In general sessions they suggested the sentence, which the count was left simply to promulgate. Inspired by a wish to provide subjects with better justice, the reform had but partial results;[54] in particular it could not prevent the count and his auxiliaries from exerting the full weight of their influence on the *mallus* and from using it as a fiscal instrument.

The remuneration of the count comprised, in reality, two essential elements: the endowment in land attached to his office (*pertinentia comitatus*), augmented by the temporary enjoyment of a part of the fiscal domains within his district; and secondly, a third of the fines imposed by the courts of justice of the county. Now, these fines (*fredae*) were considerable, being fixed in general at a third of the composition due to the adversary from the losing party. Thus the count could keep for himself the ninth part of all judicial payments. To this one must add a third of the fines which were levied for infraction of the royal ban (twenty *solidi* out of every sixty imposed) and a third of the market tolls and of the *tonlieu*. Thus abundantly provided with revenues, the counts did not hesitate to augment them through serious abuses of power: it is enough to read the capitularies issued toward the end of the reign to become fully conscious of this state of affairs.

If, in principle, the sovereign who nominated the count could similarly transfer or dismiss him at will, in reality his power to do so remained very limited. He did not have a sufficiently numerous personnel to draw good administrators from. The counts were recruited almost exclusively from the upper aristocracy, who were closely related to the royal family. They comprised several dozen great families bound to each other by marriage[55]—so much so that, even though under Charlemagne there was no hereditary succession to the office of count, the successor of a transferred or dismissed count was always related to him. A county, moreover, could be taken away from its incumbent only in the event of very serious deficiency. Also the count had come ordinarily to be kept in one place so long that he could be considered immovable: he acquired personal property in his county, established in it a clientèle of vassals, and sometimes married and founded a family there. Much more than an official, he thus figured as a local potentate. Charlemagne conceived of only two remedies for the excessive power of the counts: one consisted in the extension of immunity to nearly all the lands of the Church,[56] which device, by increasing the judicial power of the bishops and the abbots, served as a counterweight to the autonomy of the counts; the other was the establishment of the *échevins* as judges in the public tribunals, which was intended to limit the arbitrary power of the counts in judicial matters.

In connection with the counties, we must consider the more extended territorial districts which constituted duchies and marches. By the quite ambiguous term *ducatus* is understood here the national duchy, that is to say a territory which was theoretically subject to Frankish authority but which stayed outside the common law, which was not divided into counties, and was under the command of a leader who was obliged to pay tribute. Such were the duchy of Benevento in southern Italy, and Brittany, which took the form of a duchy during the very short period when it was subject to Charlemagne, and the duchy of Gascony between the Pyrenees and the Garonne, which remained nearly always independent in practice.[57] While the duchies appear as territorial units which had existed before their conquest, the marches were created by Charlemagne to assure an effective defence of the Empire against neighbouring peoples. More extensive than the county, the march (*marca, limes* or *ducatus*) was under the military authority of a chieftain, the *comes marchiae* (*marchio, Markgraf, marquis* or, in English, margrave). According to the manner in which it was formed and organized, it corresponded to two principal types. On the eastern borders of the Empire the marches were territories not yet penetrated by Frankish organization, being areas of colonization and evangelization; they were without a count, and the margrave exercised both military and civil authority in them. To this type belonged the marches of Friuli, in the kingdom of Italy, against the southern Slavs; of Austria, which we have already mentioned; of Nordgau, north of Bavaria; of Sorbia, between the Saale and the Elbe; and of Nordalbingia, against the Slavs and the Danes. The last four appear to have been primarily zones of military concentration.[58] On the western and southern borders, the marches covered territories which had been sub-jected long since and which were divided into counties. The proximity of turbulent enemies, however, had led the sovereign to place over the counts a single military commander, the margrave, who was generally a possessor of a county but was en-trusted with the defence of the whole region. Such were, on the border of Armor-ica, the march of Brittany (*limes britannicus*) between Nantes, Rennes, and Angers; in the south-west, the march of Toulouse, or Gothia, which was erected against both the Arabs and the Gascons; and, south of the Pyrenees, the Spanish March.[59] The creation of marches thus imposed between the king and the counts an inter-mediate machinery which was endowed with considerable powers: the institution contained the germ of autonomy for its holders.

Let us examine finally the manner in which communications were established between the emperor and the local administrators.

The principal contact was assured by the general assembly (*placitum generale, conventus generalis*), which was summoned each year in the spring, in May or June, at the place where the army gathered, quite often in the towns of the east (Thion-ville, Düren, Worms), sometimes in the interior of a zone which was in the process of being conquered (Paderborn in 777); from the end of the eighth century it was held mainly at Aix-la-Chapelle. At the outset it seems to have been connected with the review of the army in preparation for the opening of a campaign. As the representative assembly of the Frankish people, it included essentially the magnates of the kingdom, both lay and ecclesiastical: counts and margraves, bishops and abbots, royal vassals without public office, together with the sub-vassals whom some of them brought with them. The army, properly speaking, appeared only in the background, to be notified, eventually, of the decisions which had been taken. In addition to this general assembly there was another one which was held in autumn or in winter—a much more restricted meeting, being open only to people of very high rank who were designated by the king. It worked out with him the programme which was to be submitted to the general meeting in the spring. We can reconstruct the way in which the latter proceeded. It was divided into two groups:[60] laymen and ecclesiastics deliberated together or separately on the prog-ramme prepared by the king or his council; they were required either to reply to set questions or to pass judgment on a proposed edict which was presented to them. Both groups expressed their 'consent'; that is to say, they 'recognized that what had been presented to them conformed to the law'.[61]

The legislative acts that were drawn up in execution of the decisions taken bear the name of 'capitularies', since they were divided, in conformity with the method of deliberation practised in the assembly, into articles (*capitula*). These documents, issued not by the chancery but by secretaries who had taken part in the deliberations or had received a written draft, were of a composite character and they set forth, with remarkable lack of order, administrative and legislative provisions[62] and various measures occasioned by circumstances. In reality the term 'capitulary' covers three different categories of document, as F. L. Ganshof's research has made clear. Some were but additional material to the laws governing the peoples of the Empire, and they were drafted with the help of legal specialists called to the council. Others were instructions given to the *missi* and bearing on a wide variety of sub-jects.[63] Only the capitularies known as *per se scribenda* (having their own *raison d'être*) can be regarded as capitularies in the proper sense of the word. Although this triple distinction dates only from the time of Louis the Pious, it was already becoming gradually evident under the reign of Charlemagne.

It remained to promulgate the capitularies throughout the Empire and see to their application. Such was the task assigned to inspectors who were dispatched from the palace, the *missi dominici* (envoys of the lord, or king). This office, for which precedents can already be found in the Merovingian period, appeared during Charlemagne's reign in 789 and 793 in connection with the practice of oath-taking; it was fully functioning after 800. The *missi* (at least two in number—in principle a bishop and a count—and sometimes four or five) exercised their office in a different region from that where they held their title, though rather near to it.[64] The zone which they inspected (*missaticum*) encompassed from six to ten counties. There they made four rounds each year and each time held their assizes within the public *mallus*. Their powers were considerable: responsible at first for the proclama-tion of royal decrees and for conducting inquiries into specific questions, they extended their functions step by step to include supervision of the administration of counts and ecclesiastics, supervision of the behaviour of clerics and laymen, control of the administration of the properties constituting the fisc, and the un-covering and suppression of abuses. They were, moreover, required to submit precise accounts of their activities to the palace. The *missi* obviously represent a wish on the part of the crown to attain a unity of governmental action. Neverthe-less, there is still a question to be asked: these overworked people—we must not forget that they were at the same time *missi* and bishops or counts—who belonged to the same social milieu as those whom they were expected to control, who lacked preparatory training and the will or the capacity to correct abuses, how could they effectively accomplish their tasks? Charlemagne at least knew how to keep them busy, and as long as he lived the institution functioned somehow or other. It lost its importance after 814.

Based as it was on land, the Carolingian Empire was dominated by a rural and warlike aristocracy, which Charlemagne had tried to keep under control and to attach to himself by means of vassalage. His personnel, however, proved inadequate: the mechanism of the state, which had been perfected or created by the efforts of the emperor, had only very imperfectly fulfilled his desires. If the Empire was neverthe-less impressive during his reign, it was so, without doubt, by virtue of his excep-tional personality, of his incessant labours—labours which would later be recalled by the poet who put in his mouth the words, 'Oh God, how painful is my life'— and of his existence as a perpetual wanderer, always on the march, himself correct-

ing the abuses encountered, putting things in order for a while. In all respects he
bore the weight of the Empire which he had created and which he had wanted to
animate with high Christian ideals. But he was betrayed by men, prisoners of the
conditions in which they lived and incapable of identifying themselves with the
programme which had been proposed to them. After 808, when the emperor
ceased to travel, the governmental machine fell into disorder. And this spectacle
has inspired the notion of 'Charlemagne's failure'—the failure of an idea at grips
with the resistance of things and of men. This pessimistic view, however, should be
corrected by considering other realities. To have, if not created, at least consolidated
the bases of the civilization and culture of the West remains for Charlemagne a
title of imperishable glory, which men have never ceased celebrating. The long
survival of the emperor in the collective memory of the peoples who had belonged
to his Empire[65] is one of the most significant facts of medieval history.

Notes

1. There is a good general discussion in R. Boutruche, *Seigneurie et féodalité: Le premier
âge des liens d'homme à homme,* 2nd ed.; vol. 1 (Paris, 1968).

2. *Die Wirtschaftsentwicklung der Karolingerzeit vornehmlich in Deutschland,* 2nd, ed.
2 vols. (Weimar, 1921–22).

3. For instance, Ph. Dollinger, *L'évolution des classes rurales en Bavière depuis la fin de
l'époque carolingienne jusqu'au milieu du XIIIème siècle* (Paris, 1945).

4. Capitulary *De villis;* the *Brevium exempla;* polyptychs such as that of Saint-Germain
des Prés (about 813), that of the royal estates in Franconia in the *Codex Laureshamensis*
(about 823), those of Saint-Pierre of Ghent, Saint-Rémi of Reims, and Lobbes (about the
middle of the ninth century) and that of Prüm (about 892–93).

5. There are numerous studies available. From a general point of view see Marc Bloch,
Les caractères originaux de l'histoire rurale française, 2nd ed. (Paris, 1952–56); Marc Bloch,
'The Rise of Dependent Cultivation and Seignorial Institutions', *The Cambridge Economic
History of Europe,* 1 (Cambridge, 1941): 224–77; F. L. Ganshof, 'Medieval Agrarian
Society in Its Prime', ibid., pp. 278–322; Boutruche, *Seigneurie et féodalité,* passim; G.
Duby, *L'économie rurale et la vie des campagnes dans l'Occident médiéval* (Paris, 1962), vol. 1.
Examples of regional investigations: Ch. E. Perrin, *Recherches sur la seigneurie rurale en
Lorraine d'après les plus anciens censiers* (Paris, 1935); F. Lütge, *Die Agrarverfassung des frühen*

Mittelalters im mitteldeutschen Raum (Jena, 1937); A. Deléage, *La vie rurale en Bourgogne jusqu'au début du XIème siècle* (Mâcon, 1941); F. L. Ganshof, 'Manorial Organization in the Low Countries', *Transactions of the Royal Historical Society,* 4th Ser., 31 (1949): 29–59; W. Metz, *Das Karolingische Reichsgut* (Berlin, 1960).

6. Consult, for example, F. Lütge, 'Hufe und Mansus in den mitteldeutschen Quellen der Karolingerzeit', *Vierteljahrschrift für Sozial- und Wirtschaftsgeschichte* (1937), pp.105–28.

7. 'Observations sur le manse dans la région parisienne', *Annales d'histoire sociale,* 1 (1945): 39–52.

8. See, for example, A. Dupont, 'Considérations sur la colonisation et la vie rurale dans le Roussillon et la Marche d'Espagne', *Annales du Midi* (1955,) pp. 223–45, and the works of Ph. Dollinger and F. Lütge, cited above in notes 3 and 5. Franconia has been dis-cussed by K. Bosl, *Franken um 800: Strukturanalyse einer fränkischen Königsprovinz,* 2nd ed. (Munich, 1969), esp. pp. 13–14 and 152.

9. J. Lestocquoy, 'Le paysage urbain en Gaule du Vème au VIIIème siècle', *Annales: économies, sociétés, civilisations,* 8 (1953): 159–72. On the activity (mostly commercial) of some of these towns, see J. Dhondt, 'L'essor urbain entre la Meuse et la Mer du Nord à l'époque mérovingienne', *Studi in onore di A. Sapori,* 1 (Milan, 1957): 55–78.

10. F. L. Ganshof, *Étude sur le développement des villes entre Loire et Rhin au moyen âge* (Brussels, 1943); H. Planitz, *Die deutsche Stadt im Mittelalter* (Graz, 1954).

11. On the most important of these merchants, see E. Sabbe, 'Quelques types de marchands aux IXème et Xème siècles', *Revue belge de philologie et d'histoire,* 13 (1934): 176–87; H. Laurent, 'Aspects économiques dans la Gaule franque: marchands du palais, marchands d'abbayes', *Revue historique,* 183 (1938): 281–97.

12. R. Doehaerd, 'Ce qu'on vendait et comment on le vendait dans le Bassin parisien', *Annales: économies, sociétés, civilisations,* 2 (1947): 266–80.

13. E. Sabbe, 'L'importation des tissus orientaux en Europe occidentale aux IXème et Xème siècles', *Revue belge de philologie et d'histoire,* 14 (1935): 811–48, and 1261–88.

14. F. L. Ganshof, 'Notes sur les ports de Provence du VIIIème au Xème siècle', *Revue historique,* 183 (1938): 28–37.

15. R. Boutruche, *Seigneurie et féodalité,* p. 58.

16. The problem has been presented in full by Marc Bloch, 'Le problème de l'or au moyen âge', *Annales d'histoire économique et sociale,* 5 (1933): 1–34, and *Esquisse d'une histoire monétaire de l'Europe* (Paris, 1954). On the monetary situation of the West in rela-tion to the East, see M. Lombard, 'L' or musulman du VIIème au XIème siècles', *Annales: économies, sociétés, civilisations,* 2 (1947): 143–60; his hypotheses have been criticized especially by F. Himly, 'Y a-t-il une emprise musulmane sur l'économie des États euro-péens du VIIIème au XIème siècle?', *Revue suisse d'histoire,* 5 (1955): 31–81.

17. The basic work in this field is M. Prou, *Catalogue des monnaies françaises de la Bibliothèque Nationale,* vol. 2 (Paris, 1896). There is also R. Doehaerd, 'Les réformes monétaires carolingiennes', *Annales: économies, sociétés, civilisations,* 7 (1952): 13–20.

18. This topic has been studied by C. M. Cipolla, 'Encore Mahomet et Charlemagne', *Annales: économies, sociétés, civilisations,* 4 (1949): 5–9, and by the same author, 'Questioni aperte sul sistema economico dell alto Medio Evo', *Rivista storica italiana,* 63 (1951): 95–99.

19. The origin of nobility is a problem to which much research is now being devoted. For a general orientation consult the studies of G. Duby, 'Une enquête à poursuivre: la noblesse de la France médiévale', *Revue historique,* 226 (1961): 1–22; L. Génicot, 'La noblesse au moyen âge dans l'ancienne "Francie"', *Annales: économies, sociétés, civilisations,* 17 (1962): 1–22. More recently R. Boutruche has published relevant observations in *Revue historique,* 233 (1965): 199–203. Further, certain works dealing with the ancient French nobility should be consulted with respect to *noblesse de sang:* H. Dannenbauer,

Adel, Burg und Herrschaft bei den Germanen', *Historisches Jahrbuch, 66* (1941): 1–50; W. Schlesinger, 'Herrschaft und Gefolgschaft in der germanisch–deutschen Verfassungsgeschichte', *Historische Zeitschrift, 176* (1953): 225–75; G. Tellenbach, *Studien und Vorarbeiten zur Geschichte des grossfränkischen Adels* (Fribourg, 1957). For a general discussion of the problem see K. Bosl, *Frühformen der Gesellschaft im mittelalterlichen Europa* (Munich, 1964). For a discussion of *noblesse de service* see in particular A. Bergengruen, *Adel und Grundherrschaft im Merowingerreich* (Wiesbaden, 1958). K. Stroheker, *Der senatorische Adel im spätantiken Gallien* (Tübingen, 1948) deals with the old senatorial nobility.

20. J. Dhondt analyses this development in *Études sur la naissance des principautés territoriales en France* (Bruges, 1948).

21. The classic work of Marc Bloch, *La société féodale,* 2nd ed., 2 vols. (Paris, 1949), deals mainly with the postCarolingian period. In addition there are the works of H. Mitteis, *Lehnrecht und Staatsgewalt* (Weimar, 1933) and F. L. Ganshof, *Qu'estce que la féodalité?,* 3rd ed. (Brussels, 1957) or *Feudalism,* trans. P. Grierson, 3rd English ed. (London, 1964). By the latter author see also 'L'origine des rapports féodovassaliques' in *I problemi della civilta carolingia* (Settimane di studio del Centro italiano di studi sull'alto Medioevo, 1; Spoleto, 1954), pp. 27–45, and 'Benefice and Vassalage in the Age of Charlemagne', *Cambridge Historical Journal, 6* (1939): 149–75.

22. F. L. Ganshof, 'Note sur les origines de l'union du bénéfice avec la vassalité', *Études d'histoire dédiées à la mémoire de H. Pirenne* (Brussels, 1937), pp. 173–89.

23. See the study of E. MüllerMertens, *Karl der Grosse, Ludwig der Fromme und die Freien* (Berlin, 1963).

24. The colons and serfs are discussed in the works cited in note 5. The duties of each are evident in the polyptychs; for instance that of SaintGermain des Prés, ed. B. Guérard *Polyptique de l'abbé Irminon: ou Dénombrement des manses, des serfs et des revenus de l'abbaye de StGermain des Prés sous le régne de Charlemagne,* 2 vols. in 3 (Paris, 1836–44).

25. K. Bosl, *Frühformen der Gesellschaft,* p. 189.

26. The end of slavery has been discussed by Marc Bloch, 'Comment et pourquoi finit l'esclavage antique', *Annales: économies, sociétés, civilisations,* 2 (1947): 30–44 and 161–70; reprinted in his *Mélanges historiques* (Paris, 1963), 1: 261–85. This great historian was opposed to the view that there was a direct link between ancient slavery and medieval serfdom.

27. Let us cite, in addition, an intermediate legal category between the colons and the serfs: these were the 'lides', who had been enfranchised according to Germanic law and remained the dependants of their former masters.

28. Such was the hypothesis of Marc Bloch, which he formulated in numerous works; see his 'Liberté et servitude personnelle au moyen âge', *Añuario de historia del derecho español,* 1933, pp. 5–101, reprinted in *Mélanges historiques,* 1: 286–355.

29. L. Verriest has the merit of clarifying this issue in *Institutions médiévales: Introduction au corpus des records de coutume et des lois de cheflieux de l'ancien comté de Hainault*(Mons, 1946).

30. We draw the reader's attention at this point to general works which deal with the Emperor and his reign, such as A. Kleinclausz, *Charlemagne* (Paris, 1934); J. Calmette, *Charlemagne* (Paris, 1945); L. Halphen, *Charlemagne et l'Empire carolingien* (Paris, 1949). These works have actually been overshadowed by the remarkable collective publication, *Karl der Grosse,* 4 vols. (Düsseldorf, 1965–66), which deals with all aspects of the reign of Charlemagne and with the Carolingian Renaissance. For shorter studies see F. L. Ganshof, 'Charlemagne', *Speculum,* 24 (1949): 520–28; J. Fleckenstein, *Karl der Grosse* (Göttingen, 1962); and, quite recently published, T. Boussard, *Charlemagne et son temps* (Paris, 1968).

31. L. Auzias, *L'Aquitaine carolingienne* (Paris, 1938); R. d'Abadal, 'La domination carolingienne en Catalogne', *Revue historique*, 225 (1961): 319–40.

32. H. Waquet, *Histoire de la Bretagne*, 2nd ed. (Paris, 1948).

33. The wars against the Saxons have been presented by M. Lintzel. They are now available in his *Ausgewählte Schriften*, 2 vols. (Berlin, 1961). Cf. the summary of his views, with a few qualifying comments, in Ph. Dollinger and R. Folz, 'Histoire d'Allemagne au moyen âge: Publications des années 1960–1963', *Revue historique*, 232 (1964): 176–78.

34. The existence of the assembly of Markloo which, according to Lintzel, represented the Saxon people's highest political forum, is at the present time much debated.

35. On the progress of evangelization see H. Wiedemann, *Die Sachsenbekehrung* (Münster, 1932) and *Karl der Grosse, Widukind und die Sachsenbekehrung* (Münster, 1949); consult as well E. Müller, *Entstehungsgeschichte der Sächsischen Bistümer* (Hildesheim and Leipzig, 1938).

36. M. Bathe, 'Die Sicherung der Reichsgrenze an der Mittelelbe durch Karl den Grossen', *Sachsen und Anhalt Jahrbuch*, 16 (1940): 1–44.

37. On the problems in the South-East: I. Zibermayr, *Noricum, Baiern und Oesterreich* (Horn, 1956), passim; H. Löwe, *Die Karolingische Reichsgründung und der Süd-Osten* (Berlin, 1937); A. Brackmann, 'Die Anfänge der Slavenmission und die Renovatio Imperii des Jahres 800', *Sitzungsberichte der preussischen Akademie der Wissenschaften*, 96 (1931), report 9, reprinted in his *Gesammelte Aufsätze* (Weimar, 1941).

38. E. Delaruelle, 'Charlemagne, Carloman, Didier et la politique du mariage franco-lombard', *Revue historique*, 170 (1932): 213–24.

39. O. Bertolini, 'La caduta del primicerio Cristoforo', *Rivista di storia della Chiesa in Italia*, 1 (1947): 227–62 and 349–78.

40. This confirmation can be found only in *Liber pontificalis*, ed. L. Duchesne (Paris, 1886–92), 1: 498. According to this source (Vita Hadriani), Charlemagne had Pepin's promise of donation to Stephen II reread to him, following which he had a new one drafted in which he promised to hand over to Saint Peter the cities and territories lying south of the 'border line' indicated by Pepin, from Luni to Monselice. It encompassed the Exarchate, Istria, Venetia, Corsica, and the duchies of Spoleto and Benevento. The interpretation of this surprising text is extremely delicate. It was thought at first that the text was an immense interpolation, and recently this view has been defended by L. Saltet, 'La lecture d'un texte et la critique contemporaine', *Bulletin de littérature ecclésiastique de l'Institut catholique de Toulouse* (1940), pp. 176–206 and (1941), pp. 61–85, but the authenticity has been admitted by most contemporary historians. This being established, it is necessary to inquire about the nature of the 'donation promise' of Charlemagne. Was it a question of returning to the Holy See patrimonies which it had lost in the zone in question? Or was it rather, as has been surmised by Mgr. L. Duchesne, *Les premiers temps de l'État pontifical*, 3rd ed. (Paris, 1894) and J. Haller, 'Die Karolinger und das Papsttum', *Historische Zeitschrift*, 108 (1912): 38–76, a plan of an eventual division of the Lombard kingdom between the king and the pope? This hypothesis seems to us the more probable; it explains fully the fact that Charlemagne paid no attention at all to his 'promise' after 774, since the Lombard kingdom had not been destroyed but continued to live under a different form. For a review of the whole problem, see E. Caspar, 'Das Papsttum unter fränkischer Herrschaft', *Zeitschrift für Kirchengeschichte*, 54 (1935): 132–264, and P. E. Schramm, 'Das Versprechen Pippins und Karls des Grossen für die römische Kirche', *Zeitschrift für Rechtsgeschichte* (*Kanonistiche Abteilung*), 27 (1938): 180–217, reprinted and enlarged in his collection of studies, *Kaiser, Könige und Päpste: Gesammelte Aufsätze zur Geschichte des Mittelalters* (Stuttgart, 1968), 1:143–92.

41. E. Hlawitschka, *Franken, Alamannen, Bayern und Burgunder in Oberitalien* (Fribourg, 1960).

42. Let us recall that the duchy of Benevento, whose territory corresponded to the interior of southern Italy, had a separate existence from that of the Lombard kingdom; since 774 it had been a permanent centre of intrigues against the Frankish domination.

43. In order not to overburden these pages we have refrained from presenting the bibliography on this subject. The reader will find it conveniently arranged in R. Folz, *Le couronnement impérial de Charlemagne* (Paris, 1964), a work from which we have taken up several leading ideas.

44. This fundamental aspect of the reign cannot be dealt with in these pages; the reader is referred to our work quoted above, where he will find basic information on the subject. Also one should add to the bibliography, for certain aspects of the cultural reform, P. E. Schramm, 'Karl der Grosse', *Historische Zeitschrift,* 198 (1964): 306–45, now in his *Kaiser, Könige und Päpste,* 1:302–44.

45. This discrepancy is partially cleared up in the famous eclogue of the poet Modoin (between 804 and 814); cf. R. Folz, *Le couronnement impérial de Charlemagne,* p. 208, n.1.

46. A general bibliography of this subject will be found in L. Halphen, *Charlemagne et l'Empire carolingien* and a more detailed one in H. Conrad, *Deutsche Rechtsgeschichte: Ein Lehrbuch,* 2nd ed., vol. 1 (Karlsruhe, 1962).

47. F. L. Ganshof, 'Charlemagne et le serment', *Mélanges d'histoire du moyen âge dédiés à la mémoire de Louis Halphen* (Paris, 1951), pp. 259–70.

48. This period has been analysed by F. L. Ganshof, 'L'échec de Charlemagne', *Comptes rendus des séances de l'Académie des Inscriptions et Belle-Lettres* (1947), pp. 248–54.

49. L. Halphen, 'L'idée d'État sous les Carolingiens', *Revue historique,* 185 (1939): 59–70; Th. Mayer, 'Staatsauffassungen der Karolingerzeit', *Historische Zeitschrift,* 173 (1952): 467–84.

50. J. Fleckenstein, *Die Hofkapelle der deutschen Könige,* vol. 1: *Die Karolingische Hof-kapelle* (Stuttgart, 1959).

51. A. Dumas, 'La parole et l'écriture dans les capitulaires carolingiens', *Mélanges ... Halphen,* pp. 209–16; F. L. Ganshof, 'Charlemagne et l'usage de l'écrit en matière administrative', *Le moyen âge: Revue d'histoire et de philologie,* 57 (1951): 1–25.

52. K. Bosl, *Franken um 800,* pp. 12–37, reviews this 'state colonization' in Franconia, and points out (pp. 28–29) that the counts at this period were mere royal functionaries, with limited territorial jurisdiction.

53. The Germanic 'hundred' has been considered until recently as an offshoot of the ancient *Hundertschaft.* It is now considered to have been instituted by the Franks, but its functions are still being discussed. See, for example, Th. Mayer, 'Staat und Hundertschaft in fränkischer Zeit', in his *Mittelalterliche Studien: Gesammelte Aufsätze* (Lindau and Constance, 1959), pp. 98–138, reprinted from *Rheinische Vierteljahrsblätter,* 17 (1952): 343–84.

54. It does not seem to have been introduced generally in the Empire; for instance, it is not in evidence in Bavaria; its existence in Saxony is still being debated.

55. They formed in reality 'the aristocracy of the Empire' (*Reichsaristokratie*), a term coined by G. Tellenbach, *Königtum und Stämme in der Werdezeit des deutschen Reiches* (Weimar, 1939).

56. For this important question and the institution of 'avouerie', which is closely related to it, see the bibliography of the manual by H. Conrad, *Deutsche Rechtsgeschichte,* p. 150.

57. To the same category belonged the duchy of Bavaria before Tassilo III's dismissal.

58. E. Klebel, 'Die Ostgrenze des Karolingischen Reiches', *Die Entstehung des deutschen*

Reiches (Wege der Forschung, 1; Darmstadt, 1956), pp. 1 ff. See also from the same author, 'Herzogtümer und Marken', *Deutsches Archiv*, 2 (1938): 1–53.

59. See the works listed in notes 31 and 32.

60. At the General Assembly of October 802, which is described in the *Annales Laureshamenses,* there were in fact three, since the monks had sessions separate from the representatives of the secular clergy.

61. F. L. Ganshof, *Recherches sur les capitulaires* (Paris, 1958), p. 31.

62. They had to do with civil, penal, political, economic, moral, and religious matters. It was only gradually that there emerged ecclesiastic capitularies on the one hand and lay capitularies on the other.

63. There was also a great diversity in their presentation: reviews, more or less detailed, of the decisions which had been read or promulgated at the general sessions; résumés, article by article, of royal decisions; lists of chapter headings, which were considered sufficiently informative to refresh the memory of those who were charged with transmitting and executing the verbal orders of the king.

64. In 802, for example, the *missaticum* of the archbishop of Sens comprised the counties extending from Orléans to Troyes and from Autun to Langres.

65. See for example R. Folz, *Le souvenir et la légende de Charlemagne dans l'Empire germanique médiéval* (Paris, 1950).

edieval economic
achievement
in perspective

Sylvia L. Thrupp

WHICH PERSPECTIVE?

Medieval economic achievement has been viewed in turn in a romantic and an evolutionary light. Today it is being drawn into the more complex perspective which comparative study of 'under-developed' agrarian societies and of commerce and industry in other pre-steampower ages can offer.[1] The romantic view was attractive, none the less so because it rested on a dream which carried a built-in bias towards ignorance of facts. The dream was of a world kept essentially static by deference to religious authority and governmental power, where the mass of the peasants were enfolded in a 'cake' of custom—presumably a cake of mud—and where the sordid notion of profit was either hamstrung by canon law, or was some-how sealed off in a few picturesque towns. Early evolutionary views allowed for some ultimate movement in the direction of capitalism, but saw the greater part of Europe tied to barter as a means of exchange and ignorant of credit, until well into the twelfth century. Urban areas then entered the stage of money economy, which tended to spread; and progess thereafter was to be measured by the evolution of banking and of business techniques. The static view is obsolete, and, though our thinking is still bound to the idea of evolution, the evolutionary picture has undergone revision. Change has come by organizing enquiry so far as possible by economic theory, and by seeking to quantify the answers so far as the evidence will permit. Research focuses on the yield of land and the output of workshops in relation to population trends, on the extent to which trade or rising standards of consumption may have stimulated production, and on the extent of investment for productive purposes.

The older views shared certain psychological assumptions as to medieval man's supposed irrationality in economic matters. The new approach can afford to be neutral in this regard, to leave the fields of medieval psychology and social psychology open to research. But it takes account of the manifold uses of medieval intelligence in making economic decisions. The dullest peasant was aware that barley used for brewing could not at the same time be used for bread. Custom could have been an exact guide to the allocation of his resources only if crop returns had been constant. Actually the only fixed items in his household problems were seed requirements and rent. Since crop returns fluctuated, a peasant had each year to readjust his decisions as to how much of the disposable surplus should be eaten, drunk, or sold. The allocation of a nobleman's resources in building also involved calculation, whether the project were a church or a castle. If New Testament counsels of prudence were followed, costs would in either case be estimated prior to the start of construction. We need not envisage medieval people as wearing day and night the mask of Economic Man, that darling bogey of romantics. On the other hand, the notion that religion inhibited calculation is demonstrably an error.[2]

The sources do not of course enable us to reconstruct the economic life of the Middle Ages as neatly as they would if they included the kinds of readymade statistics which nineteenthcentury state bureaucracies compiled. We have no true totals for any country's population or for any type of productive unit. But there were many pockets of bureaucracy addicted to recordkeeping. From the twelfth century on, the results have survived in increasing quantity, exuded from law courts, from revenue offices, from the procedures of probate of wills, from the administration of great estates, and in Mediterranean areas from the public notaries who drafted private contracts and kept copies. For the early Middle Ages we have no massive body of sources save the charters by which privileges were granted or title to land conveyed. Yet to the alert eye almost any piece of writing yields some economic evidence. Even the testimony of poets may legitimately be used, when we know something about a matter already, as confirmatory evidence. Those interminable and littleread medieval romances attest, for example, to consciousness of the general scale of exchange values. When King Arthur and a thousand knights ride within sight of a prosperous farm in North Wales, in an early thirteenthcentury romance, the farmer and his sons rush to hide their most valuable portable possessions—the parts of their field implements which were made of iron.[3] Many gaps in our knowledge are being narrowed by aerial photography, by laboratory analysis of metalwork or of the pollen content of soil deposits, and by the irreverent spade of archaeology.

THE EARLY MEDIEVAL ECONOMY

If the early medieval economy is a trifle shadowy, it is mainly from long delay in reading the sources with relevant questions in mind. One good starting-point is to ask what was the ratio between available manpower and the existing supply of arable land. The late Gino Luzzatto, on reading through some thousands of documents in which large properties are described, found a superabundance of waste land and almost uniform reference to parts of the arable being out of cultivation for want of tenants.[4] On this and other evidence to the same effect, he conceded that population must have fallen in the fourth century and that it was not generally growing until the tenth. There were regional variations, but a Danish scholar's arguments in favour of a population rise in sixth-century Italy[5] have been refuted by Lellia Ruggini, in part on the grounds of a succession of epidemics.[6] The militant migrations of the earlier periods, and the constant campaigning that went on through the ninth century, could hardly have promoted population growth. The direct killing power of armies was small, but their battlefields and dirty camps no doubt spread typhus and other diseases.

The political and religious transformations of the age aggravated the situation by favouring the growth of large estates to the detriment of the small independent farms which had formerly surrounded the *latifundia*. Increasing resort to forms of dependent tenure failed to solve the chronic problem of labour shortage. For independence was not necessarily surrendered joyfully, even for the sake of children. Ruggini in this connection cites a sermon of St. Ambrose denouncing contemporary reluctance to procreate, and the desperate practice, among the poor, of exposing the new-born to die.[7] Again, as the manorial system took shape, from the seventh century on, using forced labour on the great proprietors' home farms (demesne lands), this labour may well have been so recalcitrant to efficient management as to reduce food production, thus introducing a new damper on population growth. Folke Dovring, who has lately emphasized this point, argues that all systems of agrarian bond labour have been caught in a similar vicious circle.[8] European estate management acquired more coercive power through the recasting of local custom, with the help of feudal fragmentation of regalian rights, in the ninth and tenth centuries.[9] Yet all through the Middle Ages manor lords faced both active and passive resistance to the performance of labour services.[10]

The early medieval lords' one great contribution to the improvement of productivity was to adopt, adapt, and diffuse the Hellenistic invention of the harnessing of waterpower. Ruggini, who has traced the spread of water-powered flour mills in Italy from the fourth century through the sixth, interprets the movement as a constructive reaction to labour shortage.[11] The lord's retention of a monopoly of the milling imposed on the peasants the nuisance of carriage back and forth and made them resent the surrender of a portion of their grain as a toll to the lord's miller. On the other hand, it released several hours of womanpower per household per day from the drudgery of pounding or grinding by hand. The magnitude of this released power, by the eleventh century, may be seen in *Domesday Book*. The ratio of mills to people in the England of 1086 has been estimated as one per four hundred.[12]

Early medieval trade has attracted far more attention than this impressive conquest of inanimate power. Yet it has been better described geographically, and as adventure, than functionally. Many a student is forever befogged by the impression that the laws of supply and demand were suspended, either by the fall of the Roman Empire or at the accession of Charlemagne, for some indefinite duration. Nostalgia for self-sufficient farming, on the part of intellectuals who have never tried it, combines with a shallow Marxist interpretation of feudalism to keep nobles still riding about elementary textbooks for no purpose but to eat up the produce of one manor after another, or else sitting in fatherly consensus with their peasants, apparently making do with homemade arms and homebred cart-horses in appearances at their lord's court.

In reality the proprietors of large estates lived simultaneously by three kinds of economy: by household economy, by passing trade; by local and regional exchange; and by long-distance trade.

Some of the produce of estates had always been consumed within the closed circuit of household economy, even in the heyday of commercial farming under Rome. Fixed amounts had been set aside then for seed, and for feeding the animals and the slaves. To reduce cash outlay, and to maintain labour discipline, the latter had been kept hard at work through slack seasons in making implements and containers from wood and reeds cut on waste plots.[13] Medieval lords followed the same principles. They could never run their demesne land by tenant services alone, but employed also a permanent staff of *famuli* for the purpose. Slaves are found on these staffs into the eleventh century; otherwise the *famuli* were always serfs, and they were paid, like the Roman farm slaves, in grain allowances.[14]

In respect of farm produce, the scope of household economy widened when the great proprietors forsook their town houses (which in Italy they had provisioned from the market)[15] to settle down on their estates and simplify their diet. It widened further as more and more land became the property of monks dedicated to simple living and offering hospitality to beggars and travellers. But this extended household economy coexisted with a commercial economy. Royalty and other great lords had enormous holdings, which, even when reduced by grants to vassals and to military protectors of religious houses, remained far in excess of subsistence needs. Much produce had therefore to be sold, as a matter of deliberate policy. Kings, having responsibility for army supply, and travelling always with a huge retinue, had abnormal needs which could never be supplied wholly from the market. The Carolingian regulations for the operation of the royal estates provide for the assignment of some of their produce, on order, for army supply. But they provide also for a regular accounting record of cash sales.[16] A great monastery like Westminster Abbey, with heavy entertainment demands on its abbot and its manors lying for the most part on easy transportation routes, always had a great deal of produce shipped up to headquarters, but possibly always sold some of this on the London market. Dispersed estates, as Luzzatto has shown, could be run only through considerable resort to local exchange.[17] Great monasteries regularly retained special servants to buy and sell for them, and private merchants were also on the prowl. Einhard, Charlemagne's biographer, mentions in the course of an anecdote that merchants went south from Mainz buying up grain.[18] They may have been doing so for centuries. Again, the most Gargantuan liberalization of the Rule of St. Benedict could not have enabled the monks of St Denis to drink all of the wine they produced. They produced for sale. Their famous fair successfully promoted both the cult of St Denis and the wine trade.

The same duality, the same combination of household and commercial economy, appears in such record as we have of early medieval industry. Outside Italy it was more or less completely de-urbanized—although outside Italy the Romans had probably never fully urbanized it. In North Italy both ploughshares and arms were made by rural tenants who paid their rent in this form but were otherwise free to sell.[19] Similar arrangements grew up north of the Alps for all manner of manu-factures, including the processing of dairy products.[20] Lords also retained craftsmen as *famuli*, possibly intending the products for their own use or for military supply or for distribution through the custom of gift-giving to followers. But continuous good-quality production inevitably overflowed into trade. Archaeological evidence shows the products of fifth-century Rhineland potteries, thought to have been organized on estates, overflowing into export trade to Scandinavia.[21] There is archaeological evidence also of local distribution by itinerant potters.[22]

The lay lords of the early Middle Ages were less rationally commercial than the ecclesiastics, if only because they lived so much by the excitement of war, and preferred to steal what they wanted by raiding. War-horses and arms were distri-buted also by patterns of lordly gift-giving, which continued later at tournaments. Trade itself, in so far as it drew profits from slave-running, as among the merchants of Verdun, was partly militarized. The Scandinavians—and to judge from the prominence that cattle-stealing assumes in early English codes of law, also the English—long kept a nice balance between predatory habits and peaceable trade. The main economic achievements of the early Middle Ages came through permit-ting peaceable trade to gain headway.

The continuity of marketing also calls for emphasis. Medievalists now recognize that in talking of a reversion to natural economy they were merely sweeping their economic problems under the rug of a speculative abstraction.[23] Yet by qualifying reference to sales as being only of surplus production they hedge between a truism and a fallacy. For no trade can occur until there is in some sense a surplus, and any implication that sales were haphazard is fallacious: both grain and specialized products came on the market by design. It may be useful to polarize the contrast between an increasingly commercial economy, in which it is possible to think of (and to protest against) the production of goods and services being more and more governed by price considerations, and one in which production and exchange merely serve to maintain a given social system without altering it. Yet to say that early medieval economic life approximated the latter position would again be to sweep its more interesting problems under a rug. For there was one social system in Ireland, another in Norway, and so on around the map, and each was being subtly altered by the march of Christianity; trade and enlarged communication followed the Cross. There is, however, some truth in the generalization that up into the ninth century, long-distance trade served mainly to enhance the dominance of the great lay and ecclesiastical lords: it was their demand for exotic products—for jewels, spices, incense and vestments, and fine furs—which kept that trade alive.

With the tenth century, in North Italy, we pass a decisive turning-point. The stimulus of the foreign and regional trade activated by Venice at last enables productive power to outstrip the joint effects of the absorption of wealth in the ceremonial life of the Church, and of military destructiveness.

Why had it taken so long to reach this point? Pirenne was essentially right in stressing the importance of foreign markets as a stimulus to production. Where he failed was in not sufficiently analyzing the conditions under which they will serve this function. To criticize him on any other grounds, such as for not knowing facts that were not known in his time, is ungenerous and irrelevant. Advance has come through realizing that East-West trade had already fallen off in the late Empire, and by trying to understand why it should have revived through Venetian enterprise in the tenth century. Military history only scratches the surface of this problem, and monetary history has so far proved to be a red herring.[24] Venice first raised the productive powers of North Italy by regional trade in salt, which made it possible to enrich diet by more fish and meat. What she exported to Byzantium was mainly grain and timber, demand for which was growing there due to the revival, after long suspension, of population growth. Ruggini has shown that there had been some prior export of Sicilian grain, via Ravenna, in the sixth century.[25] The resurgence of plague in the Byzantine Empire must have helped to reduce demand. Robert Lopez has long been reminding us that plague was endemic in this period over the whole area of civilization from China to Western Europe. But historians still cling, with Shakespeare and the Troy romancers, to the myth of the Gorgeous East. Study of Byzantine and Islamic economic history has had little university encouragement, but it is beginning to qualify the myth of fabulous wealth. Behind the ceremonial facade of Imperial Byzantium we have glimpses now of provincial towns that were not at all grand.[26] The political fissions of Islam fit a pattern of spheres of regional trade. The long slave-raiding from Moslem Spain in southern France had an economic purpose—to relieve labour shortage. In short, demo-graphic stagnation, the root problem of the early medieval West, was in some degree common to all of the political and monetary regimes of the time. Better understanding of it hangs on a branch of history as yet undeveloped—bacterial history, or the study of man's internal ecology.

THE AGE OF HIGH EXPECTATION

By the mid-eleventh century West Europe was launched on a series of adventures in economic growth which did not slacken until the late thirteenth. The level of expectations and of organizing energy rose on all sides. The first sign of it is in under-employed peasants obtaining the tools and the credit to carve out new farms on fertile land selected from the waste of timber or fen adjacent to their villages. Others, and the better rural craftsmen, flock to urban centres where merchant entrepreneurs enforce on them the heavy discipline required to produce standardized goods for export. The industrial town—crowded, noisy from dawn to dark with hammering, the clack of looms, and the rumble of carts over paving-stones—is born in Flanders. By the end of the period of expansion Bruges and Ghent have populations of around eighty thousand. Urbanization is most phenomenal in Italy, where Milan, Florence, Genoa, and Venice (the last two through the drawing power of their commerce and ship-building) exceed this by some 25 per cent, and where many lesser towns were larger than any elsewhere save Paris, Cologne, London, or Barcelona.

The first great export market to be opened, largely through the energy of the Genoese, is that of the Near East for Flemish textiles. One of the more fascinating questions of history is whether Italian skill could not have contrived to open this without the slaughter and the wrecking of cultural relations with Byzantium and Islam that were occasioned by the Crusades. If in 1095 the Chair of St. Peter had been occupied not by Urban II but by someone who somehow combined the wisdom of Peter the Venerable with the diplomatic skill of Frederick II, and the idealism of those French bishops who had earlier sponsored the Peace Movement with the business nose of a Genoese merchant, perhaps so. It is perhaps miracle enough that the Italians subdued the fighting spirit of their old noble families as much as they did. They tamed it to a high degree by the smell of high commercial profits, and by authority. But they allowed it some outlet in naval defence and in aggression, as in the fratricidal warfare between Genoa and Pisa. Paradoxically, the Hanseatic merchants of the Baltic zone, who were less commercially advanced than the Italians, handled the problem of intercity relations far more successfully.[27]

Home markets also flourished, expanding automatically in the wake of inter-regional export via the fairs of Champagne. Year-round business at these fairs progressively promoted specialization not only in trade and manufacturing but in finance and transport.[28] The larger towns devoured food, fuel, building materials, as well as wool and leather and the chemicals required for working them up. The merchants themselves, and the town-based specialists in administration and the learned professions, who multiplied as governmental and Church revenues and private fortunes expanded, created new demand for high-quality food, drink, clothing, furnishing, and services. The buying power of the nobility, augmented by commercial exploitation of their estates, added to such demand. In the thirteenth century the status-symbolism of consumption is not only a literary theme in Paris, where its pull is blamed on the vanity and greed of wives, but is affecting the habits of small townspeople and villagers. Common aspirations to the sense of dignity that came with better living conditions had by then spread throughout the countryside, especially among settlers attracted to new communities founded on the initiative of lords with small plots at low, fixed rents to encourage craftsmen and local trade. In both old and new villages, division of labour was making headway, with smiths, potters, weavers, dyers, leather-workers, tailors, butchers, and bakers catering to local demand. Most of these village craftsmen were not full-time specialists but did a little farming on the side; and in the north many, with the help of their wives, also made malt or beer for sale. To some extent there was a dual economy, isolated villages and the peasants of hill country having little or no connection with the network of supply and distribution channels that led in and out of the larger towns. Yet these networks were very widely ramified, leading from large towns to little ones and to country fairs where merchants and their agents came into contact with village dealers and permanently itinerant pedlars. By such means peasants were able to discard earthenware cooking and brewing vessels for metal ones made by specialists more skilled than the village smith, and village craftsmen became aware also of new textile techniques.

Inventiveness raised productivity. Twelfth-century mechanics harnessed the winds, and both windmills and watermills were adapted to new industrial uses in beating, crushing, and grinding processes. Time acquired a value, as is seen in the failure of conservative resistance to short-cut methods of preparing leather.[29]

Even spirituality became, with the Cistercian movement, more materially productive than before. The Cistercians were both humble pioneers who broke new land and ruthless uprooters of villages that stood in the way of their methods. Their methods included an extension of sheep-farming for profit and considerable recruiting of celibate lay-brothers to work other lands under a system of disciplined security which might well be the envy of Red China. It is altogether appropriate that the best medieval exposition we have of the spiritual value and necessity of work has come down to us in the writings of St. Bernard.[30]

The great question is how to find meaningful measures of the progress that had been achieved by the end of the thirteenth century, measures that will at the same time explain why expectations were then sinking. In the older views no such question presented itself. The only major general problem was to reconcile the romantic assumption that a religious society would remain economically static with the evolutionists' reasoning that the growth of towns indicated an upward move-ment through the spread of money economy. The means of reconciling the two was by accepting the idea that canon law restrictions acted as a brake on progress until the sixteenth century. Tawney, from the English point of view, and Fanfani from the Italian, made classic statements of reconciliation which meet at this point.[31] In all countries except Germany, where an academic statistical tradition flourished, medieval economic history was in consequence regarded as a branch of study confined to describing the nature and continuity of institutions. Thorold Rogers, who first opened the mine of medieval English statistical information on prices and wages, was an amateur worker, styling himself an antiquarian.

Canon law certainly affected the development of economic institutions. It affected the history of banking by deflecting commercial credit into the hands of dealers in foreign exchange.[32] It deflected twelfth-century mortgaging practice, regarded as usurious because the creditor could take the income from mortgaged property without writing it off against the principal of the loan,[33] into the channel of rent charges, that is, of borrowing through the sale of title to a fixed perpetual income, analogous to a dividend, from a given piece of land or house property. Neither of these deflections retarded the flow of credit. Title to rent charges was so firm as to be readily marketable. Records of their constitution and sale are a valuable index to the going rates of interest in this type of loan and investment market in both towns and rural areas, just as records of bankers show that exchange costs were so manipulated as to cover commercial credit costs. Otherwise usury legislation mainly wrestled, no more successfully than we do today, with the social problem of protecting the consumer-borrower from unjust exploitation in a market that is not an open one. Canon law was more successful in promoting, through the devise of property by will,[34] the transfer of wealth to charitable purposes. By the twelfth and thirteenth centuries charity included aid to hospitals and to new religious orders devoted to rudimentary nursing, aid to students and to scholarship, and aid to poor families who could not otherwise have married off their daughters. These forms of redistribution of wealth can hardly be said to have retarded economic growth.

The present position as to the spread of money economy in medieval society is less easy for the non-medievalist to understand. At first sight it seems obvious that the old generalizations must be correct, that the growth of towns and of their supply lines for cash sale must progressively have reduced the sphere of rural household economy in which there were no sales. The immediate vicinity of towns formed one sector of the economy in which this was true, and into the early fourteenth century this sector was expanding through the growth both of old towns and of many new communities founded by internal colonization in the older West and by the surge of eastward German colonization. To the extent that peasants not in the vicinity of towns sold at country fairs or to any type of merchant, we have another sector in which monetized trade was probably expanding over the same period. To the extent that division of labour was increasing within villages, local tailors and so on being paid in money, we have a third sector showing some small expansion of monetized economy.

So far, the going is easy. It becomes rougher when we look at a fourth sector of the economy, that covered by the relations of the great landed proprietors with their peasant tenants. Unfree tenants, and some of the free, traditionally paid their rent through a mixture of labour service, payment in kind, and payment in coin, in proportions that were flexibly alterable at the will of the lord. The combination of payments in money and in kind served the lord as a hedge against price fluctuations: one early twelfth-century French abbot specifically says so.[35] Labour services were regularly commutable for money, at the lord's convenience, and payments owed in money could if necessary be made in produce. The lord was thus ensured against loss of rent when his labour needs happened to fall or when peasants protested that they had no money. Finally, just at the time when the growth of rural population was pushing rents up through competition, lords were enabled to profit from the rise of food prices in urban markets by increasing the proportion of rent taken either in kind or in labour. As David Herlihy has shown, in twelfth-century Italy new commercially minded landlords were taking the first course, renewing tenant leases, as they expired, at vastly higher rents payable in kind.[36] This would have reduced buying power in the village sector of the economy. In thirteenth-century England, on the other hand, great ecclesiastical lords set the example of increasing the proportion of rent taken in labour services. This helped them to enlarge their demesne farms by new reclamation of waste land and to produce more for sale, but it must to some extent have reduced peasant capacity to produce for sale.

We are faced with the paradox that the growth of commerce in the twelfth and thirteenth centuries reduced, in certain important sectors, the play of the cash nexus. Although there is no exact parallel to this situation in any of the developing countries that are being so intensively studied today, these studies show the same trend that is apparent in current medieval research, namely, a recognition that knowledge of the money supply, in an agrarian society in which many services are paid for in kind, is of less immediate importance than knowledge of nutrition, of the adequacy of the food supply and of its distribution.

This is not to say that study of medieval money supply or of prices has been or should be dropped. More synchronic study of prices, that is, a concentration on the way in which different prices were interrelated in a given area at a given time, is needed for the study of trends in real wages and other income. But there are many problems in the interpretation of the information. For one thing, money supply was unevenly distributed. Where it ran short, coinage was flexibly supplemented by commodity money: Genoese trade continued to expand even when coinage had to be supplemented by the use of pepper.[37] It was supplemented very largely, wherever Italian merchants operated, by credit instruments. Hanseatic merchants stretched their money supply by mutual trust, often simply keeping a record of what each owed the other and periodically settling the balance. The same method was used among villagers. To quantify any part of the supply of money or credit is virtually impossible.

The problems of the age could be presented most directly and dramatically by a single four-line graph, the four lines showing the trends in the production of food and of manufactures, the trend of investment as a proportion of the total value of these two, and the trend of population growth. We have already enough data from selected areas to indicate the relative contours these lines would assume for the late thirteenth century. The curve containing the most massive productive effort—the production of foodstuffs—would, after a long slow rise, be flattening out. The curve of manufactures might still be rising slightly. The plotting of the investment curve would show a sharp decrease in the rate of mill construction, and, even were we to add some estimate of the cost of such education as children received, there would still be a generally miserable proportion of total production going into any kind of improvement of equipment or of human resources. The only curve still rising sharply would be that of population. All research shows this. To take just one example from recent work on Tuscany, Enrico Fiumi has shown the population of Volterra and its *contado* reaching its medieval maximum, which he reckons as equalling the figure for the end of the nineteenth century, towards 1340. The population of San Gimignano and its *contado* after 1290 grew more slowly but in 1332 was 12 per cent above the census figures for 1951.[38]

LATE MEDIEVAL CRISES AND RECOVERIES

The fourteenth century opens, then, to the dismal whistling of T. R. Malthus. Food supply had reached its limits, population had not; nutrition must have been deteriorating. Industrial capacity had already been strained to the utmost in enabling trade to bring Sicilian grain into Tuscany and East German grain into Flanders and the Rhineland. As it stood, the bulk of production units being little family workshops with rare recourse to power and not even a start on the complex problems of mechanizing any form of weaving, it could do no more. Nor does anyone of wealth or authority appear to have realized that only massive reorganization and investment could avert wholesale tragedy. A twelfth-century Pisan mathematician had studied the propagation of rabbits, but no one had studied human propagation. In one of his moments of practicality Roger Bacon had urged that intellectuals study agriculture, and the more progressive ecclesiastical landlords in England were trying to turn their estate accounting, traditionally used mainly as a check on the honesty of manorial servants, into a check on the efficiency of their operations. Yet early in the fourteenth century, for lack of enthusiasm, they abandoned the attempt.[39] Only the Italians had enough intelligent social conscious-ness to be aware that economic development should continue. They had up-to-date manuals on agriculture, merchants invested much of their profits in it, and the medical profession cooperated with city authorities in the policy of socialized medical aid for the poor. All of this helped North and Central Italy weather the crises that lay ahead rather better than most other areas.

The fact that the economy did struggle through, that it did not slump into the long early-medieval type of doldrums, but emerged in the 1480's better equipped, mechanically and metallurgically, in agriculture and navigation, than ever before, ready to embark on new phases of growth, makes many historians question, even in the face of statistics, the seriousness of the population crisis it had suffered. Controversy thrives, as always, on ignorance, in this case especially on the back-wardness of fifteenth-century research, and on the difficulty of interpreting the diversities of regional conditions. It thrives also on vague terminology. The term 'depression' has been hurled around without any care for the qualifications that M. M. Postan attached to it when first drawing attention to the fall in the volume and profitability of trade in this period and to the difficulties in which the falling grain market involved landlords. Most historians are, however, agreed that the heart of the problem is whether, in the face of cumulative mortality from pre-plague epidemics and repeated attacks of plague, the economy became less efficient, more efficient, or remained fairly stable, in terms of agricultural and industrial output per head. No one could yet project our hypothetical graph in these terms. To be really meaningful, it would still have to show the trend of investment as a proportion of total output, and it should also indicate changes in the age and sex structure of populations. For some areas all of this could be done but has not been done. Recent attempts to generalize the trend of agricultural production in terms of the ratio of yields to seed may soon be substantially revised by research in progress. A brief review of the kinds of evidence and argument that are being used by the optimists and the pessimists, respectively, is all that at the moment is feasible.

The optimists argue that production per head was either unchanged or actually rose, in consequence of mortality. As to food production, the argument that the survivors of an epidemic were better off because they could acquire the livestock and buildings of the dead need not be taken seriously. A few family feasts could have disposed of any surplus animals in a village, and village barns and houses were highly perishable. The more serious argument reasons that the fall in population allowed marginal land to be abandoned. Against this is the fact that soil deterioration and high credit costs had already forced the abandonment of poorer land before the major population losses occurred. Research must turn on the improvement of what was still being cultivated. In Italy there may have been real progress in this direction, since Herlihy finds that peasants were able to borrow more cheaply.[40]

As to industry, the question is complicated by competition between cities, between city and country, and between governmental areas. Gene Brucker reckons that Florentine cloth production, in relation to the city's population, fell only slightly,[41] but its competition, as Carlo Cipolla admits, had killed the Pisan industry.[42] English textile production received a boost from military and naval orders in the early phases of the Hundred Years' War, and exports continued to rise through the latter part of the fourteenth century and in some years of the early fifteenth. English historians glory in this, with typical insularity overlooking the fact that, to the extent that English cloth was merely driving Flemish products off the market, the gain was not a net gain for the European economy. Nor have they really proved a rise in English production: the increase in the number of cloths inspected and sealed as of standardized length may at least in part represent only an extension of entrepreneurial control over production that was formerly of odd lengths of cloth made by unorganized villagers. The only net industrial gain that has been proved is of German metallurgical production, which went largely into armaments to kill off more people. Cipolla remains staunchly optimistic on the grounds that areas hitherto backward were anxious to acquire industry and that governments were anxious to promote it,[43] but he has proved advance only for the regions around Milan and Pavia.

On the side of the pessimists, Postan's original argument from decline in the volume of trade and the market for foodstuffs has been extended by Lopez and Miskimin to show that decline in sea-borne trade was proportionately far greater than the decline in city populations.[44] This does not quite hit the issue to which the whole controversy has shifted, that of production per head. The excess decline in trade may conceivably have gone into home consumption, improving nutrition. Against this, a Dutch historian contends that continuing malnutrition was the cause of high plague mortality. His contention rests on the fact that fewer people died in Netherlands coastal areas, where diet included more protein and fat in the form of fish and dairy produce.[45] These areas were, however, in the later Middle Ages, subject to disastrous floods which may have had a benign aspect in drowning the rats that carried plague. Some southern Netherlands areas, where diet would have differed, also had lighter plague mortality. In all countries there was a scatter-ing of lucky places.

My own researches in the economy of English villages and small towns hold me in the pessimistic camp, for different reasons. If there is a bright side to conditions in which up to 49 per cent of the boys who were born alive died under the age of twenty-one, it escapes me. The heavy child mortality, which explains why at the end of the fourteenth century 45 per cent of London merchants left no sons, was not confined to the capital.[46] Illustrative figures from villages[47] indicate a steady fall, for any group of adult male deaths, in the number of male heirs surviving to the age of sixteen. The diminution starts in the 1270's, is pushed down by plague, and in the 1380's there is still less than one heir per death. For several decades there is then a precarious equilibrium between adult male deaths and boys surviving. Clear evidence of growth comes only with the 1470's.

A few conclusions based on comparison with other periods and other societies in which child mortality is high and adult life expectancy low can be blocked out. Health and vitality must have been wretched, continuous hard work impossible. In my opinion three-quarters of the late medieval population should have been put to bed for a thorough medical check-up while their houses were being dis-infected, their latrines cleaned out, their livestock and water-supply inspected. If the effectiveness of labour was reduced, labour per head cannot be regarded, for comparison with the preceding period, as a constant. Any increase in productivity must have depended on new technology. In England new civilian technology was virtually limited to knitting-needles, spinning-wheels, wheel-barrows, and equipment used by poachers. Examination of stewpot bones in a fifteenth-century Cistercian kitchen dump in Yorkshire shows sheep and cattle to have been stunted, having narrow bones splayed at the joints from poor feeding as lambs and calves.[48] The Cistercians are supposed to have led in the improvement of livestock, but seemingly had not led far. The Italian record is better on both the mechanical and the agricultural side.

RETROSPECT

These and other facts lead me to believe that medieval economic progress was retarded chiefly by influences extraneous to the economy itself, influences that we shall never understand until we explore bacterial history. To have maintained a viable economic organization throughout the early and late Middle Ages was in itself a great achievement, resting on the strange capacity of the human spirit to inure itself to misery, to survive hatred, to renew itself through laughter, dream, and ceremony. To have improved that organization so vastly was the achievement of a host of intelligent merchants, farmers, and mechanics, who had too little help from the nobles and the clergy. The results may seem rather poor. But let us remember that if some day the human race attains civilization, it may well wrap the twentieth century up with the Middle Ages and the Romans under the common blanket label 'The Dark Ages'.

Notes

1. See my 'The Role of Comparison in the Development of Economic Theory' [sic, for Economic History], *The Journal of Economic History*, 17 (1957): 554–70.

2. Material relevant to this point will be found in a set of articles on Asian and Western monasticism in *Comparative Studies in Society and History*, 3 (1960–61): 427–69, and in W. F. Wertheim, *East-West Parallels* (The Hague, 1964; Chicago, 1965), Chap. 7.

3. *Le roman des aventures de Fregus,* ed. F. Michel (Edinburgh, 1841), 2: 435 ff.

4. Gino Luzzatto, 'Mutamenti nell'economia agraria italiana dalla caduti Carolingi al principio del sec. XI', *I problema communi dell'Europa post-carolingia* (Settimane di studio del Centro italiano di studi sull'alto Medioevo, 2; Spoleto, 1955), pp. 601–22. Translated in Sylvia L. Thrupp, ed., *Early Medieval Society* (New York, 1967), pp. 206–18.

5. K. Hannestad, *L'évolution des ressources agricoles de l'Italie du 4ème au 6ème siècle de notre ère* (Copenhagen, 1962).

6. Lellia Gracco Ruggini, 'Vicende rurali dell'Italia antica dall'età tetrarchica ai Longobardi', *Rivista storica italiana*, 76, fasc. 2 (June 1964): 279.

7. Ibid. See also Keith Hopkins, 'Birth Control in the Roman Empire', *Comparative Studies in Society and History*, 8 (1965–66): 124–51.

8. Folke Dovring, 'Bondage, Tenure, and Progress: Reflections on the Economics of Forced Labor', *Comparative Studies in Society and History*, 7 (1964–65): 309–23.

9. See Gino Luzzatto, 'Mutamenti nell'economia agraria', trans. in *Early Medieval Society*, pp. 212–13.

10. See R. H. Hilton, 'Peasant Movements in England before 1381', *The Economic History Review*, 2nd Ser., 2 (1949): 117–36.

11. Lellia Ruggini, *Economia e società nell'* 'Italia Annonaria' (Milan, 1961), pp. 69–72.

12. Robert S. Lopez, *Naissance de l'Europe* (Paris, 1962), pp. 147–48.

13. Marcus Porcius Cato *De agri cultura*, 23, 31; Marcus Terrentius Varro *Rerum rusticarum*, i. 22. 1; Lucius Junius Moderatus Columella, *Rei rusticae*, xi. 2. 11–13, 90–92.

14. On the growing complexity of these arrangements in twelfth-century England, see M. M. Postan, *The Famulus: The Estate Labourer in the XIIth and XIIIth centuries* (London, 1954).

15. Ruggini, 'Vicende rurali', pp. 275–76.

16. Capitulary *De villis*, Arts. 28, 30, 33, in: *Monumenta Germaniae Historia: Leges, ed.* A. Boretius (Hannover, 1883–97), 1: 183. Cf. comments by Georges Duby, *L'économie rurale et la vie des campagnes dans l'Occident médiéval* (Paris, 1962), 1: 277–78.

17. Gino Luzzatto, 'Economia monetario ed economia naturale in Occidente nell'alto medioevo', *Moneta e scambi nell'alto Mediœvo* (Settimane di studio del Centro italiano di studi sull'alto Mediœvo, 8; Spoleto, 1961), 1–32.

18. Einhard, *Opera*, ed. A. Teulet, 2 (Paris, 1843): 258.

19. Georges Duby, *L'économie rurale*, 1: 78–79.

20. For some examples see F. L. Ganshof, *La Belgique carolingienne* (Brussels, 1958), pp. 104–5, 116–17.

21. Edith Ennen, 'Les différents types de formation des villes européennes', *Le moyen âge*, 62 (1956): 397–411, translated in Thrupp, *Early Medieval Society*, pp. 174–82.

22. Examples in R. Rainbird Clarke, *East Anglia* (London, 1960), p. 146.

23. Three classic articles on this subject: Gino Luzzatto (see n. 17 above); Marc Bloch, 'Économie-nature ou économie-argent, un pseudo-dilemme', *Annales d'histoire sociale*, 1 (1939): 5–16, translated in Thrupp, *Early Medieval Society*, pp. 196–205; M. M. Postan, 'The Rise of a Money Economy', *The Economic History Review*, 14 (1944): 123–34.

24. See Philip Grierson, 'Commerce in the Dark Ages: A Critique of the Evidence', *Transactions of the Royal Historical Society*, 5th Ser., 9 (1959): 123–40, and Karl F. Morrison, 'Numismatics and Carolingian Trade: A Critique of the Evidence', *Speculum*, 38 (1963): 403–32.

25. Lellia Ruggini, 'Vicende rurali', pp. 279, 282–83.

26. For several new studies see the reports of the 11th and 12th international congresses on Byzantine studies, published at Munich in 1958 and at Belgrade–Ochrida in 1961.

27. On this point see Karl W. Deutsch and Hermann Weilenmann, 'The Swiss City Canton', *Comparative Studies in Society and History*, 7 (1964–65): 393–408.

28. For new light on these fairs see R. D. Face, 'Techniques of Business in the Trade between the Fairs of Champagne and the South of Europe in the Twelfth and Thirteenth Centuries', and 'The *Vectuarii* in the Overland Commerce between Champagne and Southern Europe', *The Economic History Review*, 2nd Ser., 10 (1957–58): 427–38, and 12 (1959–60): 239–46. On business methods in general, R. de Roover, 'The Organization of Trade', in *The Cambridge Economic History of Europe*, 3 (Cambridge, 1963): 42–118.

29. David Herlihy, *Pisa in the Early Renaissance: A Study of Urban Growth* (New Haven, 1958), pp. 135–44.

30. See M. Vignes, 'Les doctrines économiques et morales de saint Bernard sur la richesse et sur le travail', *Revue d'histoire économique et sociale*, 16 (1928): 547–85.

31. R. H. Tawney, *Religion and the Rise of Capitalism* (New York, 1926), Chap. 1; A. Fanfani, *Catholicism, Protestantism and Capitalism* (London, 1935).

32. Raymond de Roover, 'New Interpretations of the History of Banking', *The Journal of World History*, 2 (1954): 38–76.

33. See F. Pollock and F. W. Maitland, *The History of English Law,* 2nd ed., 2 (Cambridge, 1898): 119–21, on the incompleteness of the deflection.

34. The early development of this is summarized in Michael M. Sheehan, *The Will in Medieval England* (Toronto, 1963), Chap. 1.

35. See Marc Bloch, 'Économie-nature', n. 14.

36. David Herlihy, 'The History of the Rural Seigneury in Italy, 751–1200', *Agricultural History,* 33 (1959): 58–71, esp. 68–69.

37. Marc Bloch, 'Économie-nature', n. 3.

38. Enrico Fiumi, 'La popolazione del territorio Volterrano-Sangimignanese ed il problema demographico dell'età comunale', in *Studi in onore di Amintore Fanfani* (Milan, 1962), pp. 250–90.

39. E. Stone, 'Profit-and-Loss Accountancy at Norwich Cathedral Priory', *Transactions of the Royal Historical Society,* 5th Ser., 12 (1962): 25–48.

40. David Herlihy, 'Population, Plague and Social Change in Rural Pistoia, 1201–1430', *The Economic History Review,* 2nd Ser., 18 (1965): 225–43. For a recent brilliant survey of the whole agricultural scene in the later Middle Ages, see L. Génicot's chapter in *The Cambridge Economic History of Europe,* vol. 1, 2nd ed. revised (Cambridge, 1966) pp. 660–741.

41. Gene A. Brucker, *Florentine Politics and Society, 1343–1378* (Princeton, 1962), pp. 14–15.

42. Carlo Cipolla, in *The Cambridge Economic History of Europe,* 3 (1963): 413.

43. Ibid., 413–19.

44. R. S. Lopez and H. A. Miskimin, 'The Economic Depression of the Renaissance', *The Economic History Review,* 2nd Ser., 14 (1961–62): 408–26.

45. Slicher van Bath, *The Agrarian History of Western Europe,* A.D.500–1850 (London, 1963), pp. 87–90.

46. Sylvia L. Thrupp, *The Merchant Class of Medieval London* (Chicago, 1948), Tables 13 and 15, pp. 200, 203.

47. Thrupp, 'The Problem of Replacement Rates in Late Medieval English Population', *The Economic History Review,* 2nd Ser., 18 (1965): 101–19.

48. M. L. Ryder, 'The Animal Remains Found at Kirkstall Abbey', *Agricultural History Review,* 7 (1959): 1–5.

he historian
and the
late middle ages
in England

Bertie Wilkinson

Of recent years, there has been a sustained and illuminating discussion, chiefly among Renaissance historians, about the transition in Europe from medieval to modern times.[1] The result has been a general tendency to reject theories of abrupt transformation, and to postulate instead a long period of transition, covering three hundred years from about 1300 to about 1600. This is a welcome tendency, though as will be seen I have reservations about it. It is much to be preferred to a view which has some popularity at the present time, and which owes a lot, I suspect, to the persuasive writing of Huizinga, to the effect that there was the death of a civilization at some time after 1200, which was the necessary prelude to the entry into the modern age.[2] Most medievalists would probably find that this extreme view has little to commend it. Yet it cannot be ignored. Some very respectable scholars have endorsed it. It makes for colourful history. And it fits in well with a contemporary mood of pessimism about the values inherent in our civilization at the present time, which easily finds application in theories of failure and decline in the medieval society from which many modern traditions were derived.

Hence, though the theories of a civilization which died have far less to commend them than those which merely see a long transition from one form of civilization to another, they have an interest of their own. At their heart, it seems possible to discern a myth—it is difficult to find any other word—about the whole nature of medieval society. This, it seems to be assumed, was not only primitive and poor, it was also based on universal injustice and oppression; it could only commend itself to a very small minority who kept down the vast majority by fear. It had no inner harmony to help it survive calamities, or challenges from without; or to save it from ultimate death, imposed by the burden of its insoluble problems.

There is no need to repeat at length my own opposition to this myth, which I would have thought to have been quite incompatible with the whole story of the medieval achievement. It seems to be most unlikely that any community held together by nothing but power and fear, and lacking any broad loyalties, could possibly have produced the material for such a story. I suspect that historians would have reacted even more sharply than they have against the myth, if they had not been influenced, however slightly, by another myth, even less defensible, to the effect that medieval men and women were actually inferior in their intellectual and moral equipment to those who succeeded them in more modern times. Thus, a distinguished historian, the late Professor Petit-Dutaillis, could write: 'Political liberty is not a natural thing. These are the natural things: violence, aggression and despotism . . . . To find the practical means of crushing down evil instincts such as the spirit of domination, there is necessary a great effort of observation, reason and material wisdom, and of this the men of the Middle Ages were not capable.'[3] All sorts of comments are suggested by this quotation. How far were men of the later Middle Ages less capable of an effort of reason and material wisdom (whatever that is) than we are today? And how unnatural is, or was, political liberty? To Jacopo Gavacciani in the Florence of 1368, 'to lose liberty is to lose everything.'[4] To Sir John Fortescue in about 1470, 'freedom was instilled into human nature by God.'[5] To the Scots, at Arbroath in 1320, 'it is not for glory, riches or honour that we fight; it is for liberty alone which no good man surrenders but with his life.'[6]

Perhaps the view of the expert on this important subject of the outlook of the late medieval man has become more favourable in the years which have elapsed since I first presented this paper. These years have seen much writing on the later Middle Ages in England, including two volumes by J. R. Lander and two of my own.[7] There is now a greater appreciation of economic well-being, and of literary and artistic achievement; but the view of the central and basic factor of political motivation is still, apparently, for the most part the same. Even the best of the more recent writers, with the notable exception of K. B. McFarlane, would seem to be agreed on this issue. All over Europe, it is said, the basis of government was 'pork barrel' morality and fear of the great. On this basis, very little in the way of constitutional principles determined the course of political events or even, according to one of the most eminent constitutionalists, of constitutional growth. Indeed, it is argued, the laity did not develop a capacity for abstract thought about the state and other problems (unspecified) until the sixteenth century. All this is not far removed from the judgment of Petit-Dutaillis. It would seem to lead straight to the sentiment expressed by a well-regarded younger historian: 'Many passages of medieval politics seem to the modern young scholar like mere feuds of bandit leaders, undignified by the national or class interests which modern politicians commonly use to justify their plans.'[8]

It is impossible to discuss the medieval outlook in detail, and it would be unwise to exaggerate the significance of a few *obiter dicta* wrenched from their context. But it seems possible to make one or two comments, preliminary to a brief survey of the period. The attitude of mind which the *obiter dicta* seem to reveal has, it may be claimed, a direct bearing on all the problems of the nature of the late Middle Ages touched on above. For my part, I must confess that I cannot share the pessimism of youth. I find myself happier in the company of writers like Jacob, McKisack and McFarlane, who know the weaknesses, but also the strength, of late medieval society, continuing the sympathetic understanding of Sir Maurice Powicke in regard to the thirteenth century. I would suggest that the only proper basis on which to judge men and women even of the fifteenth century is on the assumption that they were no better and also no worse than we are today. Their circumstances and the political conventions they grew up with were different from ours; but we have to look behind their actions to exactly the same mixture of good and evil which we find reflected in the political society of today.

With these thoughts in mind, we may venture to argue a case for seeing in the later Middle Ages neither the decline and fall of a civilization nor the bankruptcy of political motivation which was one of its portents, but rather, as we might very well expect, the broadening and expansion of a vigorous and creative society which, by virtue of its inner strength, had weathered the storms of the early feudal age, but had to struggle, as we have, with the results of its own progress and change. It was able to do all this, and to bequeath to the modern world a unique heritage, because at the deepest level its principles of thought and action were effective and enduring, not because they were outmoded or unsound. This, it may be suggested, is the proper framework for the study of the late Middle Ages in England, however much we differ in details of interpretation.

It is possible to attribute its many failures (what period is without them?) to human imperfections; but the wise historian will look also for the deeper causation, including the challenge of new and baffling situations, the difficulties and dangers of pioneering, and the temptations opened up by new forms of social and political life. On this basis, it is possible to find a touch of Hamlet even in a ruler like Edward II or Richard II; perhaps even more in Henry VI:

> *The time is out of joint; O cursed spite*
> *That ever I was born to set it right!*

The process of political change created both great progress and great dislocation and it threatened continuously to bring about an imbalance of political power. Its most important single aspect was probably the rise of the territorial state. This increased law and order and added to material wealth; but it weakened the ancient pattern of society and made feudal loyalties more complex. It thus increased political discord, weakened group life, and diminished some traditional defences against oppression. The atmosphere it created was invigorating for the strong, but bleak and occasionally disastrous for the weak. It led in the long run to progress, but created uncertainties and questionings, and demanded great powers of adaptation which were, inevitably, not always forthcoming.

Yet in spite of regicides, baronial revolts, and struggles for power, the politics associated with the rise of the territorial state present, in their sum total, a remarkably successful response to an acute political challenge, the age-long challenge of reconciling order and liberty in a bureaucratically organized and increasingly centralized state. In the final analysis, the achievement in this area was probably the greatest glory of the age.

In this connection, I cannot refrain from a word on the much debated subject of the medieval parliament. After all, it was in connection with political ideas ultimately expressed in this institution that much of the violent political conflict of the late Middle Ages in England occurred. And, despite some modern scepticism, parliament was a great and original creation, not likely to be produced without much friction, for expressing a novel relationship of co-operation between the king and the community. It fitted the changing needs of the territorial state. It was, as Otto Hintze argued, not only a novel but also a unique institution, whose creation was confined not only to one area—Western Europe—but also to one fairly brief period of time.[9] Without it, modern liberty and modern democracy might never have been achieved. It may be possible to argue that this magnificent edifice was nothing more than the accidental product of a struggle for power; though this seems to fly in the face of much evidence, to be found as far apart as the reformers of 1258 and the writings of Sir John Fortescue. But it seems utterly impossible to reconcile such an achievement with the notion of a civilization which had committed suicide or was in process of decline. The problem of creating the territorial state and at the same time preserving political liberty has always been a baffling challenge (and still is); the medieval contribution to it surely deserves a better treatment than is often accorded to it in our histories, particularly when these involve judgments on the kings and magnates of the age.

In economic and social life, the same conflicting tendencies were at work. The Black Death, for example, brought about a long-term demographic decline and great dislocation; but it also eased the problems created by an over-rapid growth of population in the thirteenth century, which was itself the consequence of greater peace and order.[10] Here again, progress created novel and unforeseen problems which were hard to understand. Other, and distant, calamities also shook the economy of Europe; though it seems to be an exaggeration to argue that they substituted closed for open frontiers. In addition to all this, the fourteenth century was plagued by the first 'national' wars—one more unwelcome, and tragic, consequence of political development and the territorial state. In spite of these adversities, a general rise in prosperity, an expansion of commerce, the rise of the cloth industry, and the emergence of the yeoman farmer, all occurred largely after 1350. Economic and social change brought about bewildering challenges and some conspicuous set-backs, in England as elsewhere; but the important fact to remember would seem to be the ability of England to emerge from the vicissitudes and losses caused by the Plague, the Hundred Years' War, and the Wars of the Roses, with the prosperity of the individual retained and expanded, and with the country ready, by the last quarter of the fifteenth century, to begin another spectacular advance.

Expanding economic life, in spite of demographic decline, brought about the rise of the middle classes (if I may still venture to use this term) and new ambitions on the part of the peasants; but it also in due course increased 'class' strife, a process of disintegration in the manor and the decline of notions like that of the just price. Other notions arising from small-scale trading, like those reflected in the apprentice system and in the regulations of guilds and crafts were also adversely affected, as indeed was the whole concept of a hierarchical society which, according to theologians, reflected the hierarchy of heaven. Many would argue now, of course, that the beginnings of a movement towards egality was nothing but an unqualified gain; but such an ideal seemed then to menace the very basis of law and order in the state. Hence, the historian must see a two-fold significance in John Ball's famous couplet:

> *When Adam delved and Eve span,*
> *Who was then the gentleman?*

It suggests the disruptive consequence that flowed from the new political order, as well as the promise it brought of a better life.

Even so, properly understood, the Peasants' Revolt of 1381 and the Revolt of Jack Cade in 1450 were signs of ambition and vitality rather than of economic decline. William Langland in the late fourteenth century, the first great social moralist produced by medieval England, also manifests this basic vitality. He castigated the social failings of his generation, but his great poem is filled with hope and courage, not failure and despair. The England which could inspire him with his vision of the ideals which had to be achieved if Christians were ever to go on the greatest of all Crusades, the pilgrimage to a heavenly Jerusalem,[11] was in no danger of succumbing to the social and economic difficulties of the age. And the same may be said, on a lower plane, of the sentiments portrayed in the *Paston Letters* half a century later, breathing the courage and ambitions of the middle class.

It is hard to say what part a rising patriotism had to play in all these achievements. Discussion of such a sentiment is not conspicuous in modern writing.[12] Nevertheless, it almost certainly had a place. Its manifestations at the royal court, in the triumph of the English tongue in government and literature, and in the translation of the Bible, are a significant part of the fourteenth-century achievement, and of the balance sheet of profit and loss in the Hundred Years' War.

The effects of the social revolution which began as a consequence of political and economic change were particularly divergent. They included the growth of individualism and secularism, often identified with progress. But in the High Middle Ages the great single cause of progress had probably been something very different—the harmony between liberty and order in the ubiquitous group, whether in the town or countryside. Hence the decline of the group, either secular or religious, presented a grave danger to the community as well as opening the way to the development of new energies and sources of strength.

This is especially true of the divergent tendencies to be seen in the rise of the so-called Bastard Feudalism. This new feudal organization brought great advantages, including a new mobility in society. It facilitated the transformation of the fighting baronage of an earlier time into the Renaissance courtiers of a later age. It helped to give a new sophistication to the magnates and a new ability to participate in the government. All this was advantageous, for a strong aristocracy was still a necessary ingredient in the nation's way of life. But it had its grave disadvantages, to be seen in such phenomena as livery and maintenance; in the danger of oligarchy resulting from the expanding powers and ambitions of the magnates; in the pursuit of aggressive wars; in the extravagances of chivalry; and in the treachery and ruthlessness of the individual, anticipating those of the Renaissance princes. None of these qualities in the aristocracy was new; but many of them were magnified by the circumstances of the age. It would be utterly misleading to paint most of the magnates either as potential saints or as degenerate sinners, with no other preoccupations except the acquisition of land and power. The wrongs committed through Bastard Feudalism were shocking enough. Men abused power then, as they do now, though in different ways. But all lords, even the greatest, had to take into account the growing power of public opinion, and all shared in a greater or less degree the notions of public good to be found in Sir John Fortescue. In one sense, the new feudalism was only the old feudalism writ large, with greater opportunities for evil but also greater opportunities for good.

The literature and art of the later Middle Ages in England had deep roots in earlier centuries; they were the product of a long evolution, with no significant break; and they probably reached their highest point, not in the twelfth and thirteenth century, but in the fourteenth. The dislocations and problems caused by progress and change were not so evident as in politics and economics; but they seem to have existed nevertheless. Much of the literature of the earlier period, apart from that of religion, had been centred on the royal court; but the court, one of the great instruments by which the territorial state had been created, was itself in process of change.

Courtly literature reached its apogee under Edward III and Richard II; but changes in the political and social scene were perhaps already reflected in the different purpose and the different audience to be associated with the writings of Chaucer and Gower, with alliterative poetry like *Sir Gawain and the Green Knight*, and with William Langland's *Piers Plowman*. The achievement of this age was great. As H. S. Bennett said, it is no longer possible to think of a 'naïve Chaucer', writing in a 'misty age'[13]; and Professor Ker long ago proclaimed the latter half of the fourteenth century as 'more conscientiously artistic, more secure in command of its resources than any other period till the time of Pope'.[14] Its literary expression was the product of a vigorous society, but it depended in part on a set of circumstances which created a special patronage and a special audience. And with the progress of society and politics, both patronage and audience began to be enlarged. This was the product of what we may call progress, though the literary revolution it heralded did not come about until the sixteenth century. Meanwhile, we may perhaps talk about a hiatus, but not at all of decadence. And at all times we must remember the contrast between the sensitivity and urbanity of the court poetry, praised by the literary critics, and the judgment of historians about the great political personages of the age.

Whilst courtly literature declined in the fifteenth century, other, more popular forms of literary expression expanded. The real strength of English writing came to reside in lyrics and plays and in miscellaneous works intended for a wider audience. The vitality of the miracle and morality plays of the century is astonishing.[15] Alongside them, Sir Thomas Malory and William Caxton with his printing press illustrate, perhaps more than anybody else, the broad process of transition from the medieval to the modern. In all this, we still need to be reminded, perhaps, of A. W. Pollard's words about the poetry of the fifteenth century: 'To say that English poetry was dead is absurd. It was not dead, but banished from court.'[16] We must talk less and less of failure in the literary expression of the century, and more and more about the literary consequences of political, economic, and social change, and about the brevity of the period which separated Chaucer, the poet of the royal court and its aristocratic circle, from William Shakespeare of the Globe.

Similar comments may be made on the subject of architectural change. In domestic architecture, both war and peace were reflected in buildings like Hurstmonceux in Sussex and Tattershall in Lincolnshire, in which beauty and comfort were transforming the homes of the great in spite of civil wars, invasions, and aristocratic feuds. In the cathedrals, parish churches, and colleges, innovation and conservatism were strikingly balanced. The basic form and inspiration remained the Gothic, consecrated by many centuries of Christian use; but this was modified by the English Perpendicular, which grew largely out of the mood of Englishmen in the fourteenth century. The Perpendicular style profoundly modified vaulting and windows. It managed to combine the Gothic curve with a great emphasis on the rectilinear, and it made much use of the ogee curve.

We cannot see evidence of conflicting forces and tendencies among the architects themselves, for the victory of the new style was sudden and complete; but it is possible to suggest that this evolution of a new style peculiar to England was deeply influenced by the conflicts which we have noticed in the field of politics, which had repercussions also in the literature of the age. The direct connection is, of course, difficult to prove; and indeed the adoption of this particular style in architecture has been explained in terms of simple artistic borrowing from France, by English master-masons. On the other hand, what G. G. Coulton called the 'miracle' of Gloucester (where the new style first made its impressive appearance) was closely connected with the burial there of the unfortunate king Edward II, regarded by some as a 'martyr' for the cause of monarchy. It was strongly encouraged by Edward III, and by builders who had been closely connected with the Court. There is a strong possibility that in the great spurt of ecclesiastical building which began in 1330 architecture, like literature, was used to extol the glory of Edward III's restoration of the monarchy. The harmony he sought with his subjects, it may not be altogether fanciful to suggest, was expressed in the harmony of the Perpendicular, with its delicacy and discipline in stone.[17]

The new style may have reflected Court influence; but it was probably accepted for its own intrinsic merits. It is difficult to find in it any trace of decadence. G. G. Coulton made a persuasive effort to see this in its repetition of pattern, its straight lines, and its traces of commercialism;[18] but its beauty and serenity are not really in question. It so caught the imagination of Englishmen that it was reflected in 90 per cent of all buildings of importance which they constructed for the next two hundred years. It was probably this broad popularity which in time made it less dependent than literature on Court patronage, and therefore less influenced by the Court's vicissitudes. Whether or not it can be fitted into the theory of three hundred distinctive years of transition is a moot question. Its appearance and popularity almost certainly cannot be used, without leaning heavily on the tag *de gustibus non disputandum est*, to support the idea of a civilization which was committing suicide.

Conflicting tendencies, largely the product of achievement and change, may be seen even in the activities of scholars. The scholastic method had produced remarkable progress between the time of Peter Abelard and that of Thomas Aquinas, dominated though it was by the syllogism and by metaphysics. In England, the great Bishop Grosseteste had shown in the thirteenth century how this might lead to the beginnings of a new scientific method, without destroying the possibility of reconciling reason and revelation, both vital elements in Christian belief. In the late thirteenth and early fourteenth centuries, further developments dominated by Duns Scotus and William of Ockham, seemed to bring Europe to the threshold of a further great advance which would bring men clear into the beginnings of modern science. Number, movement, time, and place were for the first time treated as the properties of specific beings (the words are those of Professor Leff) and as a result physics, mechanics, mathematical calculation, and geometry all reached a new flowering during the fourteenth and fifteenth centuries. If this was not comparable, Leff says, to the scientific revolution of the seventeenth century, it was still revolutionary for the Middle Ages.[19]

The new scholarship and the new outlook represented a great step forward, but they created their own difficulties. They introduced a way of thinking which was hostile to some Christian traditions which went back to St. Augustine and behind such traditions to Plato. They drove a wedge between reason and revelation and denied the capacity of the former to bring men to a knowledge of God. In the end, they threatened to denigrate faith itself. Thus they led to a strong reaction in which scholars used the same syllogism and metaphysics to defend what they considered to be the very foundation of the Christian way of life.

Here, as elsewhere, progress and achievement brought discord as well as new horizons. It even brought a tendency for scholarship to enter a cul-de-sac by continuing an excessive emphasis on logic and metaphysics and by failing to develop the promise of Robert Grosseteste. This is particularly true of the brilliant Yorkshire scholar John Wyclif, who employed the old scholastic methods to combat what he considered to be almost a new heresy, and by so doing fell into heresy himself.

Thus, circumstances combined, in spite of new ingredients, to give the old learning a new popularity among scholars, but at the same time to discredit it. The dangers which Wyclif perceived, and the conflicts stirred by Scotus and Ockham, both tended to create a reaction against the methods and priorities of the Schools, as in the case of Richard Fitzralph, archbishop of Armagh, who died in 1360. Archbishops Courtenay and Arundel introduced repression into Oxford under Richard II and Henry IV. There were no successors there to Ockham and Wyclif; though Thomas Netter, who died in 1430, was a great admirer of the latter, and was himself a well-known scholar. But Reginald Pecock in the mid-fifteenth century was only a pale reflection of the Yorkshire reformer. On the whole, we cannot seriously quarrel with H. S. Bennett's somewhat harsh judgment that after Wyclif the old learning slowly ran down, as the teachers droned on and on;[20] though there was vigour in the Inns of Court and new learning, as in the household of Humphrey of Gloucester, for example, as early as 1418.

As in literature, so in learning, the high point of achievement reached in the fourteenth century could not be maintained. Indeed, it plainly created its own difficulties. But these are not to be interpreted simply as evidence of failure. In any lively society, violent intellectual conflicts are occasionally inevitable. They may, indeed, for a time have unfortunate effects. Such conflicts were particularly harmful in the fourteenth century because the dialogue of scholars came to involve problems of far-reaching change in religion and the church and led to repression at Oxford and an unprecedented persecution of English heresy. Both were harmful: the Act *De Haeretico Comburendo* was sad evidence of a decline of intel-lectual freedom even though it was directed mainly against the Lollards. The speculations of scholars suffered much, we may suspect, from such developments because they were, and still are, one of the most sensitive and fragile elements in society. They constitute also, perhaps, an area most liable to extremes. But the extremes of this age not only created difficulites; they also made a lasting contribu-tion to both scholarship and society. As Thomas Fuller wrote, describing how Wyclif's ashes were later scattered in the river Swift, as a hostile gesture by the Church: 'This brook hath conveyed his ashes into Avon, Avon into Severn, Severn into the narrow seas, they into the main ocean; and thus the ashes of Wickliffe are the emblem of his doctrine, which now is dispersed all the world over.'[21] This was Wyclif the reformer; but Wyclif the reformer and Wyclif the scholar can never be really understood apart.

Similarly, the phenomena of religious change are not to be reduced to any simple formula. The causes of failure were infinitely complex, ranging from the institutional development of Church and State to the increased interest of the individual in secular matters. But it is doubtful, nevertheless, if we may talk of a religious decline in the later Middle Ages without qualifications which go far to rob the phrase of all meaning. It is as important to read the testimonies of McKisack and Jacob that individual piety and religion were as strong as ever at the end of their respective centuries as it is to note the well-known weaknesses in the Church.[22] Religion suffered from the failings of the centralized Papal Curia, from the growing control over the clergy by lay rulers, and from the decline of monasticism. But it found new sources of strength, including domestic piety, the participation of the educated layman in the life of the Church, the visions of the mystics, the devotion of Wyclif's poor priests, the Lollards, and the translation of the Bible. All these helped to recompense the average Christian for anything that he lost; though even his devotionalism has recently been stigmatized as stressing and perhaps increasing an emphatic and gross materialism.

It seems to be a mistake to echo the judgments of Gibbon on the difficulties created in this age by the growth of the papal and secular monarchies,[23] or to ignore the tragic dilemma of generations torn between an awareness of their great spiritual heritage and the infirmities which attended their long effort to attain the unattain-able Christian ideal. In this struggle, there were giants in the land, like John Wyclif in spite of all his shortcomings; and there were obscure parish clergy, like Chaucer's poor priest, who helped to keep the flame of Christian devotion alight. Many may have found help and strength from the mystic's vision of personal contact with Christ, propounded by such men as Walter Hilton and Richard Rolle of Hampole. Or in the writings of William Langland, the greatest religious idealist of all, who spared neither high nor low in his denunciation of spiritual weakness; yet who knew that the transcendental vision for his generation lay, not in the destruction of an age-long religious environment, but in the inspiration of the Christian truth as expounded by Holy Church.

It is difficult indeed to draw up a balance sheet of religious profit and loss. The forces at work in the Church, which caused grave stresses and strains in the four-teenth and fifteenth centuries, were also making possible the reforms and debates of the sixteenth. Lollardy is an example of the soul-searching generated by religious shortcomings even in an increasingly secularist age and persisting long after the failure of St. Giles' Field. In religion, as perhaps in literature and the arts, the continuity was in the aggregate more important than the discontinuity. Martin Luther himself was a medieval monk almost as completely as John Wyclif had been a medieval priest.

The differences between historians with regard to many of these problems, we may perhaps agree, are to be explained not by different attitudes towards evidence or towards the truth, but by different assumptions about character and motivation in the late Middle Ages as compared with our own. These differing assumptions encourage differences of opinion about the whole quality of civilization in the period from 1200 to 1500, and a tendency to deny any essential continuity of development, any uninterrupted process of evolution creating the society of today. The problem of continuity was well put long ago by a historian writing about the fifteenth century: 'Identity in difference and difference in identity might be described as the chief problem of the historian. It is easier to see the difference than the identity; but without a sense of the latter all study of history, whether political or social, is in vain.'[24] Perhaps in this context we may add words of Professor McKisack, though they were used to apply only to the literature of the period: 'With Chaucer, as with Shakespeare, whose universal quality he shares, genius is sufficient to persuade us that the children of his imagination were of like passions with ourselves and were bred in a land we know.'[25] They were not only bred in a land we know, but in a civilization which in its deepest qualities is still our own. Many of their problems have still to be faced. We may even say, in a very real sense, that many of their virtues and ideals have still to be defended and sustained.

Thus, we may finally summarize as follows. Historians should approach the later Middle Ages in England in the spirit of Kingsford and McKisack rather than that of Petit Dutaillis. They should examine this period as part of a continuous process of evolution stretching back from the present for many centuries, without any significant break; though artificial divisions are necessary for convenience. Every aspect of change in the later Middle Ages in England formed part of this general process, but at the same time was profoundly influenced by particular causes. Thus, we cannot put the same stamp on every facet of society. Nevertheless if we are driven to generalize—and generalization is part of the historian's craft—it seems wise to assume that in general terms we are dealing with a civilization which, despite minor set-backs in various aspects, achieved a progress almost unparalleled in history, a progress which, despite much poverty, violence, and oppression, was based on an almost uniquely successful way of life. The essence of this achievement is to be found above all in the reconciliation of order and liberty and the experiments and successes in this field affected almost every aspect of life. These conclusions, if they are correct, would serve to modify some modern inter-pretations of the period. In particular, they militate almost as much against the idea of a special age of transition in the fourteenth and fifteenth centuries, distinct from other periods, as they militate against what seems to be a quite untenable theory of a civilization which decayed because of a closing of its frontier or, alternatively, for internal reasons committed suicide and in any case died to make way for the modern age.

Notes

1. Denys Hay, *The Italian Renaissance in Its Historical Background* (Cambridge, 1961), and 'History and Historians in France and England during the Fifteenth Century', *Bulletin of the Institute of Historical Research,* 35 (1963): 111–27; Tinsley Helton, ed., *The Renaissance, A Reconsideration of the Theories and Interpretations of the Age* (Madison, Wisconsin, 1961); E. Cassirer, P. O. Kristeller, and J. H. Randall, Jr., *The Renaissance Philosophy of Man* (Chicago, 1948); P. O. Kristeller, *Studies in Renaissance Thought and Letters* (Rome, 1956); E. Panofsky, *Renaissance and Renascences in Western Art* (Stockholm, 1960); Lynn Thorndike, 'Renaissance or Pre-Renaissance', *Journal of the History of Ideas,* 4 (1943): 65–74; D. Durand, 'Tradition and Innovation in Fifteenth Century Italy', *Journal of the History of Ideas,* 4 (1943): 1–20. The popular writer and the expert have been happily combined in W. K. Ferguson, *Europe in Transition* (Boston, 1962); cf. his article 'The Interpretation of the Renaissance: Suggestions for a Synthesis', *Journal of the History of Ideas,* 12 (1951): 483–95. Perhaps there should be added Douglas Bush, *The Renaissance and English Humanism* (Toronto, 1939), and T. E. Mommsen, 'Petrarch's Conception of the "Dark Ages"', *Speculum,* 17 (April 1942); 226–42.

2. For example, N. F. Cantor, *Medieval History: The Life and Death of a Civilization* (New York, 1963), pp. 545–48. For variations on the theme see also Hugh Trevor-Roper, *The*

Rise of Christian Europe (London, 1965), pp. 13–21, 161–75, 180–82, and 184–86; Friedrich Heer, *The Medieval World: Europe 1100–1350*, trans. J. Sondheimer (London, 1961), pp. 6–10, 226, and 264–65; and the title of an article by H. M. Cam, 'The Decline and Fall of English Feudalism', *History*, 25 (1940–41): 216–33.

3. C. H. Petit-Dutaillis and Georges Lefebvre, *Studies and Notes Supplementary to Stubbs' Constitutional History*, vol. 3, trans. M. E. G. Robertson and R. F. Treharne (Manchester, 1929): p. 347.

4. Quoted in G. A. Brucker, *Florentine Politics and Society, 1343–78* (Princeton, 1962), p. 73.

5. *De laudibus legum Anglie*, ed. and trans. S. B. Chrimes (Cambridge, 1949), p. 105.

6. Quoted in Arthur Bryant, *The Age of Chivalry* (London, 1963), p. 215. I cannot refrain from adding the stanza from John Barbour (died in 1395), quoted by Vivian Galbraith in his essay 'Nationality and Language in Medieval England', *Transactions of the Royal Historical Society*, 4th Ser., 23 (1941): 128, as follows:

> *A! fredom is a noble thing*
> *Fredom mais man to haf liking*
> *Fredom all solace to man giffis*
> *He lifis at es that frely lifis.*

7. Wilkinson, *The Constitutional History of England in the Fifteenth Century, 1399–1485* (London, 1964), and *The Later Middle Ages in England* (London, 1969); Lander, *The Wars of the Roses* (London, 1965), and *Conflict and Stability in Fifteenth Century England* (London, 1969). An important interpretation of the Wars of the Roses is offered by R. L. Storey in *The End of the House of Lancaster* (London, 1966). A discussion of some modern views on the fifteenth century is offered in my 'Fact and Fancy in Fifteenth-Century English History', *Speculum*, 42 (1967): 673–92.

8. George Holmes, *The Later Middle Ages, 1272–1485* [vol. 3 of Christopher Brooke and Denis Mack Smith, eds., *A History of England*] (Edinburgh, 1962), p. 4.

9. For Hintze's discussion of this subject, see for example 'Weltgeschichtliche Bedingungen der Repräsentativverfassung', in his *Staat und Verfassung: Gesammelte Abhandlungen zur allgemeinen Verfassungsgeschichte*, ed. G. Oestreich, 2nd ed. (Göttingen, 1962), pp. 142–43 and 177–85. See also my forthcoming study, *The Creation of the Medieval Parliament*.

10. A. R. Bridbury, *Economic Growth: England in the Later Middle Ages* (London, 1962), pp. 23–24; J. R. Lander, *Conflict and Stability in Fifteenth Century England*, pp. 20–26.

11. D. W. Robertson and Bernard F. Huppé, *Piers Plowman and Scriptural Tradition* (Princeton, 1951) p. 235.

12. But cf. Hans Kohn, 'Genesis and Character of English Nationalism', *Journal of the History of Ideas*, 1 (1940): 69–94; V. H. Galbraith, in *Transactions of the Royal Historical Society*, 4th Ser., 23: 113–28 (cited n. 6 above); Helen Suggett, 'The Use of French in England in the Later Middle Ages', ibid., 28 (1946): 61–84. Esmé Wingfield-Stratford, *The History of English Patriotism* (London, 1913), vol. 1, has not much value for the medieval period.

13. H. S. Bennett, *Chaucer and the Fifteenth Century* (Oxford, 1947), p. 81.

14. Quoted by Bennett, ibid.

15. My *Later Middle Ages in England*, Chap. 6.

16. *Fifteenth Century Prose and Verse*, ed. A. W. Pollard (Westminster, 1903), p. xiii.

17. For recent discussion of the origin of the Perpendicular style, see Geoffrey Webb, *Architecture in Britain: The Middle Ages* (Harmondsworth, 1956), pp. 133–45; J. H. Harvey, 'The Origin of the Perpendicular Style', *Studies in Building History*, ed. E. M. Jope (London, 1961), pp. 134–65; Paul Frankl, *Gothic Architecture*, trans. D. Pevsner (Har-

mondsworth, 1962), pp. 132, 146–49, and 151–54; and my *Later Middle Ages in England*, pp. 229–33.

18. *Art and the Reformation* (Cambridge, 1953), pp. 16 and 19–22.

19. Gordon Leff, 'William of Ockham and His School', *The Listener*, 13 January, 1966, p. 68.

20. *Chaucer and the Fifteenth Century*, p. 102.

21. *The Church History of Britain from the Birth of Jesus Christ until the Year MDCXLVIII*, new ed. (Oxford, 1845), 1: 424.

22. May McKisack, *The Fourteenth Century, 1307–1399* [vol. 5 of Sir George Clark, ed., *The Oxford History of England*] (Oxford, 1959), pp. 310–11; E. F. Jacob, *The Fifteenth Century, 1399–1485* [vol. 6 of *The Oxford History of England*] (Oxford, 1961), pp. 685–87.

23. Edward Gibbon, *The History of the Decline and Fall of the Roman Empire,* ed. Oliphant Smeaton (London, 1910), 6: 362–63, 493–96, 527–36, and 544–45.

24. C. L. Kingsford, *Prejudice and Promise in the Fifteenth Century* (Oxford, 1925), pp. 29–30.

25. *The Fourteenth Century*, p. 532.

edieval heresy:
gleanings
and reflections

Vaclav Mudroch

For the ecclesiastical or intellectual historian, medieval history is chronologically coequal with the time span of medieval Christianity. The *terminus ad quem* is the Reformation in general and the nailing of the ninety-five theses on the church door in Wittenberg in particular. It is becoming increasingly clear that the *terminus a quo* can only be the origin of Christianity proper, which medieval authors incorrectly assigned to the year 1. Thus the doctrinal deviations of more than fifteen hundred years may be considered to fall within the scope of any discussion of medieval heresy.

Heresy is as old as Christianity. The name itself is even older. The Greek word αἵρεσις can be found not only in Herodotus, the father of history,[1] but also in Thucydides,[2] and in both texts it signifies 'an act of taking'. In the first century B.C., when Greek culture became fashionable in the Roman world, the word had come to mean 'a choice', and thus understood it received the freedom of Rome. In this new environment Cicero endowed the word with new meanings. It no longer meant merely 'a choice', but rather 'a sect' or 'a school of thought', and lexicographers tell us that for Cicero *haeresis* might also denote a craft, trade, calling, or profession. Most of these meanings fell into desuetude, but *haeresis*, denoting a sect, remained a part of the Latin vocabulary. In the first century A.D. Flavius

Josephus used the word in Greek to designate the doctrinal variations within Judaism.[3] We encounter the same usage in the Greek New Testament.[4]

The New Testament 'good news' depicts the unique origins of Christianity and presents the Christian message as a thing apart from other beliefs. Thus it is not surprising that the term *haeresis* acquired among the early Christians a distinctive meaning. For them it served to distinguish the other religious groups found on the Mediterranean littoral from what they, as faithful followers of Christ, regarded as the one true religion. In their vocabulary, 'heresy' was any doctrine, whether within or outside the Christian community, which was evidently irreconcilable with Christianity.

Even in apostolic times the word 'heresy' may have had this connotation for Christians. The teaching of both the Sadducees and the Pharisees is qualified in the New Testament as $αἵρεσις$,[5] in contexts which involve opposition to the apostles. Nor were the early Christians at ease with each other's attempts to solve the problems of doctrine and language that arose when their faith came into contact with the religious syncretism of the Romans and of their eastern provinces. St. Paul seems to be counselling moderation in such doctrinal disputes and temporary indecision on some points when he advises the Corinthians: 'There must be factions (heresies) among you, in order that those who are genuine among you may be recognized.'[6] But this pronouncement has a sequel in another Pauline Epistle, that to Titus, which shows the apostolic Church in a less conciliatory mood: 'As for a man who is factious (heretical), after admonishing him once or twice, have nothing more to do with him, knowing that such a person is perverted and sinful; he is self-condemned.'[7]

In this Epistle and the Epistles to Timothy, which are of the same period, something may be seen of the opposition created for the Pauline doctrine by Jewish Christian eschatological and messianic expectations. The destruction of Jesusalem in the year 70 to some extent liberated Christianity from its Jewish past. Yet heresy was by no means overcome, nor did the term fall out of use. For it was about the time of the fall of Jerusalem, as R. M. Grant has determined,[8] that Gnosticism, which was radically to intensify many a latent heterodox tendency of the expanding Church, began its career.

The adherents of the Gnostic movement laid claim to a secret knowledge, or gnosis, 'a knowledge of suprasensible reality, of that reality which within and beyond the world as seen by man constitutes the driving force behind all that occurs, eternally mysterious, knowable yet unseen'.[9] Gnosticism, with its emphasis on this hidden knowledge and on ecstatic rites of salvation, soon made inroads into the Christian communities. Gentile Christianity by now was appealing to the reasonable men of the middle class of the Empire, and these converts waged an unrelenting, and ultimately successful, war of intellectual attrition against the Gnostics. But throughout the second century A.D. the Gnostics were Christianity's most redoubtable opponents. The already familiar New Testament term *haeresis* was applied time and again in condemning the Gnostic systems, and thus it became firmly established in the Christian vocabulary as the term for condemning false doctrine.

For the Church, Gnosticism was a damnable nuisance. Irenaeus calls it 'a madness without bounds', [10] and other authors are no less scornful. We have an indication of how strenuous it was to combat the many forms and systems of this first great medieval heresy in the compendious catalogues and refutations of heresy that issued from the pens of the Christian fathers from the second to the fifth centuries, all of which devoted a large part of their space to Gnostic or related doctrines.[11] And from the time of Irenaeus, Tertullian, Hippolytus, and Clement of Alexandria to the time of Epiphanius, Filastrius, Jerome, and Augustine, the writings of the fathers convey the impression that doctrines such as those of Valentinus or Mani are a real threat, that any compromise is out of the question. Only with the barbarian invasions of the fourth to sixth centuries was Gnosticism finally driven into the Roman religious underworld, to survive only in splinter groups lacking in appeal to the populace.[12]

Meanwhile, the term 'heresy' had taken on a more precise meaning in the trinitarian and christological controversies which raged in the Church from the fourth to the sixth centuries, starting with Arius and continuing with Nestorius, Eutyches, and lesser lights of the Near East.

We have considered the origins and early use of the term 'heresy' at some length, in order to point out the fluid nature of the concept in the early Church. In the absence of a centre of authority[13] it is not surprising to find that the notion of, and criterion for, heresy were broadly conceived. Indeed, testier authors such as Tertullian might be inclined to affix the term rather freely. A heretic might be anyone who desired to introduce into the Christian communities a personal variation contrary to the traditional teaching of the Church. The criterion for heresy during this first period of its history, therefore, was the *consensus ecclesiae,* and any expression of the faith that was not in harmony with the community's way of thinking and acting might be heresy.

Before we continue our historical survey of medieval heresy, a brief digression is perhaps in order. It has been said that the criterion for heresy during the first period of its history was the *consensus ecclesiae,* and it has been implied that this first period in the history of heresy extends at least until the sixth century, when Gnosticism went underground. This reference to periods of heretical history raises the question of whether it is really necessary or possible to periodize the medieval heresies, as well as the related question of what historical scheme is best suited to this task.

The necessity of some scheme of periodization is evident to the student of the field. The Church, relying on the approach taken by Jerome in the fourth century and by Thomas Aquinas in the thirteenth, covered all heresies under a blanket moral condemnation, as species of disobedience. Such a moralizing view, unqualified by considerations of circumstances or historical development and applied equally to early as well as high medieval heresies, is a serious distortion. The forms of medieval heresy went through mutations that are incomprehensible without reference to the changing circumstantial background. The possibility of a meaningful periodization of the history of medieval heresy in a way that is not arbitrary is more open to question. We may agree that the French scholar Maurice Goguel was not indulging in an academic soliloquy when he drew our attention to the apostolic period as that in which heresy was first manifested.[14] But it is much more difficult to divide the rest of the history of medieval heresy into periods on which all would agree.

Accordingly the claim that the decline of Gnostic heresy and the prevalence of the christological controversies marks the beginning of a new period in the history of medieval heresy may seem to be a mere arbitrary convenience. In fact, however, it recognizes a profound shift in the Christian response to heresy that took place between the fourth and the eighth centuries. This change involved a clarification of the Church's understanding of heresy as a specific doctrinal opposition to the authoritative definitions of faith, especially as pronounced by the papacy and with increasing support from the civil authority.

When the Apologist fathers denounced the Gnostics and Manichaeans as heretics, they did so on their own authority, as representatives of the *consensus ecclesiae*. We look in vain for a papal or ecumenical pronouncement on these heresies. But the temper of Church and papacy changed with the times. In the trinitarian and christological disputes, formal anathemas were pronounced in ecumenical synods against false or reputedly false doctrine; in the same centuries the papacy launched the darts and barbs of excommunication against the Circumcelliones and the Donatists and all who agreed with their views. Increasingly heresy came (at least in the West) to consist in interpreting the Church's doctrine in opposition to the views of the papacy. By the end of the eighth century, when the Irish priest Clement, as well as Aldebert of Gaul, and the Spaniards Elipandus of Toledo and Felix of Urgel were accused of heresy and condemned because their doctrines did not agree with the official Roman views, we are in a new world where individuals are condemned by pope and state.

Thus in a very real sense the first age of heresy, typified by the Gnostic speculations of sects and schools, and still perhaps carried on in the popular theological strife of the Eastern christological controversies, was over before the year 800. The subsequent history of medieval heresy was quite different in character. In this sense the periodization we have adopted is fundamental.

The crisis presented by the Arian heresy, as has been pointed out above, initiated a progressive sharpening of the Christian concept of heresy. Arianism openly invaded Christian theology, inaugurating a mode of attack that was to become more and more common for heresy in subsequent centuries, particularly where civilization had enabled some degree of theological education to penetrate the lower social levels. But Arianism thus forced the Church to take more strenuous measures to clarify doctrine and protect orthodoxy. These necessities led to the involvement of the Roman state in the definition and proscription of beliefs.

Initially the principle of *consensus ecclesiae* was fully endorsed by the Roman state. Constantine, early in the fourth century, had chosen the Christian faith in his search for spiritual comfort. We may surmise, discounting the apparition of the cross in the skies on his march through Gaul, that it was precisely a concern for the unity of the Church in doctrine and organization that brought the emperor into Church matters, and into the ranks of the faithful on his deathbed. At any rate, it was Constantine, the representative of the state, who forged the bonds between Church and state and imposed a duty on Christians of remaining united for the good of the state. Thus the Council of Arles of 314, in which the Donatist heresy received its first official blow, was held to secure a condemnation which was in the interests of both Church and state in that it strove to ensure the civil and religious peace of Roman Africa. And the Council of Nicaea, summoned to deal with the Arian heresy in 325, was presided over by Constantine himself, and at his urging it strove mightily to reach a solution that would ensure peace in Egypt and the East.

At the same time, the Church was being drawn into the orbit of the state and assuming obligations that pertained to the state. Not without reason did medieval opponents of the papal rule contend that from the days of Constantine the body of the Church had been poisoned. Later emperors sought to make the Church their servant and their agent in a politic compromise with Arian doctrines. After this episode, the leaders of the Church realized that, in a state whose duty it was to protect the true belief, heresy could not be tolerated. The later Arian struggle in the West,[15] and the period of the christological controversies in the East, were accord-ingly marked by a growth in the Church's disciplinary apparatus to deal with heresy.

The christological heresies of the fifth, sixth, and seventh centuries need not detain us. Nestorian, Monophysite, and Monothelite doctrines of Christ were eastern in origin and influence, and they did not directly have bearing on the development of heresy in Europe, except insofar as they made heresy the active concern of an increasingly powerful papacy. After the Council of Chalcedon in 451 the emperors again sought to use the Church to enforce their favourite doctrine or some irenic compromise. But by this time the prestige and isolation of the papacy in the West made it largely immune to these pressures.

The persistent heresy of the Donatists and the Circumcelliones in the West, never entirely eradicated until the Muslim conquest of Roman Africa in the mid-seventh century, has already served to illustrate the growing papal role in combating heresy. As early as the second century Irenaeus had urged that the faith and usage of Rome should be the decisive criterion of orthodoxy.[16] The prestige of such popes as Leo I and Gregory I, and the active concern of Rome for right order everywhere in the Church, gave this suggestion substance. In the narrowing sphere of papal power from the sixth to the eighth centuries, it was increasingly true that *Roma locuta, causa finita est.* Thus by the time when the popes condemned the Spanish adoptionists, Elipandus and Felix, with the help of the Frankish ruler Charle-magne, a new attitude to heresy had grown up in the West. Had not the apostle Peter been given the keys to the kingdom of heaven? Was not the pope his succes-sor? Was not unity the rock upon which the Church was built? Had not the Church learned in the Roman Empire that there must be only one fold and one shepherd? Then clearly the Church could not tolerate diversity. All ought to conform to the doctrine and usage of Rome. Disobedience or opposition which the Church could not absorb was heresy.

On the other hand, the papal Church had as yet developed no really effective disciplinary apparatus against heresy. Cut off from the old Empire politically by the barbarian kingdoms, it had to fall back upon such spiritual penalties as excom-munication, which from the days of Chalcedon was used with increasing frequency and decreasing effect; in the eighth century the iconoclast Emperor Leo III accepted his condemnation by Rome with indifference and proceeded to take revenge against the pope by removing large areas from his ecclesiastical jurisdiction. It was by collaboration with the rising Frankish royal house and by foundation of a western Empire that the Church of Rome was to attain effective power in the secular arm to combat heresy in western Europe.

Thus by the year 800, which we may take as the beginning of the second major period of medieval heresy, the weight of tradition and the painful experience of the past made the Roman Church suspicious of new ideas as potential heresy, and unwilling to adapt to a changing religious world, if change should begin to stir. Also by the year 800, the Church had tested its disciplinary power and found it wanting without the participation of the state. As experience with the Arians and the Donatists and the heretics of the East had shown, the Church could correct individuals but could not suppress popular movements.

For the heresiologist, then, the transitional period between Constantine and Charlemagne is of great importance. It sets the stage, as it were, for both the intolerance of the high medieval Church toward heresy and the intimate involvement of Church and state in its suppression.

The heresies of the high and late Middle Ages are well known to scholars; some indeed have even penetrated in an emaciated form into the layman's area of knowledge. These heresies are usually treated as so many independent deviations from the doctrinal norms of the Church. Yet all the heresies of the second period of medieval heretical history share a common questioning spirit, a common temper of dissent from the 'official' faith which most Christians were taught from their childhood and considered a fundamental part of their lives. It might not be amiss for us to look at the phenomenon of heresy from Charlemagne to the Reformation, for a moment, in the most general sense; to examine this 'heresy of dissent' which was foreshadowed by the Circumcelliones and the Donatists and which blossomed fully after 1000, not as a collection of dissident notes but as a single discord in the fabric of medieval society.

Dissent is never gratuitous; it is caused. It originates in the mind which, confronted with unrehearsed data to be absorbed, rebels when it sees that those data do not conform with the ideals it already holds, from experience or education or just undiluted common sense. The dissent of heresy in medieval society therefore arose from the confrontation of medieval men with data in the Christian faith which some men felt they could not accommodate without self-betrayal. This discontent they passed on to others, pointing out the ideal standard of conduct or belief which the Christian society or its authorities were ignoring, and gathering support for their own view. In other words, the heresy of the period in question may be viewed as a consistent, albeit often misled, striving after the ideal, after a religious and social pattern which the official Church and the state had failed to recognize.[17]

But do the religious questionings of the high Middle Ages arise only from the convictions of the mind, without reference to environment and material conditions? Herbert Grundmann, the noted heresiologist, has enriched our knowledge of medieval heresy with his study *Religiöse Bewegungen im Mittelalter,*[18] which explores the heretical climate of the thirteenth century in particular. More recently, he has given us a general history of medieval heresy, *Ketzergeschichte des Mittelalters.*[19] In this work, the facts walk straight, but the interpretation limps behind. Grund-mann opposes the view that the heresies of the Middle Ages were related to social conditions, or, in a more restrictive form, to socio-religious conditions. For him the medieval heresies are purely the work of the immaterial mind reflecting upon immaterial principles. This grossly inadequate explanation openly disregards the possibility that men have eyes and ears, that they see and hear! Even a philosopher cannot avoid the world; Moses Maimonides, to take a medieval example, com-mented on the Parisian market women in one passage of his *Guide of the Perplexed,* which was hardly a travel guide through medieval Paris. Then surely the medieval heretics found the sources of their discontent in the imperfect Christian society in which they lived; surely they rejected real ways in which the Christian faith was expressed, and not merely abstract principles of belief! In dealing with the heresies of the high and late Middle Ages, the heresiologist must take the social and religious conditions of the times into account and measure these against the ideal sought by the heretics under study. Only then will the heresy be understood.

Thus, high and late medieval heresy forms an extremely complex whole. From Berengar, who denied transubstantiation in the eleventh century on theological grounds, to Hermannus Ryswick, for whom in 1502 Christ was a good-for-nothing (the translation is charitable), we meet example after example of new forms of dissent, new formulations of faith, new demands for a more Christian way of life, new understandings of dogma, new speculations about religious life, new complaints about the perversion of Christian ideals, new desires for the perfect life which the Church has failed to provide for the believer.

This panorama of medieval heresy is not made of one cloth. There are shades to the pattern of dissent, and sometimes as it were out of nowhere there appears a bright if not a gaudy colour. Some fields of the cloth are in the grey of unexplored territory. We have already heard of Berengar and his understanding of dogmatic mysteries, but who has heard of the heretics of Monteforte in Italy and their superb contempt for life? Why was the Church so alarmed by them, and what conviction led the accused heretics to commit mass suicide? We do not know. There are other heresies early in the second millenium of Christianity of which we know equally little. Éon of Étoile and Peter of Bruys traversed the regions of France followed by multitudes, among whom women played a conspicuous part. The sources we are forced to examine in the absence of fuller narratives are obstinately taciturn and unhelpful.

The twelfth century—a period of renaissance, as C. H. Haskins has made us believe[20]—yields more plentiful sources and also provides evidence of more sophisticated heretical movements. The student who sat at Abelard's feet, Arnold of Brescia, questioned the dogmas of the Church and the political aims of the Empire at the same time. The concord with which the ecclesiastical and secular powers sentenced him to death indicates to what an extent, since the age of Constantine, heresy had become a danger to both. In the second half of the same prosperous century there appeared a movement of poverty. Peter Valdes, a well-to-do merchant of Lyons, founded a sect, the Waldensians, that was to spread throughout late medieval Europe to a degree that no other sect duplicated. The case of Valdes illustrates our thesis that in the high Middle Ages it was the confrontation of the ideal in one man's mind with the existing reality that released revolutionary religious action into the world of Christendom. It also shows that heresy cannot be dissociated from the environment in which it developed, if it is to be understood. Valdes was a man of the world, but the reading of a saint's life led to his conversion; the example of St. Alexis, who had realized that wealth was really so much emptiness, led him to assume the life of a pauper and to preach poverty to the people. Valdes' new way of life caused others to pause and rethink their own. The Church, more legalistic than humanitarian at this time, refused him permission to organize his followers, and thus drove him into religious exile. The Waldensian movement was already widespread when St. Francis appeared before Innocent III with his request to organize a similar order.

The other heresy of the twelfth century that made a great impact upon the minds of believing Europe was that of the Cathars. René Nelli is, in all probability, right when he refers to them as constituting a church;[21] they differed so radically in their views from the Christian Church. Their doctrine was a new variation on an old theme, a restatement of Gnostic doctrines which can be traced to the early centuries of our era. They believed in a cosmic drama in which every individual was involved and from which he could not escape, a drama in which the world was divided into the forces of light and the forces of darkness. This dualistic conception of the world had arrived early in Languedoc and had spread widely by the twelfth century. Steven Runciman, among many others, has suggested a doctrinal relation to the Manichaeans of the third to fifth centuries.[22] In their peacefulness the French Cathars, or Albigensians, might be compared with the early Gnostics. They were the victims at last of a concerted crusading effort arranged between the Church and the northern French nobility. The Church protected its religion, and the nobles collected the spoils; the Albigensian heresy was left to die, and the southern lands were drawn closer to France.

Following the Albigensian crusade, heresy became less easy to discern, as it tended to appear under a variety of forms in many areas of Europe. The Franciscan movement especially was a hotbed of heresy. It spawned ideas that the Church had thought to be buried centuries ago, with the decline of Jewish apocalyptic elements in early Christianity. The Calabrian abbot Joachim of Flora, extolled in Dante's *Divine Comedy* as the possessor of a prophetic spirit,[23] foresaw the history of salvation entering upon an age of monastic spirituality in which the Church as an institution had no part to play. The Spirituals, those Franciscans who maintained the Franciscan ideal of absolute poverty, spread the prophetic movement to the University of Paris. There Gerard of Borgo San Donnino taught his doctrine of the Eternal Gospel and the coming end of the world so audaciously as to outrage the papacy. Nor were kings and emperors able to remain the staunch defenders of orthodoxy in papal eyes. The Emperor Frederick II was condemned by the Council of Lyons in 1244, and in reaction he declared: 'I have been an anvil long enough, now I shall be the hammer.' His heresy, which was mainly opposition to the papacy, did not find immediate followers. It was only at the end of the century that the king of France, Philip the Fair, became entangled in the strings of papal condemnation, and we know how his tumultuous conflict with Boniface VIII ended: the pope was insulted at Anagni, the king was vindicated, and the papacy was transferred to Avignon.

The defeat of Boniface marked the end of the temporal pre-eminence of the papacy, but it still remained a powerful institution. From this time on, however, the papal desire to discipline heresy assumed a new direction. In the fourteenth century and after, the popes were to be concerned with heresy in the universities and among their graduates. William of Ockham, the nominalist, then Marsilius of Padua, the political theoretician, incurred the wrath and condemnation of the papacy. A brief look at the errors of Marsilius reveals the trend of fourteenth-century heresy: the emperor, Marsilius claimed, could correct the pope; the Church could not punish a single individual without the consent of the emperor; since all clerics (whether popes, archbishops, or simple priests) owed their power to the same institution by Christ, they all had equal authority and jurisdiction. We observe here a two-pronged attack against the papacy: an attack against the papacy as an institution is now added to the attack on the supremacy of the pope as an individual within the European community of nations.

In the light of these theories, it is not surprising to find at least one author, the nineteenth-century Italian scholar Guglielmo Audisio, advancing the view that the thought of Marsilius was the model for that of the English arch-heretic of the later fourteenth century, John Wyclyf.[24] We note without surprise that English scholars have never accepted this conclusion. Wyclyf is indeed a more complex figure than the other dissidents of his century; yet he is not totally unlike them. Like Nicholas of Autrecourt or Denis Foullechat in the University of Paris, Wyclyf at Oxford sought to understand *de novo* the world around him, in a period in which the foundations of the Church appeared to be threatened. The papal captivity at Avignon having come to an end in 1378, the state of crisis assumed even more horrendous proportions with the outbreak and spread of the Schism.

Wyclyf characterizes within himself the nature of heresy in the fourteenth century, as his doctrine summarizes the heretical beliefs of that time. Whether his dissent was independent or influenced by others, there is nothing more conspic-uous about him than his volatile nature. A philosopher pure and simple at first, a royal servant, a religious and political reformer and theoretician, a dogmatic contro-versialist, an anti-papal writer, a biblical enthusiast—all these personalities he carried in his breast. Who can wonder that modern scholars have been looking for the true Wyclyf for decades and that he is still evading them? However, it should be noted that his latest biographer, Rev. John Stacey,[25] has departed from the hagiographical Protestant tradition which was still in evidence in the nine-teenth century and which can be detected in the many works that Protestant clergymen dedicated to Wyclyf at the five hundredth commemoration of his death in 1884. None of them would have concurred in Stacey's conclusion that '. . .new wine cannot be contained in old bottles. In other words John Wyclif was, as we all are, a prisoner of history.'[26]

Wyclyf, who 'could turn many a head', was *magnus et verus professor* for John Hus. The Czech reformer has been studied outside his homeland more diligently than has his English precursor. In the nineteenth century Johann Loserth contributed a study of the two men published in Prague.[27] Non-Czech scholarship, for its part, has thrown light on the life of Hus in all its aspects. The work of Ernest Denis in France,[28] of S. Harrison Thomson in the United States,[29] and of the Belgian Benedictine Paul de Vooght[30] has been especially illuminating. The biography by De Vooght is the most searching non-Czech analysis of John Hus so far to appear, and his conclusion concerning Hus is both novel and noteworthy: 'His heart always remained Catholic.'[31]

The Hussite movement of the early fifteenth century has been treated as part of an international 'Wyclyfite' movement by authors who have not studied all the available Czech texts. The reality is altogether different. Wyclyfite roots are present in the Hussite phenomenon, but they were nurtured and grew to maturity in Czech soil. Moreover, we know today that the Hussite heresy passed through stages of development. Directed against the German masters at the University in Prague, it was channelled into the streets and countryside. There it assumed new forms and developed a new doctrine which had nothing in common with the doctrine of Hus, who himself aimed at the reform of the Church. His followers were much more radical: the chiliasts and Adamites of Hussite Bohemia came from soil which the words of Hus had fertilized but had not planted. Members of these two sects honoured Hus as their leader and martyr, but they can hardly be considered as 'Wyclyfites', even though we gather from contemporary sources that they also honoured Wyclyf, referring to him as 'the fifth evangelist'.

After the execution of Hus this native Hussite movement, which was brilliantly organized and maintained a unity that the occasional campaigns against it were unable to disturb, was even recognized by the papacy, which entered into negotiations with it. This led to a weakening of the revolutionary élan of the people; fatigue caused by the wars set in, and defeat and capitulation followed.

Elsewhere in the fifteenth century heresy was not unknown, but widespread and open movements such as the Hussite revolt were not found. In England the Lollards, and notably William Swinderby, attacked the institutions of the Church in the tradition of Wyclyf and weakened the reliance which the common people placed upon them. In general, however, Lollardy was a silent movement. There was also the case of Joan of Arc; but her mistrial, execution, and vindication by the Church only showed how, towards the end of the Middle Ages, the Church was inclined to follow the secular powers and how the charge of heresy was used as a convenient political weapon.

At this point we must end our historical narrative, since to consider the next heresy would take us into an area which the religious history of the Middle Ages has never recognized as its own. Having completed this rapid survey, let us now return to a few of the medieval heresies mentioned and examine them in greater detail. We shall deal with the heresies of the 'gnostic' type: Gnosticism, Manichaeism, and Catharism.

Gnosticism is a heterodox religious movement which has only recently been rediscovered. The first German monographs on the subject date from early in the nineteenth century,[32] and in the English-speaking world Gnostic studies have

come of age only in the present century. Medieval historians tend to ignore Gnosticism altogether, on the assumption that it lies outside their chronological boundaries. Classical historians too have in general refrained from taking the movement
under consideration, although in this connection it should be noted that a description of the symbiosis of Platonic and Gnostic ideas has been attempted with
remarkable success by the French scholar Simone Pétrement.[33] Were it not for
Church historians, the Gnostics would be known to us today largely as they were
known to the Christian reading public of the first four centuries, when catalogues
of heresy compiled by such illustrious figures as Irenaeus, Clement of Alexandria,
Epiphanius, Filastrius, and Augustine were common. We must therefore be
thankful to the modern scholars who have recognized the importance of this
heresy and who continue to bring it to our attention.

Several names stand out in the history of Gnostic research, and especially that of
Adolph Harnack. Nothing surpasses a well-coined aphorism for endurance, and
Harnack's statement that 'Gnosticism was the acute Hellenization of Christianity'[34]
has worn well. Harnack's view, however, is no longer acceptable without exceptions and qualifications. Hans Lietzmann, for example, is of the opinion that
Gnosticism was 'an equally acute "re-Orientalization"',[35] and Hans Jonas speaks
of 'Harnack's half-truth'.[36] Hans Leisegang has drawn our attention to the distinction that Plato made between *mythos* and *logos* (the one term referring to
spiritual beings, the other to the abstract Ideas which man perceives behind
reality), only to warn us that the Gnostics abolished this distinction: for them the
spiritual entities of man's religious vision and the Ideas which were perceived in
man's reasonable intuition of the universe merged into one another.[37] Serge Hutin
has remarked on a variety of doctrines affecting the rise of Gnosticism, but among
them Platonic thought appears only incidentally.[38]

What, then, is Gnosticism? How is it being explained in the light of the latest
research?

Gnosticism is the result of the syncretic tendencies of that territory in Asia
which Alexander's conquests had made a part of Magna Graecia. Platonic,
Pythagorean, and Stoic ideas were transplanted into a new philosophico-religious
soil, where they were assimilated to local religions which saw the universe in terms
of opposing principles: light and darkness, God and the world. Nor were Syro-
Phoenician cosmogony and Babylonian-Chaldean astronomy without influence.
With the coming of Christianity these half-amalgamated doctrines were grafted
by various minds to the corpus of Christian teachings, with the obvious aim of
satisfying the deep desire of the pagans to have a scheme or doctrine of salvation
embracing their beliefs yet equal to the message of Christianity. This development
occurred between the years 70 and 130 of the Christian era. Jean Daniélou
admits the presence of Gnostic views in the Judaeo-Christian environment
before A.D. 70, but he emphasizes that, like apocalyptic expectations, these views
were at that time only uncongealed forms of the current messianism.[39] R. M. Grant,
who has studied the figure of Simon Magus, has determined that the early
Christian heresiologists were wrong in attributing to him the honour of being the
first Gnostic. Grant recognizes, however, that many of the disciples who developed
Simon's teaching must be labelled Gnostics.[40]

The variety of Gnostic sects is overwhelming, but there is a general uniformity to Gnostic teaching which shows that certain philosophical principles were common to all the sects. The basic principle was a definite dualism of spirit and matter. It was held that from the alien or unknown god, the highest being of the Gnostic pantheon, there came emanations, from which in turn the eternal beings called 'aeons' arose. But as the supreme god thus expanded throughout the universe, said the Gnostics, there had occurred a cosmic tragedy, an unforeseen mixture of the particles of light and spirit with the realm of matter, which was the seat of darkness and evil. This mixture had serious consequences: it yielded the matter for the creation of the world, and it also resulted in the birth or advancement to power of a perverse aeon, or secondary god, the creator. This creator god the Gnostics usually equated with Yahweh, the lawgiver of the Old Testament, whose nature was jealousy and command. In the Gnostic cosmology, there was much to be accomplished—no less than the rescue of all the light which was held imprisoned in matter, so that it might return into the *pleroma*, the kingdom of light. The great turning point of the Gnostic world drama had come only recently: into the world of the creator god had come a superior aeon, the *nous* or *logos* (often equated with Christ), to announce the coming of the most true God, the alien god until then unknown, and the advent of his kingdom of light. This superior aeon had taught a select few how to overcome the power of matter and forever eliminate it from this world. The liberation of mankind by this secret knowledge (gnosis) was at hand. The *pneumatici*, or *gnostici*, were sharers in the work of liberation and were therefore saved; the rest of mankind was divisible into two groups: the *hylici*, those given to matter, who would be destroyed, and the *psychici*, the simple Christian believers, or catholics, who would reach only inferior bliss. The goal of the cosmic drama would be attained—the return of all beings and things to their proper nature.

Karl Bihlmeyer and Hermann Tüchle, the well-known Church historians who expounded Gnostic doctrines to students at the University of Tübingen, condemned them as unchristian and naturalistic.[41] In particular, they were appalled that Gnosticism subsumed religion and morality in a process of natural development, in which the human will had no part to play. According to these two critics, the Gnostic idea of salvation was that it was only a part of the general development of the world. In their view, Gnosticism failed to realize that salvation resulted from God's love for men. Moreover, Gnostic ethics and asceticism were superficially conceived, for they demanded a purely physical mastery of matter, which was supposed originally to have had a great and unnatural strength. Bihlmeyer and Tüchle believed that such an ethical doctrine and experience could easily assume anti-ascetic values, a possibility increased by the importance—rivalling that of the god of light—which was given in Gnostic thought to the creator of the material order. They pointed out that antinomianism and libertinism were, in fact, common among Gnostics. Indeed, according to these authors, the emphasis on inner knowledge among the Gnostics led to the devaluation of external behaviour; what mattered was gnosis only, and it resided in the individual.

As has been said above, one of the first principles of Gnosticism was that the realm of matter was evil. The cosmic world of matter was therefore the den of iniquity, and it was repudiated and condemned. For the Gnostic, the fact of his own existence replaced the outside world as a frame of reference. There can be little doubt that the outlook of modern existentialism, which Sartre has expressed in the lapidary phrase 'Existence precedes essence',[42] is like to that of Gnosticism. Existence was for the Gnostic an avenue to complete fulfilment, a medium in which to assert himself and thus become completely *engagé* in the cosmic drama that was taking place around him without his full understanding.

At the same time, the dualism of the Gnostics found expression in an over-whelming variety of sects. Some held that Christ was a man and, therefore, could not have divine attributes; others denied the material existence of the aeon who had appeared as Christ. Some condemned the Old Testament god; others denied the existence of any creator-god or placed an emphasis on Sophia (Wisdom), who was opposed to the creator. Varying degrees of importance were attached to messianic hopes for an end to the earthly wandering of man. The value of baptism as the first sign of redemption was held by some and not by others. And often there was an accent upon the idea of attaining immortality, permanent existence set free from the bonds of matter.[43]

In view of these doctrines and this existential emphasis, we may conclude with Jean Doresse and Serge Hutin that Gnosticism arose from anxiety—from an anxiety, moreover, which must be linked to the disappointed expectations of the religiously motivated Jewish community, which had long awaited a Messiah and after A.D. 70 found itself facing a vacuum.[44]

The Gnostic sects, only some of whose doctrines we have passed in review, had disappeared by the time of the disintegration of the Roman Empire in the West, with one important exception. It is now recognized—and we owe gratitude to Henri-Charles Puech for his remarkable work in this area—that the Gnostic doctrines were a contributory source of Manichaeism, the religion conceived and developed by the third-century Mesopotamian prophet Mani, which exercised an extraordinary power of attraction in medieval times.

According to Puech's analysis, Manichaeism was distinguished by three principal characteristics.[45] First, its adherents understood it to be a universal religion, a unique religious belief which was capable of penetrating into the whole world. There were other religions besides that of Mani, but these were incomplete and were but fragments of the Truth. All these religions had remained separate and were geographically scattered. Mani, however, was the successor of the patriarchs and the prophets, of Buddha, of Zoroaster, and of Christ himself; he was the last link of the chain which had been forged by these celestial messengers; he was the apostle of Babylonia, the apostle of the last generation, and the seal of the prophets (a title which, as we know, was also used by Muhammad). In short, he was the supreme Revelation. The Holy Spirit which had been promised by Christ had entered Mani and made itself one with him. His revelation was therefore perfect and untouchable, a total and all-comprehensive science. Moreover, as Mani himself had said, his church was superior to all the other churches which had been chosen to rise in a particular town or in a particular country. His church would enter every city and his gospel would enter every country.

The second characteristic of Manichaeism was a remarkable missionary zeal.

Since the religion of Mani was destined to be the one religion of the whole world, a duty of propaganda for the conversion of mankind was permanently imposed on the believer. The Manichaean priest was to be a preacher; indefatigably was he supposed to launch and relaunch in space and time invitations for the Awakening and the Liberation. Each Elect, or member of the church élite, was to become a monk who, on the advice of Mani, 'was to wander in the world preaching the doctrine and guiding men in truth'.[46] As preachers they would condemn as sick all those who, like Christian monks, lived isolated from the crowds, and they would praise the Elect. They would go from place to place armed with their faith and would therefore be capable of taming ferocious beasts and hateful enemies alike. Propelled by such zeal and such energy, the expansion of Manichaean doctrine was spectacular. In the third century, communities were established in Egypt, Palestine and Rome, as well as in Mani's native Persia. From these centres new communities spread to all corners of the Roman Empire. Manichaeism continued to live in the East after the barbarian invasions, though known under different names: in the seventh century it gave rise to the movement of the Paulicians in Armenia; within the Byzantine Empire during the tenth century it engendered the Bogomil heresy of Bulgaria; and the Bogomils in turn stimulated the growth of the Cathars, or Albigensians, in southern France.

Thirdly, Manichaeism was a religion based on a book. Previous religions had relied on codifications of teaching established by the followers and disciples of a religious leader. These intermediaries, obliged to rely on their memory, had been able to recall only parts of the teaching and had deformed it by interpretations. Such hybrid, incomplete, and partially unauthentic reconstructions had given rise to conflicts and heresies. Mani, however, had avoided this scriptural jungle by collecting his views and embodying them in books, of which the *Shâbuhragân* was the most important.

The doctrine imbedded in this work and in others that claimed Mani as their author was drawn from Gnostic sources. Puech calls our attention to several important points of contact between Gnostic doctrine and Mani: the latter spent his early youth among Gnostic baptist sectaries; he openly acknowledged the influence that both Marcion and Bardesanes, two 'Christian Gnostics', exerted upon him; and he made use of Gnostic apocalypses.[47]

Like all other Gnostic doctrines, Manichaeism was born from the anxiety which is part and parcel of the human condition. In the Manichaean system (if we may follow Puech further), man found that the place he occupied on earth was of a strange nature, unbearable and profoundly evil. In such a situation he felt enslaved to his body, to time, and to the world, which, mixed with evil as they were, constantly threatened and polluted him. From this realization came man's awareness of his need for salvation. However, since man could become aware of this state of affairs and of his need to be saved, he was superior to his condition, to his own body, to time, and to this world. For this reason his condition was *not* an unbearable burden. Still it was necessary to find some explanation for the Gnostic dilemma of existence. Why had man come to be? Why was he on earth?

For the Manichaean, from the moment a man knew himself and realized that he was a stranger in this world, he came to the knowledge that God himself was a stranger, an alien God. God was but goodness and truth; He could not have willed this world of suffering and lies. God could not have been responsible for the creation of the world out of evil matter. The material creation was therefore the work of an evil principle or being who was opposed to God. Thus, as in all the other Gnostic systems, there was in Manichaeism a dualism between a transcendent and good God on the one hand and an evil, domineering creator on the other.

For the Gnostic Manichaean, the self-knowledge and the knowledge of God which we have described contained in themselves the certainty of salvation. To know oneself in the manner described was to recognize oneself, to rediscover and recover one's true self, which had been overshadowed by the ignorance brought about by the mixture of one's true self with matter. This process of recognizing oneself could be reduced to the recognition that all men, though bound to the body and matter and mixed with evil, were particles of light and part of the transcendent world, to which they were united by an immanent bond. Men who knew them-selves had it given to them to understand that there was in fact a consubstantiality between the transcendent God and the souls of men. Man's soul was a fragment of the divine substance; in each man a part of God was imprisoned here on the earth, trapped in matter. This consubstantiality was an assurance of hope to all mankind. The believer knew that God would not neglect the salvation of his followers who were engulfed in evil matter; he would take hold of them and re-integrate them with himself. Salvation was certain because, in the self-recognition of his believers, God would be saving himself.

If God was both saviour and saved, so also were the believers. Those who knew that they were part of God could save themselves. What was to be saved was the soul entrapped in matter. The agent of salvation was the spirit, or intelligence, the superior part of a man from which knowledge and self-knowledge issued. Thus to have the true Manichaean gnosis was to obtain salvation.[48]

The believer's recognition of his consubstantiality with God also solved for him the riddle of his existence. He had come to be because an evil creator had imprisoned particles of divine light in matter; he was on earth to obtain true knowledge and salvation from this state. Thus the Manichaean gnosis was able to show a man where he was and what he was, where he came from and where he was going. It was a complete Gnostic system.

But the dogma of the consubstantiality of God and man's soul meant that for the Manichaean all knowledge was self-knowledge. The self was a fragment of God's light, which knew all things; therefore the knowledge of self involved the knowledge of the world in which one dwelt. The Manichaean did not reject the knowledge of this world for the knowledge of things divine. On the contrary, his involvement on two levels, as it were, led him to develop not only theology and cosmogony but also an encyclopedic natural knowledge in which the application of reason was raised to an art.

Eventually the Manichaeans' emphasis on reason in their religious system was dissolved, and Gnostic myths of the usual type prevailed. Nevertheless, Mani-chaeism in essence remained faithful to its original doctrine. Puech occasionally speaks of puerile features of Manichaean doctrine, of its desperate rambling and its insane myths, but he ends on a note which gives to Manichaeism its due. After speaking of the Manichaean texts and hymns that have been discovered in Central Asia and in Egypt, he pronounces his final judgment: 'Here one will immediately grasp the grandeur that the dogmatic mythology of the sect occasionally assumed, and the quality of fervour with which the dualistic gnosis, despite its scholastic appearances, could imbue its believers. A deep faith, a touching lyricism, and an art of delicate beauty have grown up here, in a climate which seems abstract and unrewarding only from afar. Moreover, cannot we who live in this century of iron understand the powerful appeal, to people verging on despair, of a message which condemns material existence and the active presence of evil in the world and promises peace to men of clear conscience and a lucid, heroic understanding?'[49]

Mani died a martyr—one of the apocryphal accounts tells us that he was flayed alive—but his faith and doctrine survived. The fertile religious zone of the Near East, that region which stretches from the Persian Gulf to Armenia and from there to the Mediterranean Sea, for long continued to harbour Manichaean communities.

From the fringe of this area, at Constantinople, we learn, at the time of the eighth-century iconoclastic controversy, about the Mani-influenced Paulicians. The origins of this Armenian sect are, to use historical jargon, shrouded in the mists of controversy. But we are now certain of at least one article of the Pauli- cians' faith: they were undisguised dualists. Accordingly they have been included under the general title of 'medieval Manichees' by Steven Runciman.[50]

We are better informed about the next offshoot of dualist heresy, that of the Bogomils, which had its centre in Bulgaria. The Bogomils appeared in the middle of the tenth century, and they expressed the reaction of the Slavic peasants against their Bulgar or Graecized overlords. Their influence spread far beyond the border- lands of the Byzantine Empire. There is, for instance, documentary evidence for the presence of their bishop Nicetas at a heretical synod at St–Félix de Caraman in southern France in 1167.[51] Their doctrine, as both the Bulgar priest Cosmas and the theologian Zigabenus reported,[52] was a mixture of many a heretical tenet of times gone by which was characterized by a pronounced dualism. Their priests, the 'Elect' as they were called, boasted that they had seen God the Father as an old man with a beard: in other words, the creator was not divine.

It was, however, in southern France that the dualist doctrine achieved its fullest European development. The dualists here received the doctrine from heretical centres in Lombardy and with popular support raised it to the status of a new religion, a different creed from Christianity.

These Manichees of southern France were the Cathars, or—less correctly—the Albigensians. They have been under investigation since the eighteenth century, and the literature bearing on them continues to grow. The first scholar to consider them was the French Huguenot exile Isaac de Beausobre, who in 1734 published the first volume of an epochal study.[53] Since then, Catharism has come to be recognized as an integral part of the subject matter of medieval history. In the nineteenth century, German, French, and American scholarship provided histo- rians with accounts, now more or less dated, which paved the way for further research.[54] Subsequent work has been remarkably fruitful, so that today we are in possession of a corpus of heretical writings which enables us to examine the obscurer corners of the Catharist heresy with considerable certainty. It is very satisfying to note that some of the outstanding workers in the field are members of the religious orders. Padre Ilarino da Milano, who is a member of the Capuchin Order in Rome, and Père Antoine Dondaine, of the Dominican Historical Institute in the same city, have made very notable contributions.[55] To these scholars we must add Arno Borst, whose *Die Katharer*[56] is the most comprehensive and up-to-date account of the heretics of southern France. And this pitifully short bibliographical list would be incomplete indeed if it did not recognize the signal work of the French meridionals themselves. In southern France, the cradle of Catharism, there is a revival of interest in the religion that sprang up and grew on local soil. A journal of Catharist studies, *Cahier d'études cathares*, has been published at Arques (in Aude) since 1949, and René Nelli, who lives at Montségur, where in 1244 the last remnants of the Cathars were burned at the stake, has by his writing done much to clarify Cathar doctrine.[57]

The Cathar heresy did not arise in a vacuum. It was part of that pattern of dissent which has already been discussed, of that striving after the ideal which produced so many different heresies opposed to the structures and priorities of the Church. It is now recognized that the origins of the high medieval heretical pattern in western Europe must be sought in the declining years of the tenth century and the first decades of the eleventh. In part the new style of popular heresy was a reaction to the increasing vulgarization of the feudal world, the decline of peace, culture, and religion after the Carolingian age. The people were drawn to the stillness of monastic life, to the permanent establishment of the Peace of God, to the renewal of their religious life. And from this time on the common people carried the torch of heresy as well.

The Cathar movement had its antecedents. There was the peasant Leuthard, from the village of Vertus in Champagne, who shortly after the momentous year 1000—which, some are said to have believed, would bring the end of the world—returned home from the field where he had worked the whole day and immediately chased his wife away, then destroyed all the crosses in the village church, declared that he would not pay the tithe to the village priest, and proclaimed to all that he could not believe in the Old Testament prophets. He immediately found followers, but also accusers, who denounced him to the bishop of Châlons. Leuthard committed suicide. Herbert Grundmann, the heresiologist, considers him to have been demented.[58] Yet it is significant that in his repudiation of marriage, the cross, the Old Testament, and the secular (taxing) power of the Church, Leuthard was at one with the Bogomils.

Indeed, throughout eleventh-century western Europe there were nests of dualist heresy. The chroniclers list Italy, Rhineland Germany, Languedoc, and Aquitaine as affected, and occasionally we are told even the names of the heretics and the places where they found converts. After Leuthard came the heretics of Orléans, who maintained that God had not created the visible world and who openly disbelieved the accepted account of the physical birth of Christ, declaring 'We were not there.' They also separated the visible world from the invisible universe and held that material substance was unclean. In keeping with these views they rejected, among other things, marriage, baptism, the Eucharist, the eating of meat, the Church hierarchy, good works, and prayers. True Christians, they maintained, lived only on celestial meals.

Similar eleventh-century heretical creeds were reported by contemporaries from Arles, from Verona, and especially from Monteforte, a castle between Genoa and Turin. The doctrine of the heretics of Monteforte displays signs of doctrinal sophistication; the heretics were all members of the nobility. The repugnance of matter was emphasized, and other doctrines which we have met previously were held by these heretics. For instance, they denied that Christ was God. They condemned worldliness, and they honoured virginity as the highest ideal for human beings. Marriage, accordingly, was for them an accident; whoever had married was obliged to consider his wife as a mother or sister. The members of this community dreamed of people multiplying without sin like bees in a beehive.

In the twelfth century, non-dualist popular heresies began to appear as well, and the papacy became more actively engaged in the suppression of heresy.[59] Some representatives of the new climate of heresy have already been mentioned: the overambitious reformer Arnold of Brescia, for example, or Peter of Bruys, who, without shoes, preached to the multitudes in southern France that churches should be pulled down and prayers said in stables and country inns instead. Other examples might be cited: Henry of Lausanne or Tanchelm of Flanders.[60] But it is our purpose here to consider the growth of dualist heresy and the beginnings of the Cathar movement proper.

The commencement of the Cathar dualism seems to have coincided with the second crusade (1147–49). It is possible that the doctrine of the Bogomils was brought back with the crusaders to western Europe; another reason for the spread of dualism in western Europe at this time may have been the policy of religious persecution in the Byzantine Empire under Emperor Manuel Comnenus, in the same period. We hear of dualists, possibly Cathars, under the name *pauperes Christi* at Cologne in 1143, where they founded a church of their own. Generally, however, the Cathars lived without means, wandering from place to place, fasting, praying, and working with their hands. Their faith became the faith of others, and women from all sectors of society joined them. The faith that they held meant more to them than their own lives; in Cologne, when they were being led to the fire, they were cheerful and without fear.

It is at this time that a group of heretics, most probably peasants from the Rhineland, both men and women, landed in England. They claimed that they were Christians such as the apostles were; they refused, however, to accept the sacraments. These too were probably Cathars. The English people turned away from them, and when they were rounded up and condemned to die, they were alone and without a following. But as one of them said: 'Blessed are ye when ye are hated by men.' This condemnation took place in 1162, in the reign of Henry II.

Three years later, the Cathar crisis broke out in France at Lombers, ten miles south of Albi, where churchmen, nobles, and followers of the Cathar doctrine met to engage in a verbal duel in which the merits of Christianity and Catharism were to be decided once and for all. But the Cathars were opposed to a public disputation; they refused to be questioned by the prelates, whom they described as 'wolves', 'hypocrites', and 'seducers' who wore richly decorated robes and carried diamonds on their fingers. This, they asserted, Christ had not taught them.[61] The encounter was indecisive.

It was within the next three years, in 1167, that the die was cast. In the presence of Nicetas, the Bogomil bishop of Constantinople, the Cathar southerners of France affirmed dualism as their creed, erected an organization, and rigidified their beliefs into dogmas.

The Cathar movement was launched. In less than one hundred years it was no more. It was banned by the Church and attacked by voracious crusaders, who are still remembered because a Montfort led them and because of such events as their massacre of the mixed Cathar-Christian population of Béziers, when they followed the advice of their leaders: 'Kill them all, for God knows his own.'[62] The survivors withdrew to Montségur, a Cathar shrine according to Fernand Niel,[63] where they were starved into surrender and then delivered by a fiery death from the crusaders.

What was the doctrine of the Cathars? There is no doubt that they were dualists —many of them unmitigated dualists, for whom the existence of evil on earth posed an ever-present problem of excruciating pain. This is how their creed was formulated in a confession of faith of certain Florentine Cathars in Italy: 'In the beginning there were two principles, that of good and that of evil, and from eternity two gods, that of light and that of darkness. The god of light made all light and things spiritual; the god of darkness made the devil, all evil, and all darkness.'[64]

Because of their identification of evil with matter, some Cathars refused to be-lieve in the real existence of the material world. The world was a negation for them, an emptiness created without God. True creation resided only in God, and only the spirit expressed reality. The material world, being the cause of evil in life, could only be the work of Satan. This view of material creation was utterly pessimistic.

As far as the heavenly world was concerned, Cathar views present a complexity which few systems can match. It was peopled with spiritual, created beings. They were made up of the same three components that were in man: that is, body, soul, and spirit. However, whereas the body of man was matter, the body of the spiritual beings, or celestial emanations, was of the same nature as 'the glorious body' of the resurrected Christ.

The Cathars further had a well-developed concept of the end of the world, which they anticipated as their final victory. The waters, they believed, would cover the earth; the sun, the moon, and the stars would cease to shine, and darkness would reign. Next fire would engulf the waters, and the waters would then extinguish the fire—such is the paradoxical explanation we find in Cathar writings.[65] The final stage of the world's end would be the appearance of hell, in which the devils would perish and with them all those who had been unable to purify themselves during the many lives which, according to Cathar doctrine, each man lived. In this way the work of Satan would finally be destroyed forever.

Cathar religious practice was irreconcilably opposed to that of the Catholic Church. The Cathars had no understanding of sacraments, of the symbol of the cross, of churches, of Catholic rites, of the Old Testament. Their moral doctrine enjoined an asceticism without parallel, which it was possible for only an élite to practise. Thus we find the Cathars divided, like their precursors the Manichees, into two classes—the Auditors, or Believers, and the Perfect. The Perfect were not to indulge in carnal pleasures of any sort or possess private property. In Cathar doctrine, moreover, it was wrong to kill, because the act of killing could interrupt the process of expiation between reincarnations, in which they believed, and thus bring to naught the course of penance of a believer. For this and other reasons, Cathars were not to eat meat or eggs, although they might eat fish in moderation.

To undergo death was for the Cathars an act of belief. Their faith was stronger than death. We know, for instance, that the Cathars in Goslar marched volun-tarily into the prepared fire rather than kill a single chicken. And at Minerve in France, the Cathars threw themselves into the fire chanting. Finally, there was the *endura*, the practice of self-imposed death by starvation. The *endura* has been exploited ad nauseam by those who want to emphasize that Catharism was an anti-social movement which deserved the treatment it received. It has, however, been shown that the *endura* was practised in only one section of the Cathar territory, in the valley of the Ariège from Toulouse to Ax-les Thermes.[66]

A few more words about the Cathar rites. They were unbelievably simple. They consisted of prayers, chants, long fasts, and, above all, sermons in which the doctrine was explained to the Auditors. There was no special place for holding prayers. Since the Cathars disapproved of all sacraments and of sexual inter-course, they allowed marriage only to the Auditors, and such marriage was a civil ceremony in which a priest never took part. Included in the Cathar liturgy was a rite of public confession, called the *apparellamentum*.

Finally, there was the *consolamentum*, the rite by which a Believer was initiated as a Perfect. Many Believers might ask for the *consolamentum* to be administered to them only when death was near. The ceremony has been preserved in Cathar writings; it consisted of promises rendered to a Perfect never to eat meat, eggs, or cheese, never to lie, swear, or live carnally, never to abandon the Cathar com-munity for fear of fire or water or any other means of death. Then the Believer recited the Cathar *Pater* and the Perfect laid his hands on him—an act which symbolized the giving of the Holy Spirit. It must be emphasized that the Cathars strictly adhered to the promises which they had made during the *consolamentum*. Of all the medieval heresies, no other inspired such allegiance or made its faith play such a part in the life of the individual.

We have seen but a little of the great variety of dissenting beliefs and hopes that make up the panorama of medieval heresy from the earliest days of Christianity until the fifteenth century. A few general reflections on the subject, however, may be appropriate.

Heresy of the type that we have examined in detail impresses us with its honesty. It is an act of faith, an assertion of ideals sincerely held by sincere men and women. It does not lie, it does not seek approval. It springs from the conscience of the individual, whose mind lives a lonely life. But the mind expresses the man, whose only inalienable possession is the freedom to think. A man of conscience cannot lead separate lives on different levels; there comes a time when he has to decide which of the various lives that he can lead in his mind is his own and thus assert his freedom, whatever the cost. Decisions of that heroic quality were clearly present in medieval heresy.

Notes

1. *Histories,* 4. 1.
2. *History of the Peloponnesian War,* 2. 58. 2.
3. *Antiquities of the Jews,* 13. 5. 9; *Jewish War,* 2. 8. 1–2.
4. St. Jerome, in his fourth-century translation of the Bible into Latin, used the Latin words *haeresis* and *secta* interchangeably for the Greek word employed in this sense: *haeresis* four times, *secta* five times.
5. Acts 5:17 and 15:5.
6. I Cor. 11:19.
7. Titus 3:10–11. Attempts have been made to reconcile this statement with the conciliatory policy suggested by the previous quotation, with only limited success. To explain the conflict between them one must take into account the different dates of the two epistles, and the change in circumstances. According to the French patristic scholar Daniélou, the first Epistle to the Corinthians originated sometime between 54 and 57, while the Epistle to Titus at the earliest dates from 63, following Paul's release from surveillance at Rome. In the later circumstance Paul is faced with a resurgence of Judaizing tendencies and is advocating stern measures to guard the young Christian community from Jewish 'myths and false apostles'.
8. R. M. Grant, *Gnosticism and Early Christianity* (New York, 1959), p. 89.

167

9. Loosely translated from the definition given by the German scholar Hans Leisegang in his *Die Gnosis*, 3rd ed. (Stuttgart, 1941), p. 1.

10. In his *Refutation and Overthrow of the False Gnosis,* usually referred to simply as *Adversus haereses,* 1. 25. 4.

11. In his *Adverses haereses,* which is devoted almost entirely to the Gnostic heresy in its many forms, Irenaeus feels constrained to apologize for having to write so much in order to combat the heresy: 'Just as our Lord used many words to proclaim the truth about one and the same God, his Father, the Creator of the world, so we must employ a multitude of proofs to confound those who are confused by any number of errors, in the hope that, defeated by the very number of our arguments, they will return to the truth and be saved.' This is a loose translation of 4. 41. 4, based upon the reliable French version in *Sources chrétiennes,* 100 (Paris, 1965): 993.

12. Catalogues of heresy did continue to be written, but in the sixth and seventh centuries they bear witness to a growing interest in the victorious past, for at this time the Church had relatively little heretical opposition. The sources of the time are widespread both chronologically and geographically, but a close reading of Sulpicius Severus, Gregory of Tours, or the Venerable Bede will leave little doubt that Gnosticism had been driven underground.

13. Many Roman bishops of the first and second centuries, for instance, are known to us only because Irenaeus has bequeathed their names to us in *Adversus haereses* 3. 3. 2–3; so little was the importance of the future papacy.

14. Maurice Goguel, *The Birth of Christianity,* trans. H. C. Snape (London, 1953), pp. 393–432.

15. The Arian controversy obtained a new lease on life in the West after 400, because some of the barbarian invaders had already been converted to Arianism in their homelands.

16. *Adversus haereses,* 3.3.1.

17. Even the earlier Gnostic heresy fits this pattern to some extent, although it was inward-looking and not socially aggressive, as were the later medieval heresies. For example, the Gnostic believer Theodotus held that the gnosis that liberated men was an ideal and complete knowledge of the world, not merely a state of grace following the washing of baptism—a knowledge 'of who we were, and what we have become, where we were or where we were placed, whither we hasten, from what we are redeemed, what birth is and what rebirth', as quoted by Clement of Alexandria in the *Excerpta ex Theodoto,* ed. and trans. R. P. Casey (London, 1934), 78.2, pp. 88–89.

18. Herbert Grundmann, *Religiöse Bewegungen im Mittelalter,* 2nd ed., revised (Hildesheim, 1961).

19. Herbert Grundmann, *Ketzergeschichte des Mittelalters* (Göttingen, 1963).

20. C. H. Haskins, *The Renaissance of the Twelfth Century* (Cambridge, Mass., 1927).

21. See René Nelli, ed. and trans., *Écritures cathares: la cène secrète; le livre des deux principes; le rituel latin; le rituel occitan; textes précathares et cathares ... avec une introduction sur les origines et l'esprit du catharisme* (Paris, 1959), pp. 11 and 28.

22. Steven Runciman, *The Medieval Manichee: A Study of the Christian Dualist Heresy* (Cambridge, 1947), pp. 117–18.

23. *Paradiso* 12. 141–42; cf. the commentary on these verses in Dante Alighieri, *Divine Comedy,* trans. J. D. Sinclair (London, 1939), 3 (*Paradiso*), 186–87.

24. Guglielmo Audisio, *Droit publique de l'église et des nations chrétiennes,* trans. Canon Labis (Louvain, 1865), 2: 102–105.

25. John Stacey, *John Wyclif and Reform* (London, 1964).

26. Ibid., p. 164.

27. Johann Loserth, *Hus und Wiclif: Zur Genesis der Husitischen Lehre* (Prague, 1884).

28. Ernest Denis, *Huss et la guerre des Hussites* (Paris, 1878).

29. S. Harrison Thomson, ed., 'Four Unpublished *Questiones* of John Hus', *Mediaevalia et humanistica,* 7 (1952): 71–88, and also his ed. of Hus: *Tractatus De ecclesia* (Cambridge, 1956).

30. Paul de Vooght, *L'hérésie de Jean Huss,* Fascicule 34 in Bibliothèque de la revue d'histoire ecclésiastique (Louvain, 1960).

31. Ibid., 481.

32. Such works as F. C. Baur, *Die Christliche Gnosis oder die Christliche Religionsphilosophie in ihrer geschichtlichen Entwicklung* (Tübingen, 1835); J. Horn, *Über die biblische Gnosis: Pragmatische Darstellung der Religionsphilosophie des Orientes zur Erklärung der Heiligen Schrift* (Hannover, 1805); A. J. W. Neander, *Genetische Entwicklung der vornehmsten gnostischen Systeme* (Berlin, 1818).

33. Simone Pétrement, *Le dualisme dans l'histoire de la philosophie et des religions: Introduction à l'étude du dualisme platonicien, du gnosticisme et du manichéisme* (Paris, 1946).

34. Adolph Harnack, *History of Dogma,* trans. Neil Buchanan (London, 1895–1900), 1: 226.

35. Hans Lietzmann, *A History of the Church,* trans. B. L. Woolf, vol 1: *The Beginnings of the Christian Church,* 3rd ed., revised (London, 1953), p. 295.

36. Hans Jonas, *The Gnostic Religion: The Message of the Alien God and the Beginnings of Christianity* (Boston, 1958), p. 36.

37. Hans Leisegang, *Die Gnosis,* p. 12.

38. Serge Hutin, *Les gnostiques* ('Que sais-je?', No. 808; Paris, 1959), pp. 82–93.

39. Jean Daniélou and Henri Marrou, *The First Six Hundred Years,* trans. Vincent Cronin [L. J. Roger and others, eds., *The Christian Centuries: A New History of the Catholic Church*] (New York, 1964), p. 55.

40. R. M. Grant, *Gnosticism and Early Christianity,* pp. 70–96.

41. Karl Bihlmeyer, *Church History,* revised by Hermann Tüchle, trans. from the 13th German ed. by V. E. Mills, vol. 1: *Christian Antiquity* (Westminster, Md., 1958), p. 148.

42. Jean-Paul Sartre, *Existentialism,* trans. B. Frechtman (New York, 1947), p. 15.

43. With the Gnostic Carpocrates a new approach to the affirmation of existence is introduced: man cannot be liberated from the gods of the material world without first becoming a slave of the vices over which they preside.

44. Jean Doresse, *The Secret Books of the Egyptian Gnostics: An Introduction to the Gnostic Coptic Manuscripts Discovered at Chenoboskion,* trans. Philip Mairet (New York, 1960), pp. xvi and 110–13; Serge Hutin, *Les gnostiques,* pp. 10, 20, 24, 107, and 126.

45. For what follows I depend closely on H.-C. Puech, *Le manichéisme: son fondateur— sa doctrine* (Paris, 1949), pp. 61–68.

46. Ibid., 64, quoting al-Biruni.

47. Ibid., 40–42 and 69–70.

48. Ibid., 70–72.

49. Ibid., 92.

50. S. Runciman, *The Medieval Manichee,* pp. 26–62.

51. D. Obolensky, *The Bogomils: A Study in Balkan Neo-Manichaeism* (Cambridge, 1948), pp. 288–89.

52. Ibid., 117–38 and 205–29.

53. Isaac de Beausobre, *Histoire critique de Manichée et du manichéisme* (2 vols; Amsterdam, 1734–39).

54. C. U. Hahn, *Geschichte der Ketzer im Mittelalter, besonders im 11., 12. und 13. Jahrhundert* (3 vols.; Stuttgart, 1845–50); C. G. A. Schmidt, *Histoire et doctrine de la secte des*

Cathares ou Albigeois (2 vols.; Paris–Geneva, 1848–49); H. C. Lea, *A History of the Inquisition of the Middle Ages* (3 vols.; Philadelphia, 1888).

55. See, for example, Ilarino da Milano, 'Il *Liber supra stella* del piacentino Salvo Burci contro i Catari e altre correnti ereticali', *Aevum*, 16 (1942): 272–319, 17 (1943): 90–146, and 19 (1945), 281–341; Antoine Dondaine, *Un traité manichéen du XIIIe siècle, le 'Liber de duobus principiis' suivi d'un fragment de rituel cathare* (Rome, 1939), and also 'La biérarchie cathare en Italie', *Archivum Fratrum Praedicatorum*, 19 (1949): 280–312, and 20 (1950): 234–324.

56. Arno Borst, *Die Katharer* (Stuttgart, 1953).

57. See René Nelli, *Écritures cathares;* also, *Le phénomène cathare* (Paris, 1963).

58. Herbert Grundmann, *Ketzergeschichte des Mittelalters*, p. 10.

59. It is now generally agreed that the attention of the papacy, which had unleashed the political storms of the preceding hundred years, was largely responsible for the violent developments in heretical history in the twelfth century and later.

60. In Flanders, Tanchelm was followed by great crowds. Purity, he said, was the one goal of man; a pure man was as close to God as Christ was; he had the Holy Spirit and was husband to the Virgin Mary. Tanchelm's popularity was undeniable; he had his own bodyguard, and he preached his gospel in a robe of gold, surrounded by armed men. His life ended, however, like that of Peter of Bruys; both were murdered by priests.

61. C. G. A. Schmidt, *Histoire et doctrine de la secte des Cathares ou Albigeois*, 1: 71–72.

62. H. C. Lea, *A History of the Inquisition of the Middle Ages*, 1, 154.

63. In R. Nelli, F. Neil, and others, *Les Cathares* (Paris–Alençon, 1965), pp. 381–89.

64. Quoted in G. R. Ristori, 'I Paterini in Firenze nella prima metà del secolo XIII', *Rivista storico-critica delle scienze teologiche*, 1 (Rome, 1905):16.

65. H. Söderberg, *La religion des Cathares: Étude sur le gnosticisme de la basse antiquité et du moyen âge* (Uppsala, 1949), p. 262. Söderberg is slightly abridging statements by Cathars before the Inquisition, such as that found in J. J. I. von Döllinger, *Beiträge zur Sektengeschichte des Mittelalters*, vol. 2; *Dokumente vornehmlich zur Geschichte der Valdesier und Katharer* (Munich, 1890), 'Confessio Petri Maurini de monte Alionis', p. 210.

66. D. Roché, *Le catharisme*, revised ed. (Toulouse, 1947), pp. 43–44 and 85–86. Roché quotes as his authority C. Molinier, 'L'*endura*, coutume religieuse des derniers sectaires albigeois', *Annales de la Faculté des Lettres de Bordeaux* (1880), p. 282 ff.